"With myriad insights and examples, *From Rural Village to Smart Village: Digital Connectivity for Development* provides detailed accounts of how digital technologies are closing communication gaps and enhancing development in rural and remote regions of the world. The book is an important contribution to the field of development communication and social change."

John K. Mayo, *Dean Emeritus, College of Communication, Florida State University, USA*

"This book is an important source for researchers and those working for change in developing economies. It is a comprehensive review of current trends and of communication technologies over the past several decades and their contributions in promoting that change. It is a must read!"

Emile McAnany, *Emeritus Professor, Santa Clara University, USA*

"Drawing on her extensive experience in field research, policy engagement, and program evaluation, Professor Hudson offers a comprehensive guide to the role of digital connectivity in rural development. Truly global in scope, the work analyses the opportunities and tensions shaping digital societies from Alaska to the Global South."

Rob McMahon, *Associate Professor, Communications and Technology, University of Alberta, Canada*

"Heather Hudson's book takes a masterful look at the difficult task of assuring the digital viability of rural areas. While new technologies are disruptive it is arguably even more disruptive to disconnect parts of societies. This wide-ranging book is a cogent roadmap on how to achieve a digital development that reaches all."

Eli Noam, *Professor of Economics and Finance Emeritus, Columbia University, USA*

FROM RURAL VILLAGE TO SMART VILLAGE

This book investigates how the rise of information and communications technologies is transforming life for Indigenous communities and those living in rural and developing areas.

The global reach of the internet and the proliferation of mobile phones, broadband, and social media have created an interconnected global village of communicators able to access and share information almost instantaneously. More recently, the COVID-19 pandemic has further increased reliance on online services for access to education, health, and e-commerce, especially in rural areas. This book provides an essential overview of the impacts of digital technologies, including recent case studies and research, and key policy issues for planners, policymakers, and researchers to consider concerning information and communication technologies in rural and developing regions. It concludes by examining policy solutions and strategies to help to address barriers in availability, affordability, and digital skills, in order to make universal access to the electronic means to create, locate, and share information a reality.

Written by renowned international expert Heather E. Hudson, this book will be ideal for researchers or students of communications and development and for practitioners and policymakers working for governments, consultancies, international organizations, and development agencies.

Heather E. Hudson is a leading global authority on communications for development. She is Professor Emerita at the University of San Francisco and former Director of the Institute of Social and Economic Research (ISER), University of Alaska Anchorage and was previously Associate Professor in new communication technology and policy at the University of Texas at Austin.

Her research focuses on applications and impacts of communication technologies for socioeconomic development, regulatory issues, and policies and strategies to extend affordable access to digital connectivity in rural and developing regions. She has planned and evaluated communication projects in northern Canada and Alaska and in more than 50 developing countries and emerging economies in Africa, Asia, the Caribbean and the South Pacific. She has consulted for government agencies, consumer and Indigenous organizations, the private sector, and international organizations including USAID, the World Bank, the ITU, UNDP, UNESCO, CIDA, IDRC, and the Commonwealth of Learning.

Professor Hudson has held a Fulbright Policy Research Chair and a Fulbright Asia-Pacific Distinguished Lectureship, as well as a Sloan Foundation Fellowship at Columbia University's Institute for Tele-Information (CITI) and fellowships in Australia, the University of Hong Kong, and the East-West Center in Hawai'i. She has published numerous articles and written or co-authored eight previous books on information and communication technologies for development, international communications, communications policy, and communication satellites.

Rethinking Development

Rethinking Development offers accessible and thought-provoking overviews of contemporary topics in international development and aid. Providing original empirical and analytical insights, the books in this series push thinking in new directions by challenging current conceptualizations and developing new ones.

This is a dynamic and inspiring series for all those engaged with today's debates surrounding development issues, whether they be students, scholars, policymakers, or practitioners internationally. These interdisciplinary books provide an invaluable resource for discussion in advanced undergraduate and postgraduate courses in development studies as well as in anthropology, economics, politics, geography, media studies and sociology.

Community-Led Development in Practice
We Power our Own Change
Edited by Elene Cloete and Gunjan Veda

Post-Development from the Global South
Radical Alternatives or Ambivalent Engagements?
Edited by Sally Matthews and Alba Castellsagué

Digital Inclusion in an Unequal World
An Emancipatory Manifesto
Tim Unwin

Poverty in Polycrisis
Dynamic Pathways for Lasting Change
Vidya Diwakar

The Decentralization Delusion
Challenging the Underlying Assumptions of Development
Ruby Dagher and Nana Afia Aku Ofori-Yentumi

From Rural Village to Smart Village
Digital Connectivity for Development
Heather E. Hudson

For more information about this series, please visit: www.routledge.com/Rethinking-Development/book-series/RDVPT

FROM RURAL VILLAGE TO SMART VILLAGE

Digital Connectivity for Development

Heather E. Hudson

Routledge
Taylor & Francis Group
LONDON AND NEW YORK

Designed cover image: Photography by L. Manuel Baechlin for Farm Radio International

First published 2027
by Routledge
4 Park Square, Milton Park, Abingdon, Oxon OX14 4RN

and by Routledge
605 Third Avenue, New York, NY 10158

Routledge is an imprint of the Taylor & Francis Group, an informa business

British Library Cataloguing-in-Publication Data
A catalogue record for this book is available from the British Library

ISBN: 9781032556659 (hbk)
ISBN: 9781032517070 (pbk)
ISBN: 9781003431602 (ebk)

DOI: 10.4324/9781003431602

Typeset in Times New Roman
by KnowledgeWorks Global Ltd.

To the many people in the Far North and the Global South from whom I have learned so much.

CONTENTS

KEY ABBREVIATIONS AND ACRONYMS

2G	second generation mobile network (for voice and text)
3G	third generation high-speed mobile network
4G	fourth generation high-speed mobile network
5G	fifth generation high-speed mobile network
6G	sixth generation high-speed mobile network
AI	artificial intelligence
Analog	a signal that varies continuously
API	application programming interface
ATM	automatic teller machine or bank machine
B2B	business-to-business
B2C	business-to-consumer
B2G	business-to-government
Bandwidth	the capacity of a communications channel, expressed in hertz, cycles per second
Bit	binary digit, i.e. either 0 or 1
BPL	broadband over powerline
BPO	business process outsourcing
Broadband	high-speed, high-capacity transmission systems such as microwave, coaxial cable, optical fiber, or satellite
C2C	citizen-to-government
C2G	consumer-to-consumer

C-band	band of radio frequencies; satellite uplink transmissions are generally around 6 GHz, and downlink transmissions around 4 GHz
Capex	capital expenditure(s)
Cellular	A wireless communications system in which the coverage area is divided into small sections called cells
CRTC	Canadian Radio-television and Telecommunications Commission
Digital	a discrete or discontinuous signal that transmits audio, data, and video as bits (binary digits) of information
Downlink	transmission from a satellite to Earth
DSL	Digital subscriber line
ECG or EKG	electrocardiogram
EMR	electronic medical record
Encryption	transformation of data for transmission so that it cannot be understood if intercepted
ERP	enterprise resource planning
FCC	[U.S.] Federal Communications Commission
Fiber optics	*see* optical fiber
fintech	financial technology
Footprint	the geographical coverage area of a satellite
Frequency	cycles per second, expressed in hertz
Frequency spectrum	the range of frequencies useful for radio communications, from about 10 KHz to 3,000 GHz.
FRI	Farm Radio International
G2C	government-to-citizen
GB	gigabytes: billions of bytes
Gbps	gigabits, billions of bits per second
GDP	gross domestic product
GDPR	General Data Protection Regulation (European Union)
GED	General Educational Diploma, the equivalent of a high school diploma

GEO	geostationary satellite, a satellite with an equatorial orbit 22,300 miles (36,000 kilometers) above the Earth; the satellite revolves around the Earth in 24 hours, and thus appears stationary when viewed from Earth
GHz	gigahertz, billions of cycles per second
GII	Gender Inequality Index
GIS	global information systems
GNI	gross national income
GNP	gross national product
GPS	Global Positioning System
GPU	graphics processing unit
GSM	Global System for Mobility, a second-generation mobile standard
GSMA	Global System for Mobile Communications Association
GSO	geostationary or geosynchronous orbit; *see* GEO
HCI	human capital index
HF	high frequency
ICTs	information and communication technologies
IEEE	Institute of Electrical and Electronics Engineers
IMF	International Monetary Fund
IoT	internet of things
IP	Internet Protocol
ISP	internet service provider
IT	information technology
ITU	International Telecommunication Union, the UN agency responsible for telecommunications
IVR	Interactive Voice Response
K–12	kindergarten through 12th grade
Ka-band	Portion of the electromagnetic spectrum in the 20 to 30 GHz range, used for satellite communications
Kbps	kilobits, thousands of bits per second
KHz	kilohertz, thousands of cycles per second
KMS	knowledge management systems
Ku-band	band of radio frequencies: satellite uplink transmissions are generally around 14 GHz, and downlink transmissions around 11–12 GHz

LDC	least developed country
LEO	Low Earth Orbit [satellite] – in contrast with GEOs, LEOs appear to move across the sky, and are located at lower altitudes; a series of satellites is required to provide continuous coverage of a given geographical area
LMIC	low- and middle-income country
LTE	Long Term Evolution, a 4th generation high-speed mobile technology
MB	megabytes, millions of bytes
MHz	megahertz, millions of hertz, cycles per second
Microwave	radio transmissions in the 4 to 28 GHz range, requiring antennas located within line-of-sight
MIS	market information systems
Modem	modulator/demodulator; a device that enables digital data to be transmitted over analog telephone lines
MOOC	massive open online course
MSMEs	micro, small, and medium enterprises
NGO	non-governmental organization
OECD	Organisation for Economic Co-operation and Development
Opex	operational expenditure(s)
Optical fiber	a communications medium made of hair-thin glass that conducts light waves
Photovoltaic	a material that develops voltage and electrical current when light shines on it; used for solar power systems
QoS	quality of service
S-band	frequencies in the 2.5 GHz range, used for community reception from satellites and for fixed wireless community networks
SD	secure digital [memory cards]
SDGs	[United Nations] Sustainable Development Goals
SMMEs	small, medium and micro enterprises
SMS	text messaging
STEAM	science, technology, engineering, art, and mathematics
STEM	science, technology, engineering, and mathematics

Teledensity	telephone lines per 100 population
Telemedicine	Use of telecommunications for health care and health education
UNDESA	United Nations Department of Economic and Social Affairs
UNDP	United Nations Development Program
UNESCO	United Nations Educational, Scientific and Cultural Organization
UNHCR	United Nations High Commissioner for Refugees
UNICEF	United Nations Children's Fund
Universal service	the goal of providing a communication service to everyone, traditionally by providing voice telephone service to every household; may now include internet access or broadband
Uplink	transmission to a satellite from Earth
USAID	United States Agency for International Development
USF	Universal Service Fund
VoIP	voice over internet protocol
VR	virtual reality
VSAT	very small aperture [satellite] terminal
WFP	World Food Program
WHO	World Health Organization

ACKNOWLEDGMENTS

I owe a great deal to the insights and encouragement of many friends and colleagues including Clifford Block, Dennis Foote, John Gilbert, Doug Goldschmidt, Michel Guité, John Mayo, Emile McAnany, Rob McMahon, Bill Melody, Bella Mody, and Doug Ward.

I also want to recognize the contributions to my understanding of the role of connectivity in development and its policy challenges from colleagues and mentors who are no longer with us, including Richard Butler, Richard Gwyn, Meheroo Jussawalla, Gerry Kenney, Tony Meyer, Donna Pace, Ed Parker, Walter Parker, Pat Pearce, Wilbur Schramm, Robert Walp, Tony Williamson, and Martha Wilson.

In addition, I appreciate the assistance of colleagues in government departments, foundations, non-profit organizations and development agencies, including the Aspen Institute, the Canadian Department of Communications (subsequently Industry Canada and now Innovation, Science and Economic Development Canada or ISED), Farm Radio International (FRI), the Ford Foundation, the Fulbright Foundation, the International Development Research Centre (IDRC), the International Telecommunication Union (ITU), the Internet Society (ISOC), the Sloan Foundation, the United States Agency for International Development (USAID), and the World Bank.

And I especially want to recognize the people in rural and remote areas of the Far North and the Global South who helped me to understand how communication contributes to development.

PROLOGUE

This book is the third in a series I have written on the role of communications in development over the past 40 years. My early field research was in the Canadian North. In remote communities, people invariably said that their first priority was for reliable communication to get help in emergencies, order supplies, track down funding promised by government officials, and stay in touch with family members studying or working in distant cities. In Alaska, I helped to evaluate a telemedicine experiment using a NASA satellite to link health aides in remote villages to doctors at regional hospitals. We found that daily reliable communication with a doctor significantly improved diagnoses and treatment outcomes of patients in the "satellite villages."

From the Far North, I was recruited to work on communications projects in the Global South for USAID, the World Bank, the ITU, UNDP, and other development agencies. What I learned in the North turned out to be valid throughout rural and remote regions in the developing world. From the South Pacific to southern Africa, and from Belize to Borneo, people said that they wanted reliable telecommunications for all the reasons that their northern counterparts had given.

Based on this experience and findings from researchers, my first book, *From Rural Village to Global Village: The Role of Telecommunications in Rural Development*, was published in 1984. So much has changed in the field of development communications since I wrote that first book! Then, mobile phones were brick-sized car phones, and the internet was a closed network linking a few American research universities and institutes. Telephones in the developing world were primarily in government and business offices and the homes of the elite. Some 20 years later, *From Rural Village to Global Village: Telecommunications and Development in the Information Age* (2006) was published. By then, telephony was expanding into rural regions, the internet was becoming accessible through telecenters and other community facilities, and tutors were using audio teleconferencing to help distant students with correspondence courses.

A further 20 years later, this third book examines the applications and impacts of digital connectivity for internet access and widespread adoption of mobile devices, increasingly smartphones. Now, digital connectivity is enabling rural residents to use smartphones for video chats as well as for transferring money and studying online, with broadband being extended to their communities via small satellite antennas, wireless networks, or optical fiber.

What has not changed is the importance of information in the development process. Information is obviously central to education, but also to health services and to economic activities, ranging from agriculture to manufacturing and services.

This book explores these applications of digital technologies and their contributions to current and future rural development, as well as the challenges they pose. Of course, these transitions are not universally positive. Gig workers may toil for low wages and long hours while being monitored electronically. Digital illiteracy can result in internet and social media users being misled or swindled. Digital gaps remain, as broadband availability and affordability become the benchmarks for universal connectivity. And while AI offers promise, such as for medical and other discoveries and for eliminating tedious administrative tasks, it also poses potential threats.

A woman using a rural telecenter in Africa wrote in the logbook "Information is the key to all doors." I share her optimism. Despite challenges, information and communication technologies will continue to provide new means to open these doors.

1

INTRODUCTION

Digital Connectivity and Development

> "Information is the key to all doors."
>
> – Woman using a rural telecentre in Africa

The end of the twentieth century was marked by dramatic technological developments in computers and telecommunications and the emergence of the internet. It took 75 years before 50 million customers had telephone service, but only 4 years for the internet to reach 50 million users. In the first two decades of the twenty-first century, mobile phone access expanded so that there are now more than 5 billion mobile subscribers, and the majority have smartphones that access the internet as well as communicate by voice and text.[1] Technology has effectively erased distance barriers, as members of rural cooperatives in Latin America check futures prices and exchange rates, African farmers find information about crop prices and techniques to improve crop yields on their mobile phones, and Inuit in Arctic communities market their handicrafts and ecotourism online.

As the woman noted in the logbook at an African telecentre, access to information is critical to development. The classifications of "information rich" and "information poor" mean more than distinctions based on gross national product (GNP) or other traditional development indicators. Information and communication technologies (ICTs) used to produce, store, and transmit information, are vitally

DOI: 10.4324/9781003431602-1

important development tools. Voice, text, social media, and internet resources are creating a global village of communicators able to access and share information almost instantaneously.

The Historical Context

Studies on the impact of communication technologies on development focused almost exclusively on mass media until the 1980s. While interest in educational radio in the industrialized world declined with the growing popularity of television, radio in the developing world continued to offer, for both content producers and listeners, an inexpensive means of transmitting information and educational content. Development agencies such as the United Nations Educational, Scientific and Cultural Organization (UNESCO) and the U.S. Agency for International Development (USAID) funded educational radio projects to teach children directly or to upgrade teachers' knowledge and skills, and to reach youths not in school as well as adults at home and at work.[2]

Radio remains an important development tool today, often complemented with interactive feedback or advice via mobile phone.[3] For example, in East Africa, radio broadcasts are popular across all ages and economic groups. Farmers listen to programs about improving and marketing their crops. Vehicle drivers listen to the radio for music and news, and young people are attracted to radio for music and sports. Thus, in addition to analyzing the impacts of the internet and mobile phones, it is necessary to include the ICTs that are most used by households.[4]

As television became available in developing countries, its educational potential was explored and evaluated in early projects in American Samoa, El Salvador, and Senegal, and eventually in many more developing regions. Yet two-way or interactive communications were generally ignored except by a few pioneering technical scholars such as Colin Cherry, who sought to understand the social and economic impacts of telecommunications in the industrialized world.[5]

During the mid-1970s, studies on interactive applications such as telemedicine and teleconferencing began to appear, many of which were funded as part of technical trials on experimental communications satellites.[6] Beginning in the late 1970s, studies examined the impact, or potential impact, of interactive telecommunications, primarily instigated by the International Telecommunication Union (ITU) and the World Bank. Much of the early research was synthesized in one of the first comprehensive reviews, *When Telephones Reach the Village* in 1984.[7] In the next two decades, the diffusion of personal computers coupled with the introduction of online data services and the internet led to adoption of these tools for development as well as to further research on their impact. Research on these innovations and on policies that could help to extend affordable access to online connectivity was the focus of *From Rural Village to Global Village: Telecommunications and Development in the Information Age*, published in 2006.[8] The purpose of this book is to review what we have learned since that time, as mobile phones have become almost ubiquitous, internet access is considered a "basic service," and expectations for connectivity now include broadband.

The Technological Context

The technological context may seem like a whirlwind that tosses up tantalizing but confusing arrays of equipment and services, resulting from breakthroughs in the speed of transmission and processing of data and in storage capacity. The transformation from analog to digital communication has made possible the convergence of services that were once considered completely separate, including transmission of data, but also voice, music, graphics, and video. Terrestrial wireless and satellite technologies make possible communication anywhere, any time The expansion of the internet as a global web enables content to be transmitted between individuals or among groups or to be "broadcast," i.e. disseminated to any and all connected to the network. Social media has emerged as a powerful tool for sharing information and organizing activities ranging from cultural gatherings to protests.

The telecommunications sector itself has been restructured in much of the world through the privatization of formerly government-owned networks and liberalization, allowing competition among services and across technologies. This restructuring is reflected in industry transformation, with new entrants as well as mergers and acquisitions creating vertically and horizontally integrated providers of both conduit and content, hardware and software. Privatization brought greater efficiency in operations and investment in infrastructure to expand and upgrade networks. Competition brought more choices and lower prices in many regions, including for mobile phone service in much of the developing world. Technological convergence merged voice, data, and video onto single digital networks, but has resulted in restructuring competitive providers in some cases into fewer and more powerful platforms.

There are several significant implications resulting from these technological trends, particularly for rural and developing regions:

- *Distance is no longer a barrier to accessing information.* Satellite and terrestrial wireless technologies have extended the range of networks to rural and remote areas, rather than depending solely on wires or cables across vast expanses or difficult terrain.
- *Costs of providing services are declining.* Satellite transmission costs are independent of distance as distance to and from satellites is virtually the same from any location, rather than being measured in geographical distance. Transmission costs using other technologies have also declined dramatically. Thus, communications services can be priced not according to distance, which penalizes rural and remote users, but per unit of information (message or bit) or unit of time.
- *Affordability remains a challenge.* Despite technological advances, users in rural regions may still find connectivity unaffordable because of data caps or other charges from providers.
- *Broadband is becoming a basic requirement.* The proliferation of broadband-based services has increased demand for affordable bandwidth and high-capacity infrastructure.
- *Distinctions are disappearing.* Distinctions between the traditional sectors of telecommunications, data processing, and broadcasting are disappearing with digitization of voice services and streaming of video content.
- *Users are now producers of content.* Digital convergence has contributed to the rise of social media, in which voice, data, and images may be combined according to the needs of users, and users can create and share their own content.

- *Investment in infrastructure is critical.* Despite the advances in these technologies, there are still requirements for funding to extend their range or upgrade their capacity. Networks may have insufficient capacity for new digital services, especially to reach rural areas and low-income communities.
- *The potential for competition is increasing.* Lower technology costs make rural/remote areas more attractive to service providers. New competitors can offer multiple infrastructure solutions, including wireless, satellite, and optical fiber.
- *Opportunities exist for small providers.* Some small and local providers, including Indigenous providers, can now offer services to their communities using these technologies, but regulatory constraints may hinder the ability of these providers to offer affordable services.

The Global Context: Toward a Digital Economy

The global economy is becoming increasing dependent on digital communications and processes, not only in services but in manufacturing, logistics, transportation, and resource industries. The digital economy refers to "that part of economic output derived solely or primarily from digital technologies with a business model based on digital goods or services."[9] However, some researchers suggest that

> it is more useful to think of the emerging digital economy more broadly as the contemporary global economy, with aspects of … the "old" economy and physical labour being facilitated by online sourcing, use or delivery, together with purely digital products and services, online work and production.[10]

Countries without sufficient digital infrastructure and workers with digital skills are at risk of falling further behind nations with greater investment in connectivity and related technologies and a more educated population. The process of integrating digital technologies across sectors and human activities is referred to as *digital transformation*, or simply *digitalization.*

The Digital Divide

The digital divide itself has evolved since the gap in access to telecommunications was first publicized more than four decades ago. In the 1980s, the ITU's Maitland Commission highlighted the "missing link," the gap between access to telephone services in developing and industrialized countries.[11,12] Researchers also documented the lack of reliable telephone services in rural areas and low-income urban areas of industrialized countries.[13] A decade later, policymakers were calling for a "global information infrastructure" that would link everyone into a worldwide network, or, more likely, a network of networks.[14] By the turn of the century, world leaders were committing themselves to bridge "digital divides" between the industrialized and developing worlds. Now the quest is for "broadband for all."

Today, innovations in technology mask both old and new disparities. While voice and text are almost ubiquitous, the internet is still not available in some rural and developing regions. Two-thirds of the world's population were using the internet in 2023. However in Africa just 37 percent of the population use the internet, and, across all low income countries, just 17 percent of people in rural areas are online.[15]

> The barrier to use for many people [in Africa] is therefore not that they are not covered by a signal, but that people do not have the resources to get online – the primary barrier being the cost of devices as well as the price of data. But another barrier for some is lack of awareness. For example, researchers found that in Ghana and Nigeria, 43 percent and 40 percent, respectively, of those who do not use the internet, also do not know what the internet is.[16]

As the Secretary General of the ITU points out:

> [T]o a large extent, the link is still missing. A full one-third of the world's population remains *totally* offline, and many among the online population are not "meaningfully connected" because of connectivity that is too slow, or unreliable, or costly, or because they lack the digital skills needed to get the most out of devices and services.

> At the same time, the "missing link" has morphed into multiple divides: across and within countries; between men and women; between youth and older people; between cities and rural areas."[17]

Mobile phone penetration has increased dramatically, and almost half of the global population now access the internet using a smartphone; yet mobile broadband coverage remains limited in many developing regions, particularly in rural areas. While 95 percent of the population in high-income and middle-income countries is covered by 4G or 5G mobile services, coverage drops to 39 percent in low-income countries, where 3G, with much more limited bandwidth, is often the only technology available to connect to the internet.[18] Some 400 million people (about 5 percent of the global population) live in areas without broadband coverage, and more than 20 percent living within mobile broadband coverage are not using mobile internet. The majority of these non-users do not own a mobile phone.[19]

Some 15 percent fewer women than men own smartphones or access the mobile internet in low- and middle-income countries.[20] Women may face barriers of structural inequalities in education as well as income, and restrictive family or cultural norms. Yet young people are increasingly likely to go online even in low-income countries, where 15- to 24-year-olds are almost twice as likely to use the internet as older populations.[21] With half of the population of these countries being 20 years of age or younger, as more go online, they will become an increasingly technology-savvy workforce.

More than 25 years ago, Frances Cairncross wrote "The death of distance as a determinant of the cost of communications will probably be the single most important economic force shaping society in the first half of the next century."[22] In many ways, she was right. Most charges for voice are now based on flat rates or minutes regardless of distance, and prepaid services allow people in developing countries and other low-income users to buy small increments of time. News and opinions are shared across the globe almost instantly.

But other challenges remain. Users now need broadband to access websites and many online services, and, where available, broadband pricing may include high monthly fees and expensive overage charges for data in excess of specified limits. Internet access may not be *affordable* for rural and low-income populations. The ITU has set an aspirational goal of pricing for entry-level broadband subscriptions at less than 2 percent of income per capita. However, in low-income economies, the median price of an entry-level mobile-broadband subscription amounts to 8.6 per cent of average income, a share 22 times larger than in high-income countries (0.4 percent).[23] And internet-capable phones remain expensive. In low- and middle-income countries (LMICs) the price of an entry-level device is equivalent to 17 percent of the average monthly income for men, and 24 percent for women.[24]

Elder and colleagues refer to "first order" digital divides, lack of infrastructure or connectivity to online services, and "second order" digital divides, the ability to use ICTs.[25] A wide digital skills and digital literacy gap excludes some population groups in rural and developing regions from the benefits of a digital economy. As the World Bank notes, "digital skills are a prerequisite for citizens, professionals, civil servants and policy makers to reap digital economic dividends across all sectors of the global and regional economy."[26] Digital literacy can range from basic skills to go online or access the internet from a smartphone to understanding how to assess the credibility of online information or to protect personal privacy.

The following sections of this chapter provide an overview of the critical role of connectivity in development and introduce key theoretical concepts. The chapters that follow explore the impact of connectivity in various social, economic, and cultural contexts, as well as barriers to achieving the benefits of universal connectivity and of policies and research initiatives that could help to address these challenges.

The Development Connection

Information is critical to the social, cultural, and economic activities that comprise the development process. If information is critical to development, then digital communications as a means of sharing information form not only a connection between people but also a link in the chain of the development process itself.

The internet provides the means to access and share information (or knowledge, which we may consider to be an organized body of information). Digital connectivity is especially valuable for small and isolated communities without local access to information resources (whether they be medical specialists, teachers, or elders living in distant communities). Access to information is critical for education and training as well as for health services – for example, to obtain advice on diagnosis and treatment of cases beyond local expertise or the capacity of local facilities. Information is also critical to running organizations and businesses and preserving and enhancing endangered languages and cultures. The ability to share information online can open new markets for local products and services. And sharing Indigenous knowledge about climate and the environment can contribute to strategies to manage and maintain land and water resources.

Internet access can enable workers to learn new skills through training videos, while students can benefit from online courses and materials, as was demonstrated in many countries during the COVID-19 pandemic. Telemedicine networks can help community health workers to get advice from urban physicians and enable distant specialists to interpret patient data and images. Telehealth services can also help to monitor patients where they live and provide in-service training for health care providers. These advances may be particularly beneficial for rural residents who typically have much more limited access to health care than their urban counterparts because of a lack of health workers, medical supplies, and clinics, resulting in lower life expectancy and higher infant mortality rates in rural than in urban areas.

Distance represents time in an increasingly time-conscious world. In countries where economies depend heavily on agriculture, fisheries, or the extraction of resources (such as lumber and minerals), distance from urban markets has traditionally been alleviated with the installation of improved transportation facilities, typically roads. Yet transportation links without reliable communications leave industries without access to up-to-date information, which is increasingly important for production and marketing of their commodities in the global economy. Now, with timely access to information, it is possible for products ranging from shade-grown coffee to Indigenous art to compete for global customers. Also, as the World Bank notes, digital technologies can promote development and generate digital dividends by reducing the costs of accessing information, thereby lowering the costs of economic and social transactions. In addition to boosting efficiency, cheaper and faster access to information and collaboration promotes innovation.[27]

The growth in the service sector is one of the features of the global economy. Information-based activities account for the largest part of the growth in services, and other sectors are becoming increasingly information intensive. While services tend to be a more visible component of urban economies, this structural shift is mirrored in rural economies of industrialized countries, where public and private services increasingly supplant agriculture and manufacturing. Economic development depends on human resources as well as economic diversification. Thus, basic education of children and adults as well as specific skills training are vitally important.

Concerning the COVID-19 pandemic, the ITU and UNESCO state:

> The events of the last three years have yielded unique insights into just how critical stable, broadband access is and will continue to be. As a knock-on effect of the digital transformation and pivot from the pandemic, new internet devices and applications, growing broadband penetration into developing markets, there is a stronger demand than ever for digital products and services."[28]

The ITU adds: "The pandemic has driven a remarkable discontinuity in digital adoption: a global disaster has generated a leap forward for the digital economy. The pandemic has generated a once-in-a-generation shift in connectivity demand and supply." Between 2019 and 2023, mobile- and fixed-broadband traffic had an estimated annual average growth of 30 percent with a peak rate of growth at the start of the COVID-19 pandemic in 2020.[29]

However, networks in many rural regions of both industrialized and developing countries could not keep up with demand from teleworkers, home-bound students, health care providers and others suddenly dependent on internet access.

Major Benefits of Connectivity

In general, the ability to access and share information electronically can contribute to the development process by improving:

- *Efficiency*, such as: savings in time or money (for example, treating patients locally rather than transporting them to a hospital); submitting grant and tax forms online rather than through the mail; ordering spare parts and other items online to save time and money.
- *Effectiveness*, or the quality of products and services, such as: improving health care through telehealth consultations; augmenting in-person instruction with online materials.
- *Equity* and *inclusion*, or the distribution of development benefits throughout the society, such as: providing government, banking and other services online to remote and Indigenous communities.
- *Reach*, or the ability to contact new customers or clients, such as: using the internet to reach global markets for crafts and ecotourism.

The following are examples from research on the benefits of internet access after broadband became available to the villages of southwestern Alaska, where the population is primarily Indigenous (Yup'ik):

- *Efficiency*: Economic development and local government agencies previously had to use facsimile or air courier via small aircraft to get documents to isolated villages without road access. The ability to email scanned documents including those requiring signatures was both faster and more reliable than faxing. Also, submitting applications online for funding enabled organizations to save time and money.

  Online banking and bill paying were obviously much faster than mailing checks to a distant bank; these services also gave more timely access to funds for merchants and customers. Store managers could now take a photo of a check on their smart phones to deposit the funds, and customers could use online bill paying and automatic bank machines to deposit or retrieve funds.

  Ordering spare parts online for public works saved both time and money for local governments, while online shopping allowed both small businesses and non-profit organizations to get access to supplies and equipment at better prices and with more choices than available locally.

- *Effectiveness*: Both commercial and non-profit organizations began to arrange webinars and to share training videos with village staff rather than relying on in-person sessions that required expensive travel by plane, often with delays because of poor weather. Also, e-government services (such as provision of hunting and fishing licenses and online application forms for government benefits) improved the effectiveness of government services in reaching citizens in rural areas.
- *Equity*: In remote southwest Alaska, improved equity for rural residents compared to their urban counterparts included access to online financial and government services that were not available locally and more timely access to training and funding opportunities. Students could take online high school courses not available in village schools, and outpatients could be monitored using telemedicine in their home communities rather than staying in distant hospitals.
- *Reach*: Tourist-related businesses (such as hunting and fishing lodges and guiding services) used websites and social media to reach new markets: "When you get the word out online using Facebook a lot more people can see what you are doing businesswise; if one person 'likes' it on Facebook, you can get word out quickly to a lot of potential customers."[30]

Additional examples of rural development benefits from digital connectivity in many rural and developing regions are discussed in the following chapters.

Identifying Impacts: The Chain of Inference

Policymakers and project funders often look for immediate benefits of connectivity. However, although there may be numerous examples of online activities, their impact may be harder to determine or may require a substantial time period. Sometimes many factors are involved besides access to information. Bad weather or other problems may delay delivery of vital spare parts ordered online. Local people may not have adequate training to take advantage of employment opportunities. Also, the impacts of connectivity may take time to be realized. For example, high school dropouts may complete high school equivalency online but may not be able to find jobs or apprenticeships immediately.

It is therefore important to understand the "chain of inference" – that is, the connections between the internet or other online services and eventual social or economic benefits. For example, more adults earning high school diplomas online may result in more local people being employed or eligible for skills training. Access to videoconferencing for social contact with distant families and for continuing education may result in reduced turnover among outsiders employed in the community. Online meetings and working groups taking place in local governments may generate increased applications for development funding, resulting in investments and employment. This chain of inference must be made explicit to trace any causal connection between provision of the facilities and outcomes, which may extend beyond the timeframe of short-term evaluations. These issues are discussed further in Chapter 9, "Field Research and Evaluation."

Connectivity as Complement: Necessary but not Sufficient

Digital connectivity can contribute significantly to rural development, but investment in connectivity alone is not likely to be sufficient for development to occur. Thus, online networking may be seen as a *complement* to other infrastructure required for development, such as transportation, electrification, and a clean water supply. Effectively managed operations may also benefit more from improved connectivity. For example, a well-managed entity such as a tribal government or tourism enterprise will likely derive greater benefits from online services than a poorly managed or understaffed operation. Online training may benefit participants if they can then qualify for available jobs or apprenticeships.

Online access may also serve as a *catalyst* for development if certain conditions are met. An artist who wants to stay in their community may generate income from selling their artwork online. A start-up business can take advantage of online resources for payroll and taxes. A mechanic may expand their business by finding how-to videos and schematics online.

To summarize, access to digital connectivity is generally a *necessary but not sufficient* condition for socioeconomic development.[31] Other factors may facilitate or hinder the impact of the internet and other online services, referred to by the World Bank as "analog complements":[32]

- *Context*: It is important to understand the social, cultural, and economic context. For example, if transportation is infrequent or very expensive, local people may not be able to benefit significantly from online ordering or from selling their wares online. Unreliable electric power may make it difficult to charge communication devices.
- *Content*: People who primarily speak minority languages may not benefit from online materials in major languages such as English, French, or Spanish. Texts and written content will not help the illiterate, although AI-enabled translation may overcome these barriers. Also, the potential of digital resources will be realized only if content is both relevant and actionable for minority and Indigenous users. For example, African farmers may not be able to take advantage of recommended hybrid seeds if they do not have enough money to buy them and credit is not available.
- *Capacity*: Effective use of the internet requires digital literacy[33] – skills in finding information, using popular software, and assessing the context and veracity of information from various sources. Training in accessing and evaluating online sources may be necessary; "infomediaries" or digital navigators could also help to find and explain online information. As Research ICT Africa points out:

> The ability of citizens to deploy these technologies and digital services to enhance their livelihoods and wellbeing will be determined not only by affordable access or even their digital literacy to consume the service, but the education and skills to do so productively.[34]

Adera and colleagues suggest:

> Rather than being an unqualified benefit to those who are poor, it seems probable that the impact of ICTs will be determined by the context in which these technologies are deployed, the preparedness of the users, and the opportunities that exist for their application.[35]

Warschauer refers to these additional requirements as digital resources, human resources, and social resources:[36]

> Three types of resources are needed in addition to the physical or supply side factors … First, there is a need for *digital resources*, which refers to the content that is available through the new technologies, and whether this is relevant, comprehensible, and responds to the needs of the new users. Second, the use of ICTs requires *human resources*, i.e. the knowledge and skills necessary to use the tools in a meaningful way. This includes traditional literacy that allows you to read and write, but also a range of other literacies, such as computer literacy, information literacy, multimedia literacy, and computer-mediated communication literacy. Finally, there is a need for appropriate *social resources*, which refer to the social relations, social structures, and social capital that are required to support meaningful use of ICTs in families, communities, and institutions.[37]

Contributions to Sustainable Development

Development strategies now emphasize sustainability, both in environmental terms and in implementing policies and strategies that are sustainable and scalable means of achieving development goals. In 2015, the United Nations adopted 17 Sustainable Development Goals (SDGs) for the year 2030 as a blueprint for a better and more sustainable future for all. The examples above and throughout the following chapters demonstrate that ICTs are essential to achieve these SDGs, which address poverty, education, health care, gender equality, clean water, climate action, and other development priorities.[38]

BOX 1.1 THE UNITED NATIONS SUSTAINABLE DEVELOPMENT GOALS (SDGS)

- **Goal 1**. End poverty in all its forms everywhere.
- **Goal 2**. End hunger, achieve food security and improved nutrition, and promote sustainable agriculture.
- **Goal 3**. Ensure healthy lives and promote wellbeing for all at all ages.
- **Goal 4**. Ensure inclusive and equitable quality education and promote lifelong learning opportunities for all.
- **Goal 5**. Achieve gender equality and empower all women and girls.
- **Goal 6**. Ensure availability and sustainable management of water and sanitation for all.
- **Goal 7**. Ensure access to affordable, reliable, sustainable, and modern energy for all.
- **Goal 8**. Promote sustained, inclusive and sustainable economic growth, full and productive employment, and decent work for all.
- **Goal 9**. Build resilient infrastructure, promote inclusive and sustainable industrialization, and foster innovation.
- **Goal 10**. Reduce inequality within and among countries.
- **Goal 11**. Make cities and human settlements inclusive, safe, resilient, and sustainable.
- **Goal 12**. Ensure sustainable consumption and production patterns.
- **Goal 13**. Take urgent action to combat climate change and its impacts.
- **Goal 14**. Conserve and sustainably use the oceans, seas, and marine resources for sustainable development.

- **Goal 15**. Protect, restore, and promote sustainable use of terrestrial ecosystems, sustainably manage forests, combat desertification, and halt and reverse land degradation and halt biodiversity loss.
- **Goal 16**. Promote peaceful and inclusive societies for sustainable development, provide access to justice for all, and build effective, accountable, and inclusive institutions at all levels.
- **Goal 17**. Strengthen the means of implementation and revitalize the global partnership for sustainable development.[39]

The goals are integrated, in that action in one area could affect outcomes in others. Each goal has specific subgoals, targets and indicators. For example, Goal 9 includes reference to universal and affordable access to the internet:

> 9.c Significantly increase access to information and communications technology and strive to provide universal and affordable access to the internet in least developed countries by 2020.[40]

As with most SDG goals, this target is still aspirational. However, the significance of digital connectivity is primarily in contributing to achievement of other SDG goals and targets, such as universal health care, women's empowerment, universal education and lifelong learning opportunities, and management of natural resources. As the German Development Fund points out,

> ICTs are crucial for achieving all of the SDGs as they are catalysts that not only accelerate all three pillars of sustainable development (economic growth, social inclusion and environmental sustainability), but also provide an innovative and effective means of implementation in today's interconnected world.[41]

Risks and Challenges

Of course, the benefits associated with increased reliance on digital technologies and services are accompanied by risks. The World Bank notes:

> Quickly expanding automation, even of mid-level office jobs, could contribute to a hollowing out of labor markets and to rising inequality. And the poor record of many e-government initiatives points to high failure of ICT projects and the risk that states and corporations could use digital technologies to control citizens, not to empower them.[42]

Competition, regulation, and education are all elements of strategies required to mitigate risks and extend benefits. Competition can help to maximize access and affordability, by creating incentives to provide multiple information sources and applications. Even where there is competition, regulation will still be required to protect users from misuse of their private information, erroneous content, and misleading marketing practices. There will be ongoing requirements for consumer education including digital literacy to enable users to benefit from digital resources and to identify and avoid fake content and illegal online business practices.

Another risk is that digital technologies can contribute to erosion of minority and Indigenous languages and cultures. Western entertainment and popular culture reached global audiences through television and film and, more recently, social media. But low-cost audio and video production tools, including smartphones and online distribution through social media, have made it possible to create and share multicultural music and Indigenous language lessons, games, and stories. And innovative applications continue to appear, as discussed in the following chapters.

The coming "youth bulge" will exacerbate the need for accelerated economic activity, as Africa's youth population is expected to double to over 830 million by 2050, while currently two-thirds of non-student youth are "unemployed, discouraged, or marginally employed." Many young people in these regions are finding work in the "gig economy," a labor market characterized by freelance, flexible, on-demand work facilitated by digital technologies. Self-employed gig workers earn income as drivers, delivery people, freelancers, and other "on-demand" services. Yet, as Research ICT Africa points out, while offering income opportunities to the jobless, the growth in the gig economy comes with the risk of exploitation of workers through a lack of labor regulation and the irregularity of employment. They cite examples of gig workers in South Africa who are minimally paid, undertake dangerous tasks, and have no protection from exploitation.[43]

Although the ICT sector is a major contributor to transport substitution and economic efficiency, it also consumes energy. It must therefore accelerate its transition to renewable energy to meet the computing demands of data centers that will be critical in the era of "big data" and artificial intelligence (AI). While AI is the latest challenge, its potential contribution to many development priorities is already evident. Health care providers can access findings from huge data sets to identify diseases and possible treatments; agronomists can search global data to identify plants suitable for changing climates; and automatic speech recognition is being used to transcribe messages from African farmers to producers of agricultural radio programs.[44] These opportunities and caveats are explored in Chapter 12, "The Era of Artificial Intelligence."

Commentary

The following chapters examine research and innovation in digital applications for health care, education and training, commerce and entrepreneurship, agriculture and natural resources, cultures and minorities, and governance. This book reviews our knowledge about how new information and communication technologies and services can contribute to social and economic development, particularly in rural and developing regions. It reviews key studies and identifies research findings concerning rural, remote, and Indigenous regions in both developing and industrialized countries, because conditions in remote regions of industrialized countries (such as northern Canada, Alaska, and outback Australia) are often similar to those of developing regions in terms of poor connectivity and relatively low incomes and/or high costs. It is based on the premise that despite differences in climates and cultures, the Far North and the Global South provide valuable insights and lessons that can enhance our understanding of rural connectivity.

A review of field research methodologies is included to suggest techniques that can be applied to evaluation of impacts of digital connectivity. Chapters on communication technologies and the potential of AI explore current and future technological contexts. The chapter on policies and strategies addresses issues such as digital inequities in access, affordability, and skills as well as the privacy and security required to help to close digital connectivity gaps and to open broader opportunities, so that universal access to the electronic means to create, locate, and share information will become a reality.

Readers should keep in mind that the references are intended to be illustrative rather than exhaustive, as the literature on information and communication technologies in many development sectors is very extensive – and continues to proliferate. Also, several references include major studies and reports which themselves include extensive bibliographies.

References

1. GSMA Intelligence. See https://www.gsmaintelligence.com/data/.
2. See, for example, McAnany, Emile G. (Ed.) (1981), *Communications in the Rural Third World*, Praeger; and MacBride Commission (1981), *Many Voices, One World*, UNESCO.
3. See, for example, Farm Radio International: www.farmradio.org.
4. Adera, Edith Ofwona, Waema, Timothy M., May, Julian, Mascarenhas, Ophelia, & Diga, Kathleen (Eds.) (2014), *ICT Pathways to Poverty Reduction: Empirical Evidence from East and Southern Africa*, International Development Research Centre, Ottawa.
5. Cherry, Colin (1971), *World Communication: Threat or Promise? A Socio-Technical Approach*, Wiley-InterScience.
6. See, for example, Parker, Edwin B., & Hudson, Heather E. (1995), *Electronic Byways: State Policies for Rural Development Through Telecommunications* (2nd edition), Aspen Institute.
7. Hudson, Heather E. (1984), *When Telephones Reach the Village*, Ablex.
8. Hudson, Heather E. (2006), *From Rural Village to Global Village: Telecommunications and Development in the Information Age*, Routledge.

9. Economic and Social Research Council of the United Kingdom, quoted in R. Bukht & R. Heeks (2017), Defining, Conceptualising and Measuring the Digital Economy, *International Organisations Research Journal*, 13, 143–72. 2017.
10. Razzano, G., Gillwald, A., Aguera, P., Ahmed, S., Calandro, E., Matanga, C., Rens, A., & Van Der Spuy, A. (2020), *SADC Parliamentary Forum Discussion Paper: The Digital Economy and Society*, Research ICT Africa, Cape Town, South Africa.
11. ITU (1984), *The Missing Link: The Maitland Report*. International Telecommunication Union.
12. The author was a contributor to *The Missing Link* report.
13. See, for example, Hudson, Heather E., Parker, Edwin B., Dillman, Don A., & Roscoe, Andrew D. (1989), *Rural America in the Information Age: Telecommunications Policy for Rural Development*, University Press of America.
14. See Hudson, Heather E. (1997), *Global Connections: International Telecommunications Infrastructure and Policy*, Wiley.
15. ITU (2023), *Measuring Digital Development: Facts and Figures 2023*, International Telecommunication Union.
16. Razzano, G., Gillwald, A., Aguera, P., Ahmed, S., Calandro, E., Matanga, C., Rens, A., & Van Der Spuy, A. (2020), *SADC Parliamentary Forum Discussion Paper: The Digital Economy and Society*, Research ICT Africa, Cape Town, South Africa.
17. Bogdan-Martin, Doreen (2022), in *ITU Global Connectivity Report 2022*, International Telecommunication Union. https://www.itu.int/itu-d/reports/statistics/global-connectivity-report-2022/.
18. GSMA (Global System for Mobile Communications Association) (2023), *The State of Mobile Connectivity Report 2023*. https://www.gsma.com/r/somic-2023/.
19. GSMA (2023), *The State of Mobile Connectivity Report 2023*. https://www.gsma.com/r/somic-2023/.
20. GSMA (2021), *Connected Women: The Mobile Gender Gap Report 2021*. https://www.gsma.com/r/wp-content/uploads/2021/06/The-Mobile-Gender-Gap-Report-2021.pdf.
21. ITU (2022), *Global Connectivity Report 2022*, International Telecommunication Union. https://www.itu.int/itu-d/reports/statistics/global-connectivity-report-2022/.
22. Cairncross, Frances (1997), *The Death of Distance*, Harvard Business School Press.
23. ITU (2023), *Measuring Digital Development: Facts and Figures 2023*, International Telecommunication Union.

24. GSMA (2023), *The State of Mobile Connectivity Report 2023*. https://www.gsma.com/r/somic-2023/.
25. Elder, Laurent, Emdon, Heloise, Fuchs, Richard, & Petrazzini, Ben (Eds.) (2013) *Connecting ICTs to Development: The IDRC Experience*, International Development Research Centre, Ottawa.
26. Melhem, Samia & Jacobsen, Astrid Herdis (2021), *A Global Study on Digital Capabilities*, World Bank, Washington, DC. https://documents1.worldbank.org/curated/en/959181623060169420/pdf/A-Global-Study-on-Digital-Capabilities.pdf.
27. World Bank (2016), *World Development Report 2016: Digital Dividends*. https://www.worldbank.org/en/publication/wdr2016.
28. ITU/UNESCO (2023), *The State of Broadband 2023: Digital Connectivity. A Transformative Opportunity*, ITU/UNESCO Broadband Commission for Sustainable Development. https://www.itu.int/dms_pub/itu-s/opb/pol/S-POL-BROADBAND.28-2023-PDF-E.pdf.
29. ITU (2022), *Global Connectivity Report 2022*, International Telecommunication Union, p. 133. https://www.itu.int/itu-d/reports/statistics/global-connectivity-report-2022/.
30. Hudson, Heather E. (2015), *After Broadband: An Analysis of Organizational Use of Broadband in Southwest Alaska*, Institute of Social and Economic Research, University of Alaska, Anchorage.
31. Parker, Edwin B. & Hudson, Heather E. (1995), *Electronic Byways: State Policies for Rural Development Through Telecommunications* (2nd edition), Aspen Institute.
32. World Bank (2016), *World Development Report 2016: Digital Dividends*. https://www.worldbank.org/en/publication/wdr2016.
33. See, for example, McMahon, R., McNally, M., Fraser, C., Pearce, H., & Fontaine, T. (2018), Supporting Digital Literacy Learning and Resources with Gwich'in Tribal Council, *Northern Public Affairs*, 6(2); and McMahon, R., Gurstein, M., Beaton, B., O'Donnell, S., &Whiteduck, T. (2014), Making Information Technologies Work at the End of the Road, *Journal of Information Policy*, 4(1).
34. Razzano, G., Gillwald, A., Aguera, P., Ahmed, S., Calandro, E., Matanga, C., Rens, A., & Van Der Spuy, A. (2020), *SADC Parliamentary Forum Discussion Paper: The Digital Economy and Society*, Research ICT Africa, Cape Town, South Africa.
35. Adera, Edith Ofwona, Waema, Timothy M., May, Julian, Mascarenhas, Ophelia, & Diga, Kathleen (Eds.) (2014), *ICT Pathways to Poverty Reduction: Empirical Evidence from East and Southern Africa*, International Development Research Centre, Ottawa, p. 16.

36. Warschauer, M. (2004), *Technology and Social Inclusion: Rethinking the Digital Divide*, MIT Press.
37. Warschauer, M. (2004), *Technology and Social Inclusion: Rethinking the Digital Divide*, MIT Press.
38. https://www.un.org/sustainabledevelopment/.
39. *Transforming Our World: The 2030 Agenda for Sustainable Development*. https://sdgs.un.org/2030agenda.
40. *Global Indicator Framework for the Sustainable Development Goals and Targets of the 2030 Agenda for Sustainable Development*. https://unstats.un.org/sdgs/indicators/indicators-list/.
41. *Harnessing the Chances of Digitalization for Rural Development: Lessons-Learnt in German-Funded Rural Development Projects* (2018), Deutsche Gesellschaft für Internationale Zusammenarbeit (GIZ) GmbH, Bonn.
42. World Bank (2016), *World Development Report 2016: Digital Dividends*. https://www.worldbank.org/en/publication/wdr2016.
43. Razzano, G., Gillwald, A., Aguera, P., Ahmed, S., Calandro, E., Matanga, C., Rens, A., & Van Der Spuy, A. (2020), *SADC Parliamentary Forum Discussion Paper: The Digital Economy and Society*, Research ICT Africa, Cape Town, South Africa.
44. See https://www.comminit.com/policy-blogs/content/using-automatic-speech-recognition-transcribe-voice-messages-african-farmers.

2

THE INFORMATION SOCIETY AND THE DIGITAL ECONOMY

> "With the advent of … the fourth industrial revolution … societies have truly entered the digital era. This era is, in many ways, different from the previous industrial paradigm and different from the earlier phases of digitalization in terms of reach, complexity, technology, and outcomes."
>
> – The World Bank[1]

The Emerging Digital Economy

The transition to a "postindustrial" or "information society" was proposed by Japanese and U.S. researchers in the 1960s and 1970s. Machlup's 1962 monograph *The Production and Distribution of Knowledge in the United States*[2] and Daniel Bell's book *The Coming of Post-Industrial Society*[3] attempted to quantify the size of the "knowledge industry" and its workforce (the "post-industrial society"), and to relate them to GNP. The concept of a *joho* (or *johoka*) *shakai* or "informationalized society" became a Japanese government goal as early as 1971: "a new national target, 'Realization of the Information Society'."[36] The creation, distribution, use, integration, and manipulation of information are key; information technologies have made possible this transition to what has been called the information society or knowledge society. As the World Bank points out, the current stage of digitalization, however, differs in terms of reach, complexity, technology, and outcomes.

DOI: 10.4324/9781003431602-2

In the 1970s, pioneering research by Marc Porat[4] developed a typology of information divided between primary and secondary information sectors. The primary information sector included communications technologies, mass media, telecommunications, print, and other producers of information. The secondary information sector included those industries and activities that use information as an input, such as banking and finance, insurance, education, administration and management, logistics, and many others. Today, virtually all social and economic activities require information inputs. This combination of primary and secondary information sectors has become known as the digital economy. Bukht and Heeks define the "digital economy" as "that part of economic output derived solely or primarily from digital technologies with a business model based on digital goods or services."[5] However, that definition may be expanded to include much of the global economy, with activities such as agriculture and manufacturing now including digital functions such as logistics and e-commerce, as well as purely digital products and services. The terms digitalization or digital transformation can be defined as the use of digital technologies to change business models, or more broadly "the integration of multiple technologies into all aspects of daily life that can be digitized."[6]

The Power of Networking

Access to communication services can magnify the power of information-sharing: a property of information networks is that each user's welfare rises with the number of users who can access the network. A basic principle of connectivity known as Metcalfe's Law (referring to Robert Metcalfe, one of the inventors of the internet) is that the number of connections and thus the potential value of the network increases almost as the square of its users,[7] so that the more users of a network, the more useful it becomes. The more people who have mobile phones or are on social media, the more valuable these services are to each user. Coupling these tools with the vast number of websites and other online information sources, digital networks have enormous potential to facilitate the sharing of ideas and, through them, communication, the expansion of knowledge.

This networking effect can also strengthen social inclusion. Adera and colleagues point out that users feel more connected with friends and family immediately through the use of ICTs. "This feeling of connectivity immediately increases social capital and reduces vulnerability."[8] The beneficiaries range from dispersed family members, workers, and students away from home, to individuals looking to connect with others with shared interests in their profession, hobbies or other activities who can now stay in touch and make new contacts through social media and video chats.

Externalities and the Role of "Infomediaries"

Information also has unusual properties in that it may be shared without being transferred: when you tell your friend a secret, you both know it, whereas when you give your friend a present, she now has it and you do not. Also, the benefits may extend to those who have not directly participated in information acquisition, processing, or dissemination. Thus, information or knowledge can be considered a "public good" (in economic terms, non-rivalrous and non-excludable), i.e. use by one person neither prevents access by other people nor reduces availability to others. These characteristics may affect both how the benefits or information are shared and how they may be overlooked by policymakers.

Some benefits may accrue to individuals who use the internet, such as finding information online to solve a problem, and saving time by using online services to arrange transport or to substitute for travel. Other benefits may require more complex types of information-seeking or use by people with institutional affiliations, such as businesses or social service organizations. For example, a patient would benefit if a health worker were able to find out how to treat her rare disease by searching on the internet or could manage her care without transferring her to a distant hospital. Artists would benefit if their local librarian could help them search online for markets for their work. Indigenous guides would benefit if an ecotourism lodge can promote its wildlife expeditions online. These indirect benefits are also known as *externalities*: lives may be saved, travel costs eliminated, incomes increased.

It is also important to recognize that beneficiaries who do not themselves use the internet such as the patient or the artist in the examples above may be helped by resource people to find the information they need. These intermediaries are sometimes called *infomediaries* or *digital navigators*. They could include teachers, librarians, local government or NGO (non-governmental organization) staff members, and digitally savvy teenagers – for example, those who helped elders to find appointments and register online for vaccinations during the COVID-19 pandemic in North America.

Many online activities generate substantial benefits such as time saved, consumer convenience, expanded choice, and access to more knowledge. In economic terms, these benefits are known as *consumer surplus*: the difference between the price individuals are willing to pay and the actual price for the product or service.[9] While apparently obvious, consumer surplus and the power of networking and are often overlooked in assessing the value of investments in connectivity. As discussed in Chapter 11, "Digital Policy Issues and Strategies," these concepts are critical for formulating policies – for example, to extend broadband, as they imply that building out the network and connecting more subscribers, including those in remote and Indigenous communities, should be a priority for rural development. Infrastructure funders and policymakers must therefore look beyond the costs of installation facilities and the revenues from subscribers to the social and economic benefits that digital connectivity can generate.

The Question of Causality

Numerous studies using national- or international-level data have attempted to measure some impacts of the digital economy through analysis of data on broadband, the internet, and mobile phones. Their findings have been cited by development organizations, policymakers and the ICT industry as evidence that investment in communications infrastructure contributes to economic development.[10] Examples of these cross-sectoral and national-/international-level studies on the role of information and communication technologies in development are discussed below. However, most do not explain why or how this investment could impact national economies. For this interpretation, micro-level studies, including field research, are needed. Also, as discussed below, macro-level studies may not control variables to explain causality – does ICT investment "cause" development? Or does economic growth "cause" (i.e. contribute to) more infrastructure investment? Or both? For example, does the availability of broadband result in more jobs or income for rural residents, or does the availability of educated rural workers result in increased investment in rural communications infrastructure for these potential customers? Both results may occur, such as with the expansion of rural broadband, which can generate revenue for providers and income-based activities for users.

A frequently cited study by the World Bank estimated that, for developing countries, each 10 percent increase in fixed broadband penetration appeared to boost the average annual GDP growth rate by 1.2 percent. However, the authors acknowledged that demand for broadband services rises with wealth and that their model did not deal with this problem explicitly, so that there could be reverse causality, i.e. that increase in GDP contributed to increased broadband penetration.[11]

An earlier study on telephony and development by Hardy using a methodology that identified bidirectional causality found that, while economic growth led to increased access to telephones, there was also a significant contribution of telephone penetration to economic growth.[12] In other words, increases in GDP "led" to (i.e. preceded) more investment in telecommunications, but access to telephones also "led" to economic development.[13] To isolate the impact of telecommunications on GDP, Roller and Waverman developed a model to deal with the possibility of reverse causation, i.e. increase in GDP "causing" more investment in telecommunications.[14] They found that density of telecommunications (at that time, telephone lines per 100 population) was important in estimating contribution to GDP. They concluded that a 10 percent increase in the penetration rate of telecommunication infrastructure would create a 2.8 percent increase in GDP, but growth was only generated once a minimum threshold of telecommunication density was achieved. This threshold was found to be at around 24 percent, meaning that only once 24 percent of the population has access to telecommunications might economic growth be generated.

A study that applied this approach to examine the impact of broadband found economically significant effects, also depending on penetration levels. Research on 22 Organisation for Economic Co-operation and Development (OECD) countries grouped them by their broadband penetration levels. The study was designed to identify the effect on GDP of an incremental change in broadband penetration, depending on the current penetration level. It concluded that for each 10 percent increase in fixed broadband penetration, the effect on GDP per capita was an increase of 0.08 percent for countries with low levels of broadband penetration, 0.14 percent for countries with medium penetration, and 0.23 percent for countries with high levels of broadband penetration, respectively.[15]

In a review of studies on the impact of broadband, Bertschek and colleagues found that, on a macroeconomic level, increased broadband deployment translates into higher economic growth and productivity but also helps to create new jobs and, at least partially, facilitates economic development in rural areas. However, the microeconomic studies they reviewed "paint a more differentiated picture. Most notably, broadband adoption is accompanied by a pronounced skill bias regarding workers' labor market outcomes that strongly favors highly skilled workers."[16]

Some studies have attempted to isolate economic impacts in developing countries. Arvin and colleagues examined broadband and economic growth using a panel data set covering the G20 countries for the period 1998–2011. (The Group of 20 (G20) is an intergovernmental forum comprising 19 countries, the European Union, and the African Union.) They found a network of G20 causal connections between the variables including short-run bidirectional causality between broadband penetration and economic growth among the more developed countries within the G20. For the developing countries within the G20, they found evidence of unidirectional causality from economic growth to broadband penetration. In other words, for the developing countries economic growth contributed to infrastructure investment that increased broadband penetration.[17] However, a study by García Zaballos and López-Rivas found that a 10 percent increase in broadband penetration brought about an average increase of 3.2 percent in per-capita GDP across 26 Latin American and Caribbean countries.[18] Also, an analysis of the impact of the introduction of broadband in 12 African countries through submarine cables and domestic fiber networks showed large positive effects on employment rates. The sample-wide impact was driven by increased employment in higher-skill occupations, but with lower employment gains for less-educated workers. Firm-level data available for some countries indicated that increases in firm entry, productivity, and exporting contributed to higher net job creation.[19]

Researchers for consulting firms have used these studies and findings to project potential benefits for developing regions of technologies. For example, a report on the potential benefits of submarine cables in Southeast Asia references several studies on the economic benefits of connectivity and concludes: "Submarine cables improve the connectivity environment, to the [economic] benefit of individuals, businesses and governments."[20]

Few researchers have focused on adoption (for example, of broadband) rather than availability, such as wireless coverage or extension of local terrestrial connections. A study on the rural United States used data from the National Broadband Map (NBM) and the Federal Communications Commission (FCC) to assess the potentially causal relationship between broadband availability/adoption and measures of economic growth. The growth rates of a variety of economic development variables between 2001 and 2010 were compared across groups of rural counties. The results demonstrated that "high adoption" non-metro counties had faster growth in median household income and lower growth in unemployment rates, while "low adoption" non-metro counties saw lower growth in both the number of firms and total employment. The authors concluded that "In general, thresholds for broadband *adoption* are shown to be more important to economic growth measures than those for *availability*."[21] This study indicates that adoption rather than solely availability of infrastructure contributes to economic growth. However, they noted that they could not make strict claims of a causal relationship, because of the potential influence of unobservable factors and data limitations.

A systematic review of the econometric literature exploring the relationship between broadband and economic growth conducted in 2016 by the World Bank points to the consensus in the empirical literature that a certain penetration threshold is necessary before a significant economic impact is discernible from fixed broadband investment.[22] It is difficult to extrapolate the findings from these studies to regions with different demographics and rural economies. Also, such studies do not explain the "chain of inference" – what information-related activities actually contributed to increases in economic indicators? For example, Hudson found from research in northern Canada that Indigenous communities that had previously participated in regional collaboration were more likely to make constructive use of telecommunications, such as for business- or government-related purposes, than those with little earlier regional or external activity.[23]

Many arguments have been put forward for how ICTs can impact economic growth. Katz and Callorda point out that network effects (benefits from more connected users) are likely to help explain that the effect of fixed broadband penetration on GDP increases with the country's broadband penetration level, up to about 40 subscriptions per 100 inhabitants.[24] Jalava and Pohjola suggest that the production of ICT goods and services can directly contribute to national GDP.[25] Also the use of ICTs as an input in the production of other goods and services can have growth-enhancing effects. The theories on the contribution of information to development discussed in Chapter 1, "Introduction: Digital Connectivity and Development," can also explain the contribution of connectivity to economic growth. A reduction in information asymmetries can enhance the efficiency of resource allocation and decrease the chances of well-informed large firms extracting economic rent (such as excess revenues) from less-informed small firms. On a macro-level this broader access to information can create faster growth and diversify the economy. The OECD also reports that research has shown that an increase in internet penetration has a positive correlation to growth in businesses, has an impact on the types of business that are created, and ultimately affects economic growth and national income.[26]

While investment in ICTs may contribute to increase in GDP at the national level, it is difficult to determine whether or under what conditions low-income populations may benefit financially. Research by Mora Rivera and Garcia Mora indicates that internet access helps reduce poverty levels in Mexico, and that the impacts on reducing extreme income poverty and extreme multidimensional poverty are more significant for the rural sector than for the urban sector.[27] Two studies by PICTURE Africa also address poverty reduction. A panel study consisting of 1,600 household interviews across four African countries (Kenya, Rwanda, Tanzania, and Uganda) found that, controlling for other dimensions of poverty, gaining access to ICTs by poor households resulted in a statistically significant reduction in economic poverty levels among the benefit group. In the survey, which was carried out two years after the interventions were introduced, the proportion of poor households had decreased to 16 percent among the benefit group, whereas it was about 38 percent among the control group.

Another study among two groups of small and micro urban enterprises in Tanzania found that increased use of mobile phones and the internet resulted in a significant reduction in financial poverty.[28] These analyses indicated that benefits are mediated through a range of uses, providing insights into the mechanisms of how ICTs contribute towards poverty reduction. As Adera and colleagues point out:

> Rather than being an unqualified benefit to those who are poor, it seems probable that the impact of ICTs will be determined by the context in which these technologies are deployed, the preparedness of the users, and the opportunities that exist for their application.[29]

They add:

> In the case of financial capital and physical capital, the link is indirect – ICTs enhance the capacity of the user to increase or expand income (through getting a new job or through getting more business clients resulting in bigger sales and increased income). The increased income can then be used to acquire durable assets (economic capital) and enhance physical capital (improved housing or increased access to basic services).[30]

E-Readiness

The countries with the highest average daily time spent on social media in 2023 were Brazil, Nigeria, and the Philippines. Other developing countries in the top ten were South Africa, Kenya, Ghana, and Indonesia.[31] Yet, although many activities in developing and emerging economies now include use of digital technologies, their context may lack the conditions needed to transition to a more digital economy. At the national level, these conditions may be called "e-readiness," with two main categories: those that focus on basic infrastructure or a nation's readiness for business or economic growth and those that focus on the ability of the overall society to benefit from ICTs. These two categories have also been called the "e-economy" and "e-society."[32]

To address the factors that can influence the extent of economic and social benefits of connectivity, the ITU proposed the ICT Opportunity Index (ICT-OI), now referred to as the ICT Development Index. It noted that the "bigger picture" includes consideration of cause-and-effect relationships in the information society:

- Factors that influence ICT use and development; and
- Influences that ICT has on society, the economy, and (to a lesser extent) the natural environment.[33]

Also emphasizing context, *The Economist* proposes an "e-Readiness Index" with the following primary categories:

- Consumer and business adoption
- Connectivity and technology infrastructure
- Business environment
- Social and cultural environment
- Government policy and vision
- Legal environment.[34]

For example, Ireland has implemented strategies to benefit from e-readiness and to attract ICT business by investing in educational programs to build a labor supply with core ICT and electronic or electrical engineering skills. Ireland also introduced complementary initiatives to bolster this strategy and make the country more attractive for foreign investment, including keeping the corporate tax rate low, and investing in property for business and technology parks. These strategies contributed to the relocation of multinational corporations to Ireland, bringing both economic activity and intellectual property.[35] Several developing countries are attempting to emulate this approach, but struggle to build the skilled labor force and legal framework to attract necessary investment to digitize their economy.

Commentary

Studies over the past several decades have attempted to define the "information economy" or more recently "digital economy" and to quantify its contribution to national economies. While several findings indicate that increased investment in communications infrastructure leads to economic growth, most do not explain why this growth may occur, or what other factors besides technology may influence the rate and extent of growth. Despite variations, factors highlighted in some studies do appear relevant in understanding the impact of connectivity in all contexts:

- *Adoption*: high adoption rates rather than simply availability of connectivity appear necessary for positive rural economic impact.
- *Education and skills*: employees and business owners with more education and skills are likely to benefit more in terms of employment and business revenue that less educated or less skilled workers.
- *Industry sectors*: information-intensive sectors such as finance, professional and public services, education/training, and health care benefit from better connectivity; manufacturing or resource industries benefit as well by employing information technologies to improve efficiency, output, and revenue, but management and administration of the latter (such as mining, agriculture, and fisheries) could also benefit.

References

1. Melhem, Samia & Jacobsen, Astrid Herdis (2021), *A Global Study on Digital Capabilities*, World Bank. https://documents1.worldbank.org/curated/en/959181623060169420/pdf/A-Global-Study-on-Digital-Capabilities.pdf.
2. Machlup, Fritz (1962), *The Production and Distribution of Knowledge in the United States*, Princeton University Press.
3. Bell, Daniel (1973), *The Coming of Post-Industrial Society*, Harper.

4. Porat, Marc (1977), *The Information Economy: Definition and Measurement*, Government Printing Office, Washington, DC.
5. Economic and Social Research Council of the United Kingdom (2017), quoted in R. Bukht & R. Heeks (2017), Defining, Conceptualising and Measuring the Digital Economy, *International Organisations Research Journal*, 13, 143–72. 2017.
6. Gray, J. & Rumpe, B. (2015), Models for Digitalization, *Software and Systems Modeling*, 14, 1319–20. https://doi.org/10.1007/s10270-015-0494-9.
7. Metcalfe, Robert (2013), Metcalfe's Law after 40 Years of Ethernet, *Computer*, 46(12), 26–31.
8. Adera, Edith Ofwona, Waema, Timothy M., May, Julian, Mascarenhas, Ophelia, & Diga, Kathleen (Eds.) (2014), *ICT Pathways to Poverty Reduction: Empirical Evidence from East and Southern Africa*, International Development Research Centre, Ottawa.
9. World Bank (2016), *Digital Dividends*, World Bank Development Report. https://www.worldbank.org/en/publication/wdr2016.
10. See for example, META, UN Broadband Commission, Microsoft. https://farmradio.org/?s=How+to+use+information+and+communication+technologies+%28ICTs%29+to+interact+with+your+listeners%3A+Three+methods.
11. Qiang, C.Z.W., Rossotto, C.M., & Kimura, K. (2009), *Economic Impacts of Broadband. Information and Communications for Development*, World Bank. https://documents1.worldbank. org/curated/en/645821468337815208/071652160_201407217023713/ additional/487910PUB0EPI1101Official0Use0Only1.pdf.
12. Hardy, Andrew P. (1980), The Role of the Telephone in Economic Development, *Telecommunications Policy*, 4(4), 278–86.
13. See also Hudson, Heather E., Hardy, Andrew P., & Parker, Edwin B. (1982), Impact of Telephone and Satellite Earth Station Installations on GDP, *Telecommunications Policy*, 6(4), 300–7.
14. Roller, Lars-Hendrik & Waverman, Leonard (2001), Telecommunications Infrastructure and Economic Development: A Simultaneous Approach, *American Economic Review*, 91(4), 909–23.
15. Koutroumpis, Pantelis (2009), The Economic Impact of Broadband on Growth: A Simultaneous Approach, *Telecommunications Policy*, 33(9), 471–85.
16. Bertschek, I., Briglauer, W., Hüschelrath, K., Kauf, B., & Niebel, T. (2015). The Economic Impacts of Broadband Internet: A Survey, *Review of Network Economics*, 14(4), 201–27. https://doi.org/10.1515/rne-2016-0032.

17. Arvin, B.M. & Pradhan, R.P. (2014). Broadband Penetration and Economic Growth Nexus: Evidence from Cross-Country Panel Data, *Applied Economics*, 46(35), 4360–9. https://doi.org/10.1080/00036846.2014.957444.
18. García Zaballos, A. & López-Rivas, R. (2012), *Socioeconomic Impact of Broadband in Latin American and Caribbean Countries*. https://doi.org/10.18235/0009082.
19. Hjort, J. & Poulsen, J. (2019). The Arrival of Fast Internet and Employment in Africa, *American Economic Review*, 109(3), 1032–79. https://doi.org/10.1257/aer.20161385.
20. Abecassis, David, Kende, Michael, Teo, Dion, & Hussain, Nabeel (2021), *Economic and Social Impact of Meta's Submarine Cable Investments in APAC: Report for Meta*, Analysys Mason. https://www.analysysmason.com/consulting/reports/meta-submarine-cable-investments-asia/.
21. Whitacre, B., Gallardo, R., & Strover, S. (2014), Does Rural Broadband Impact Jobs and Income? Evidence from Spatial and First-Differenced Regressions, *The Annals of Regional Science*, 53(3), 649–70. http://dx.doi.org.ezproxy1.apus.edu/10.1007/s00168-014-0637-x.
22. Minges, Michael (2015), *Exploring the Relationship Between Broadband and Economic Growth*, World Development Report 2016 Background Paper, World Bank.
23. Hudson, Heather E. (1984), *When Telephones Reach the Village: The Role of Telecommunications in Rural Development*, Ablex.
24. Katz, R. & Callorda, F. (2018). *The Economic Contribution of Broadband, Digitization and ICT Regulation*, International Telecommunication Union. https://www.itu.int/en/ITU-D/Regulatory-Market/Documents/FINAL_1d_18-00513_Broadband-and-Digital-Transformation-E.pdf.
25. Jalava, Jukka & Pohjola, Matti, 2002. Economic Growth in the New Economy: Evidence from Advanced Economies, *Information Economics and Policy*, 14(2), 189–210.
26. OECD (2019) *Southeast Asia Going Digital – Connecting SMEs*. https://www.oecd.org/goingdigital/southeast-asia-connecting-SMEs.pdf.
27. J Mora-Rivera, J. & García-Mora, F. (2021), Internet Access and Poverty Reduction: Evidence from Rural and Urban Mexico, *Telecommunications Policy*, 45(2).
28. Adera, Edith Ofwona, Waema, Timothy M., May, Julian, Mascarenhas, Ophelia, & Diga, Kathleen (Eds.) (2014), *ICT Pathways to Poverty Reduction: Empirical Evidence from East and Southern Africa*, International Development Research Centre, Ottawa, p. 234.

29. Adera, Edith Ofwona, Waema, Timothy M., May, Julian, Mascarenhas, Ophelia & Diga, Kathleen (Eds.) (2014), *ICT Pathways to Poverty Reduction: Empirical Evidence from East and Southern Africa*, International Development Research Centre, Ottawa, p. 16.
30. Adera, Edith Ofwona, Waema, Timothy M., May, Julian, Mascarenhas, Ophelia, & Diga, Kathleen (Eds.) (2014), *ICT Pathways to Poverty Reduction: Empirical Evidence from East and Southern Africa*, International Development Research Centre, Ottawa, p. 236.
31. https://www.statista.com/statistics/270229/usage-duration-of-social-networks-by-country/.
32. Bridges.org (2005), *E-Readiness Assessment Tools Comparison 28 February 2005* (updated), Bridges.org. Accessed at http://www.bridges.org/files/active/0/ereadiness_tools_bridges_10Mar05.pdf.
33. ITU (n.d.), *The ICT Development Index*. /https://www.itu.int/en/ITU-D/Statistics/Pages/IDI/default.aspx. https://www.itu.int/hub/publication/D-IND-ICT_MDD-2025-1.
34. Economist Intelligence Unit. *E-Readiness Index*. https://www.eiu.com/public/topical_report.aspx?campaignid=TechReadiness.
35. OECD (2016), *OECD Economic Surveys: Ireland 2015*. https://www.oecd.org/en/publications/oecd-economic-surveys-ireland-2015_eco_surveys-irl-2015-en.html.
36. Duff, A. (2000). Joho shakai: The Japanese Contribution to Information Society Studies. Keio Communication Review, 22, 41–77.

3

DIGITAL LEARNING

Education and Training

> "The ability of citizens to deploy … technologies and digital services to enhance their livelihoods and wellbeing will be determined not only by affordable access or even their digital literacy to consume the service, but the education and skills to do so productively."
>
> – Razzano et al., *The Digital Economy and Society* (2020)[1]

Overview

Communications technologies have been used in education for decades. As Wilbur Schramm pointed out years ago, motivated students can learn from anything (teachers, books, radio, television, etc.).[2] In the 1940s, farmers gathered on the Canadian prairies to discuss radio programs about how to improve their crops. In Australia in 1950, teachers on the School of the Air began to communicate via two-way high frequency radio with children studying by correspondence on family sheep stations (ranches). Development agencies funded projects in the 1970s to reach schools in developing countries via radio and television broadcasts. Today, motivated learners around the world can now access online training, continuing education and university-level courses, often for free. But as Razzano and colleagues point out, they will need the education and skills to take advantage of these digital opportunities.

DOI: 10.4324/9781003431602-3

The following are the most common goals of digital learning in education and training:

- To augment classroom instruction, for example by adding supplemental materials, research resources, opportunities to practice skills, etc.
- To provide instruction in schools without qualified teachers (for example, to teach foreign languages or advanced science or mathematics courses).
- To provide continuing education and training, such as for high school completion for adults who have dropped out of school; to offer college courses in remote communities and at job sites; to provide training to qualify for jobs or promotions, etc.

These goals may also be combined with the need to save *time* and/or *money*: for example, to enable employees and teachers to upgrade qualifications in their communities rather than traveling to classes or taking leave of absence to attend distant meetings; or to stretch limited educational funds by teaching students simultaneously in several separate locations.

These various models of instruction are also classified as *formal education*, i.e. within existing institutional education systems, and *non-formal education*, i.e. outside these institutions – for example, community education, adult education and lifelong education. An analysis of digital connectivity use in distance- or e-education and training can also include the following categories:

- *Target population*: for example, school students; school teachers; adults who have not completed high school; adults seeking training; adults taking college-/university-level courses;
- *Content*: for example, required curriculum; elective content (art, music, languages, etc.); STEM (science, technology, engineering, and math); training- and employment-related content;
- *Technology:* internet/broadband; broadcast radio or television; devices: tablets or computers, mobile phones, or a combination of these;
- *Access:* free; payment required (by individual or institution such as school district or college); payment required to receive academic credit for completion.

Completion of courses, certificate programs, or degrees is generally a necessary step in the chain of inference to evaluate impacts of connectivity from online instruction to obtaining jobs and increasing income. But when motivation drops, or seemingly insurmountable barriers, such as family commitments or confusing content, discourage students, they tend to drop out. Traditional correspondence courses typically have low completion rates, as do online courses and free online university classes. As discussed below, interactivity, in the form of local or online tutors, study groups, and interactive instruction can improve completion rates.[3]

The COVID-19 pandemic dramatically increased use of the internet to reach students locked down in their homes in industrialized countries. Analysis at the state and national level in the United States found that three years after the pandemic lockdowns, many students still lagged behind, and average test scores were lower than before the pandemic. The U.S. National Center for Education Statistics (NCES) found that average test scores for 13-year-olds in reading and mathematics administered in 2022–2023 declined 4 points in reading and 9 points in mathematics compared to the previous assessment administered during the 2019–2020 school year.[4]

This macro-level analysis did not include variables such as internet access and speed at home, digital literacy skills, family size and distractions, etc. Evidence from research on effectiveness is mixed, with some students unable to access online instruction because of lack of available or affordable internet service, as well as reports of loneliness and boredom, and lower achievement on standardized tests for those studying remotely. Researchers found that in rural Michigan, many associations between broadband and educational outcomes (test scores, educational ambitions) were indirect. For example, fast broadband access was associated with higher rates of homework completion, which in turn was associated with higher grades (explaining about one-third of the variation in grades). Better home internet access was also associated with higher digital skills, which, in turn, were associated with better performance on standardized tests. The researchers point out: "These insights show that it is important to understand broadband as part of a broader ecosystem of teaching and learning that includes other media uses and activities."[5]

Technologies for Instruction: From Radio to Mobile Phones and Satellites

Interactive radio instruction (IRI) or interactive audio instruction (IAI) are effective means to use inexpensive technologies in education. IRI uses one-way radio to reach both students and their in-class teachers. Pre-recorded audio programs are delivered via mobile phones or MP3 players connected to a speaker or CD players. The radio or audio teacher delivers content and directs the in-class teachers to apply a variety of interactive instructional approaches such as singing songs, participating in individual and group work, answering questions, and performing certain learning tasks.[6] These radio projects use strategies similar to those pioneered in developing countries in the 1970s with radio used for direct instruction or for teacher training, often with interactive components.[7]

Cape Verde has used radio for instruction at both primary and secondary school levels. IRI programs provided Portuguese-language and mathematics instruction to Grade 4 to 8 students and teachers. Radio segments were 20 minutes in length and highly interactive, involving games, physical movement, and music. Evaluation data showed that children who had access to IRI tested better in Portuguese and math than children who did not. Radio Escola (School Radio) offered radio classes for secondary-school-age students who had left school. Students were sent printed materials to use with the radio programs to learn secondary-school subjects. Cape Verde has also used radio broadcasts to support teacher professional development, as well as to help the general population with Portuguese skills, environmental education, and other subjects.[8]

The proliferation of mobile phones and commensurate decreases in prices for devices and mobile broadband have enormous potential benefits for educational content design and delivery, data collection, distance learning, and support and coaching for teachers and students through text messaging (SMS) and VoIP (Voice over Internet Protocol) applications such as FaceTime and Skype. For example, in several African countries, "Instant Schools" provide a free digital learning platform without data charges for anyone on the Vodafone/Vodacom networks, hosting digital educational content in local languages and reaching more than 750,000 learners. In South Africa, where it is known as eSchool, the platform provides video lessons, homework questions, and interactive quizzes, along with tools for evaluating and rewarding progress.[9] Also in South Africa, Idea Digital Education has created core curriculum content for device-agnostic (mobile, tablet, and computer) delivery including STEM courses, virtual high school, and professional development for teachers. Its partners include national and state departments of education.[10]

Text2Teach, initiated in the Philippines in 2003 as Bridge IT, was designed to reach underfunded and neglected state primary schools and their communities, especially those in remote areas. Text2Teach provides full-access interactive multimedia packages in English, science, and math for Grades V and VI pupils as well as teacher training. Teachers are given mobile phones with pre-installed multimedia and video clips; a 29-inch color television; print-based teacher guides and folios in English, science, and math; and in-person training. Phones are connected to television via cable, and the teacher uses the multimedia and video clips and follows the guide to teach the lessons.[11] A summative evaluation found that exposure to Text2Teach as an intervention led to significantly higher learning gains in English, science, and math at both grade levels, although improvements varied across provinces, and girls improved more than boys.[12]

Indonesian students are among the world's highest users of technology in education, with more than two-thirds of Indonesian students using smartphones for studying in class and an even larger total (more than 80 percent) using smartphones to do their homework.[13] Ruangguru, a for-profit venture, is the largest marketplace for private tutoring in Indonesia, connecting prospective students with more than 80,000 private tutors.[14] Ruangguru states that 70 percent of its users in Indonesia come from middle- to low-income families and had no previous access to after-school instruction.[15]

Students in isolated Alaska villages and in the Australian outback now take courses online and communicate with distant teachers via satellite. In Alaska, local wireless or optical fiber networks connect schools to satellite earth stations serving the village, whereas in Australia individual farms have small satellite antennas communicating via Low Earth Orbiting (LEO) satellites.

Reaching Remote Students

A pioneer in distance education, Australia's Alice Springs School of the Air continues more than 70 years after its founding to teach children who live in an area of more than 1.3 million square kilometers in remote outback Australia. "The world's largest classroom" offers a wide range of educational services and activities from pre-school to Year 9. Students are supervised at home by home tutors, typically parents or guardians. Instead of using two-way radios, today the students and teachers communicate online, with most students using LEO satellite internet technology to access their online lessons and resources via high-definition videoconferencing.[16]

High school graduation or equivalent certification (often also called GED, General Educational Diploma) is typically a requirement for many jobs and an entry requirement for any postsecondary education or training. Some free sites offer reviews and practice tests to prepare for GED examinations. Online help and in-person tutoring can be critical for some students to succeed. For example, in northern Ontario, Canada, there are no high schools in the remote First Nations communities; teenagers must leave home to attend high school in distant towns or cities. The Keewaytinook Internet High School (KiHS) is a partnership between an Indigenous communications provider and the Ontario education ministry for students who did not complete high school. KiHS provides conferencing, email, and other online services for students studying to receive their high school diplomas in these Ojibway and Cree communities.[17]

Begun with a handful of students in 1999, KiHS is now an asynchronous online high school with a range of more than 80 courses that range from applied to academic, and from workplace preparation to university preparation.[18] Local mentors in the remote Indigenous communities have helped the students to qualify for jobs or training in health care, education, and local government. KiHS has also partnered with the Cisco Online Academy to offer computer and network-based training for a variety of skill levels.

Although faced with similar isolation, students in Alaska villages face a different problem. All Alaska communities with at least 10 students must offer kindergarten through grade 12 so that students do not have to leave home to complete high school. However, the result is that village schools may have only a couple of teachers who must teach students at all grade levels. Teachers use online sources to supplement their lessons and materials. High school students may take online courses in sciences, mathematics, foreign languages, and other subjects as part of their high school curriculum. "Schools have embraced webinars; students can take courses from Pennsylvania or Wyoming; students can [even] take music lessons online."[19] Some high school students also take college classes before they finish high school. A school district in southwestern Alaska is on a standards-based system, so that once students finish a standard they can move on, and many complete high school early. If students want to continue schooling, they can take online courses for college credit. Teachers also often require students to use the internet outside of class to complete homework or projects. One teacher noted: "Most of the students are required to go online to finish up homework projects online. We … require students to download their assignments and then send them to the teacher."[20]

Indigenous organizations may also share training materials online. For example, KNet in northern Ontario, which manages KiHS, uploads training videos to YouTube and archives webcasts that can be streamed by remote communities as needed. Alaska Native organizations also share training materials for village governments on YouTube. The First Mile Connectivity Consortium (FMCC), representing Indigenous communications providers, argued that YouTube is an important development tool and not a luxury at regulatory hearings on broadband as a basic service in Canada.[21]

After the pandemic, rural schools across the United States faced a shortage of teachers in specialized subjects. Recruiting agencies now supply virtual teachers in subjects such as world languages, special education, science, and math. These agencies recruit teachers from retirees and those who want to work part time, as well as those with U.S. teaching credentials from other countries such as Mexico, the Philippines, and South Africa. For example, students in rural Arizona take Spanish lessons via interactive video from a teacher working from home in North Carolina, helped by a local classroom coach. Also, some states have designed facilities to transmit STEM courses to disadvantaged rural students. In Alabama, a non-profit and architectural firm created what they call the Connected Rural Classroom, a high-tech room designed to provide STEM classes virtually to some of Alabama's poorest regions. Anecdotal feedback from teachers who have taught classes remotely was that the format has promise but will never fully replicate teaching in person. Teachers said that the quality can vary widely, based on whether the district hires a consistently available adult to help inside the classroom.[22]

Teacher Training

Digital technologies can also help to upgrade teachers' skills and aid them with adoption of digital tools and resources in the classroom. For many teachers, mobile-based professional development can provide a lifeline to learning. Applications on mobile phone apps, such as social media, messaging apps, video, and audio can be used for professional development that can be personalized and available to teachers where they work in place of, or to augment, in-person training.

Research in South Africa examined how teaching and learning were affected in rural schools after a three-year mobile technology implementation project. The project involved providing mobile tablets to all teachers and schools, training the teachers through a university accredited course, training ICT technicians to support teachers, and doing a baseline and endline survey. Results indicated that 97 percent of the teachers would continue to use mobile technology for teaching rather than traditional teaching. The teachers also indicated that, for them, the most outstanding benefit of the training was to learn new teaching strategies. Teachers reported an 80 percent improvement in school attendance and that learners were much more involved and eager to learn when using mobile tablets in the schools.[23]

In rural Papua New Guinea, few students could read at grade level, and teachers often did not know what lessons they were to cover in a given week or how to teach them effectively. However, most of the teachers in the target rural area had mobile phones. The SMS Story project sent daily text message stories and teaching tips to teachers as an aid to help improve student reading. The SMS messages reminded and motivated teachers to teach reading every day. The results were that while comprehension did not noticeably improve among literate students, the intervention halved the number of children who could not read at all.[24]

Community Access to E-learning

In Mauritius, The National Computer Board operates two "Cyber Caravans" that travel to communities to provide ICT training. The Cyber Caravans are equipped with laptops and broadband internet. Free training is available to the community at large on topics such as ICT literacy, use of common software packages, coding, and ICT awareness for senior citizens.[25]

Cape Verde has also provided ICT training in the form of WebLab, an after-school program operating in its secondary schools. WebLab activities are held in a secure solar-paneled shipping container on the school grounds. The containers have high-speed internet connectivity and are outfitted with a smartboard, laptops, tablets, technology repair kits, and other technology components.

In remote regions of Alaska, a project called OWL (Online with Libraries) has upgraded village libraries with broadband connectivity and videoconferencing equipment. Librarians help residents to find and download materials: "Since we have broadband and then wireless, kids have been coming up [to the village library] a lot … Instead of books, we provide Kindles. We download different sets of materials geared toward different ages … kids love using the Kindle books."[26] Residents can also access webinars, videoconferences, and online instruction. For example, an adult took a Yup'ik course online, and did coursework in the library. Some older students have taken online courses at the library to get their high school diplomas. A teacher of a popular aviation class offered the course over the OWL network from the library in his community. Residents can also use the OWL network to complete online classes required for occupational endorsements for jobs in their communities.

The Indigenous Havasupai village of Supai, Arizona, is the most remote community in the contiguous United States, at the bottom of the Grand Canyon. Supplies are flown in by helicopter or transported by mule train. The tribe deploys their own community wireless network so that now residents can pursue teaching degrees and training at home. Havasupai Elementary School teachers stated that access to the high-speed wireless network significantly decreased the time they need to obtain credentials from Northern Arizona University. Tribal leaders assume that these teachers with access to online resources will be able to provide more effective instruction and support for expectant mothers, young children, and kindergarten through to 12th Grade (K–12) students.[27]

In rural and developing regions around the world, where the internet is accessible, motivated individuals may also take advantage of online tutorials and videos to gain or improve their skills. For example, a young IT manager at an adult education center in Soweto (South Africa) completed a Microsoft certification course online. A mechanic in an Alaska village learned how to repair appliances from online videos.[28] A young piano student from Pakistan taught himself percussive guitar from online videos, and used the internet to showcase his music. One of his songs went viral, and, the following year, he shared a stage in Edinburgh with one of his online idols.[29]

Reaching Displaced Persons, Refugees, and Conflict Zones

Interactive radio instruction has been used to reach internally displaced persons (IDPs), particularly children and youth. For example, for the Somali Interactive Radio Instruction Program (SIRIP), community educators, and leaders developed instructional content to replace and supplement formal education in math and reading for approximately 330,000 IDP students on the outskirts of Mogadishu, as well as out-of-school students and those in alternative schools (for example, Qu'ran and community schools) across Somalia.

Mobile connectivity provides access to education for IDPs and refugees in the "Instant Network Schools" project established with collaboration of the Vodafone Foundation and the United Nations High Commissioner for Refugees (UNHCR) in seven refugee camps in Kenya, Tanzania, South Sudan, and the Democratic Republic of Congo (DRC). Instant Network Schools connect classrooms to the internet and provide equipment, software, and teacher training to deliver digital educational content to around 50,000 students each within refugee camps.[30]

In rural Burkina Faso, "Local children did not go completely without education after the jihadist incursion thanks to the Radio Education Programme (REP), which provides educational material for young people who cannot attend school due to the insecurity."[31] A regional radio station broadcasts educational programs that can reach 200,000 to 300,000 students, many without access to classrooms. A pilot scheme supported by the United Nations Children's Fund (UNICEF) provided 70 families in a village with a radio, flash drive, and solar panel so that teachers and students could listen to the radio and access recorded materials. Students could listen at home or at school, where the teacher listened with the students and helped them with the lessons in math, reading and writing.[32]

In 2021, about 1.1 million Afghan girls attended secondary school. Then, under Taliban rule, girls in Afghanistan were prohibited from attending school past sixth grade and were banned from universities and from working at most jobs. In 2023, the World Economic Forum ranked Afghanistan last of 146 countries in a study on gender gaps.[33] Several organizations now offer clandestine online education to reach these isolated girls and women in their homes. SOLAx is a WhatsApp-based online academy operated by the School of Leadership, Afghanistan (SOLA), a boarding school for girls originally based in Kabul that now operates from Rwanda. SOLAx offers asynchronous classwork in three languages (English, Pashto, and Dari) by texting the SOLAx chatbot on WhatsApp. Since SOLAx requires only a smartphone and a basic mobile connection, it is intended to provide equal access to education for girls from lower-income families and from rural areas.[34]

Herat Online School offers online live and recorded classes in Persian through a network of more than 400 volunteer teachers and administrative staff from around the world.[35] The Afghanistan Law & Political Science Association (ALPA), an association of Afghan scholars in exile, offers free college-level courses to Afghan girls and women in tenth grade through graduate school and beyond. Topics range from the hard sciences to the arts, human rights, critical thinking, gender studies, and scholarship preparation.[36] These clandestine online classes rely on access to connectivity which may not be available to all Afghan households, and they have been occasionally disconnected by the Taliban. They also rely on donations of time by volunteer instructors and funds to cover administrative and operational costs.

Digital Skills

Lack of digital literacy – understanding the basic uses of computers, for example – or fear of trying new technologies can discourage teachers from adopting digital tools in the classroom, and discourage adult learners. Digital literacy is therefore the primary focus of some online training programs, to prepare teachers and others expected to use digital services, while other programs are designed to provide training to children and to adults in general.

The technology start-up Pinnguaq teaches computer and coding skills to residents of Inuit communities in Canada's far north. To cope with connectivity challenges and lack of devices, Pinnguaq developed offline open-source training programs for coding that are stored on USB flash drives and provided to training participants.[37] Today, the staff act as digital stewards who facilitate Pinnguaq's digital skills workshops, camps, and classroom visits. They provide training in coding, digital arts, 3D arts, and digital storytelling.[38]

Online training is also used in business. For example, the Mobile Internet Skills Training Toolkit (MISTT) was developed by GSMA for mobile operators. Available in Bengali, English, French, Hindi, and Kinyarwanda, MISTT uses a "train the trainers" approach; staff from the mobile operator train sales agents who then teach customers. MISTT has been used in countries throughout South Asia and Africa. South Africa-based operator MTN offers MISTT in eight African countries and has trained over 18 million people.[39]

Some online training resources are designed specifically for employees and others who want to improve professional and business skills. Codeacademy is an online interactive platform that provides coding classes in several programming languages as well as other

IT topics such as cybersecurity, data analytics, game development, and web design. It was founded in 2011 and then acquired by Skilsoft, which "partners with enterprise organizations and serves a global community to prepare today's employees for tomorrow's economy." It offers subscription plans for individuals, students, and teams.[40]

University Courses

Universities have offered extension courses since the days when students received study materials and sent in assignments by mail, often with long delays in receiving corrected assignments and test results. In the 1960s, some universities began to transmit lectures over public or educational television channels. This model for distance higher education builds on existing institutions to extend their geographical or demographic reach. Another higher education model is an independent open university. There are now at least 65 open universities throughout the world, including in South Africa, India, and the Philippines, with most offering online or hybrid instruction as well as online materials and interaction or tutoring.[41]

Instead of extending the outreach of existing universities, the Open University (OU) in the UK was established as a separate educational institution. Since it was established in 1969, more than 2.3 million students have taken its distance education courses with video materials co-produced by the BBC. More than two-thirds of the students work full or part time; the OU is also a major provider of higher education for people with disabilities.[42] Its OpenLearn is a free learning resources website that offers short courses as well as study materials in a variety of formats.[43]

The University of South Africa (UNISA) is Africa's largest distance education institution. More than 370,000 students enroll annually; 71 percent are women; and 62 percent are "mature students" between the ages of 25 and 39 years. UNISA offers a wide range of study fields at levels from certificate to degree.[44] UNISA traces its history to the founding of the University of the Cape of Good Hope in 1873. In 1959, it became the world's first dedicated correspondence university; until 1994, it was the only way most Black South Africans could access higher education.[45] UNISA Open Learning provides free access to introductory modules; students then pay tuition fees for modules to complete their qualifications.

In Canada, Athabasca University in Alberta is also a stand-alone open university. Established by the Alberta government in 1970, Athabasca began as a traditional campus-based institution, but early on shifted primarily to distance education, initially with printed materials, televised lectures, and taped audio and video content. In the 1980s, Athabasca pioneered the offering of computer-based online courses, and today it is one of the world's major distance education universities with more than 40,000 students worldwide.[46] The university also enables Indigenous residents in remote communities to study online and offers Indigenous-focused courses as well as support to assist Indigenous students.[47]

In the Caribbean and the South Pacific, regional universities offer distance education courses online and through extension centers. The University of the West Indies (UWI) has campuses in Jamaica, Barbados, Trinidad and Tobago, and Antigua and Barbuda. The University of the West Indies Distance Teaching Experiment (UWIDITE) was an initiative funded by USAID to link its campuses and extension centers.[48] The telecommunications system was first used in St. Lucia, Dominica, Antigua, and Grenada to provide access to courses in non-campus territories. The Open Campus (UWIOC), approved in 2007, has facilities in 17 English-speaking countries and territories in the Caribbean. Tutors online and at extension centers help students with their coursework. Some courses are also taught online. The Open Campus offers distance and face-to-face mode certificate, diploma, and degree programs.[49]

The University of the South Pacific (USP) serves a population spread over 33 million square kilometers of ocean.[50] Its main campus is in Fiji and its agricultural school is located in Samoa. In addition to these locations, it has local campus centers in 10 countries and territories across the South Pacific islands. USP states that it has more than "30 years' experience in digital delivery," but its (analog) connectivity began in the 1970s with satellite-delivered tutorials and administrative support to reach students throughout the region, who gathered at their local USP extension centers.[51] Today, USP offers online and hybrid courses throughout the South Pacific. Evidence from both UWI and USP has shown that interactivity with local and online tutors and with other students can contribute to a reduction in dropout rates.[52]

Traditional universities may also offer degree and continuing education programs primarily for working adults. Some, such as Stanford, began by offering specialized technical courses. Fifty years ago, Stanford established the Honors Co-op Program in its engineering school at the request of tech companies (in what became known as Silicon Valley) to enable their employees to complete master's degrees without wasting time commuting to campus. The approach was what the director called "candid classroom"; regular on-campus courses were televised over special frequencies to employees at their workplaces.[53] Two-way audio enabled remote students to ask questions and participate in the class. Today, the program has evolved into Stanford Online,[54] which offers graduate courses in engineering worldwide, as well as continuing and professional education in many fields through the Stanford Engineering Center for Global & Online Education.[55]

MOOCs

Several institutions, including universities, non-profit organizations, and for-profit businesses, now offer postsecondary education and training courses to students worldwide. Globally available free online courses are known as MOOCs, Massive Open Online Courses. Examples discussed below include Khan Academy, Coursera, Udacity, and Udemy, several of which allow free access to courses but charge for certificates or other completion credentials.

Khan Academy

Khan Academy's mission is "to provide a free, world-class education to anyone, anywhere." It provides free online lessons and practice in math, sciences, and humanities from kindergarten through early college. Teachers can also use the content to personalize learning and increase student engagement. Khan Academy is also using artificial intelligence to provide a tutor and teaching assistant called Khanmigo to help students with content and practice exercises and guide them through structured problem solving.[56]

With about 150 employees and $64 million in expenses, Khan Academy relies primarily on funding from foundations and large corporations, particularly in tech-related fields, as well as individual donors and trusts. About 15 percent of the budget is spent on administration, including fund raising.[57] It claims to have more than 150 million registered users in 190 countries, using 56 languages. Outside North America, 19 percent of users are from Asia, 14 percent from Latin America, but only 3 percent from Africa.[58] Translating and adapting curricula to local contexts appears necessary to achieve significant course utilization and impact. Khan states that they are adapting curricula in countries including India, Brazil, Peru, and South Africa.

Research at Peru's Daniel Alcides Carrión National University (UNDAC) found that persistent use of Khan Academy materials had a meaningful and positive impact on mathematics learning among university students at UNDAC. The study found that the platform both improved content mastery and fostered learning autonomy.[59]

Research including 157 elementary schools in Brazil found that weekly usage of Khan Academy resulted in positive effects on math scores and attitudes towards math when implemented *with adequate support* (italics added).[60] A randomized-control trial with about 3,500 third- through sixth-grade students in El Salvador found that supplemental use of Khan Academy resulted in better math scores than teacher-only interventions.[61] The World Bank observes that the success of the program [in schools] is a function of teacher skills and engagement; schools and government administrations should support teachers throughout the period of implementation.[62]

Khan Academy itself states:

> Every year, more than 100 million people come to Khan Academy to learn. By using Khan Academy for 30 minutes a week over the course of the school year, students can completely change their academic trajectory. Last year, 1.5 million people reached that level of learning.[63]

However, the implications of these data are not clear. Do they imply that more than 98 percent of those who register do not achieve that level? Do these learners benefit anyway?

Coursera

Founded in 2012 by two Stanford professors, Coursera's goal is to "provide universal access to world-class learning." With more than 136 million registered learners, it is one of the world's largest online learning platforms. Its clients include individual students as well as businesses, governments, and universities.

Its strategy is to partner with leading university and industry sources to offer a wide range of content as well as credentials including specializations, certificates, and bachelor's and master's degrees. Coursera is a for-profit enterprise. Learners can watch video lectures for free and then pay to earn course certificates upon completion. Institutions can pay for seat license subscriptions or enterprise license agreements.[64]

Udacity

Udacity is another for-profit training platform offering courses in artificial intelligence, cloud computing, cybersecurity, data science, product management, and executive leadership. Udacity was founded after two (other) Stanford University instructors offered a free online course in "Introduction to Artificial Intelligence," and found that more than 160,000 students enrolled from more than 190 countries. Clients include national governments as well as businesses and individuals. Striving to be "audacious for you, the student," Udacity offers "nanodegrees," i.e. certificates for completing course sequences. Udacity is now owned by Accenture.[65]

Udemy

Udemy is also a for-profit online platform for skills development, targeting organizations and enterprises as well as individuals. It offers content provided by "real world experts." For example, in the year following the launch of ChatGPT in November 2022, Udemy stated that about 800 instructors created and published more than 1,000 courses related to ChatGPT on its platform, with more than 2.2 million enrollments. Courses were developed in 25 languages, with the largest number of learners from India, the United States, Japan, Mexico, and the UK.[66]

Udemy relies on individual instructors to provide content. Instructors set the prices for their courses within Udemy's tier guidelines, and receive compensation based on number of enrollments as well as a share of total revenue and other incentives.

Commentary

The lack of evaluation of most of the projects and applications described above – and many others – hinders efforts to identify both the best practices and the problems and strategies to overcome them. For development projects, part of the reason for limited research appears to be lack of funding for evaluation by donors. Funders such as USAID and the Gates Foundation have required independent evaluation, but many others, including the private sector, do not. Also, researchers who find separate funding for project evaluation may initiate data collection only after the project is underway, which eliminates the opportunity to use before/after research designs. They may also face limitations on access to existing data or restrictions on field research. And, as Burns and Santally point out, at least in sub-Saharan Africa, research that does exist has not been widely disseminated among educators and policymakers, and national and regional educational technology initiatives have failed to incorporate research findings.[67]

There is sufficient evidence, however, to support the following generalizations:

Projects that focus primarily on providing technology are not likely to succeed. It is important to relate content and approach to established curricula and the local context. For example, the importance of addressing priority teaching needs and providing adequate teacher training and support was illustrated in the much publicized but generally unsuccessful One Laptop per Child (OLPC) initiative. Founded at Massachusetts Institute of Technology (MIT) in 2005, OLPC has distributed more than 3 million laptops with the goal of empowering children by providing digital devices at an affordable price.[68] Although they increased access to digital technologies, the OLPC programs varied in their implementation and impacts on learning.

> In a meta-analysis of 15 studies of OLPC programs in five countries (China, Colombia, Ecuador, India, and Peru), only the programs that accompanied the distribution of laptops with some level of guidance, from providing training courses to using adaptive software for weekly sessions, improved learning.[69]

OLPC now states: "Today we have gone back to our core fundamentals which are learning through technology, not the technology in itself. Technology is a means, not an objective."[70]

Interactivity aids motivation and retention. Whether it be incorporating student activities, questions from teachers or local tutors, or online interaction, interactivity can improve motivation and learning outcomes. Interactive support from local tutors or online assistance and study groups can reduce dropout rates among adult learners. AI applications are now being introduced to interact with students to help them practice skills and solve problems.

Engagement of teachers is critical. For classroom instruction, at all phases from pre-project planning to training in technology and from use and pedagogical techniques to ongoing support, the engagement of teachers is likely to be critical for short-term success and longer-term adoption.

Online content can enrich and expand school curricula. This is especially the case in regions with a shortage of specialized teachers. Telecourses, in which one teacher would teach a course that could be transmitted to several schools, were initially rejected by many classroom teachers as a threat to their jobs. Today, telecourses help to fill gaps where there are teacher shortages, especially in STEM fields and additional languages.

Content quality varies. Among adult education platforms such as MOOCs, the content quality can be uneven with some platforms adapting or disseminating online courses from accredited institutions, while others simply offer a list of topics from self-appointed instructors.

Demand for skills credentials is growing. Some MOOC providers generate income by charging for certificates or other credentials for successful completion of courses or modules. The "e-credential" market is estimated to reach $20 billion by 2028, with a compound annual growth rate exceeding 13 percent.[71]

References

1. Razzano, Gabriella with Alison Gillwald, Pablo Aguera, Shamira Ahmed, Enrico Calandro, Cecilia Matanga, Andrew Rens and Anri Van Der Spuy (2020), *The Digital Economy and Society*, Research ICT Africa. https://researchictafrica.net/research/sadc-pf-discussion-paper-the-digital-economy-and-society/.
2. Schramm, Wilbur & Chu, Godwin (1975), *Learning from Television: What the Research Says*. National Association of Educational Broadcasters (NAEB).
3. Hudson, Heather E. (2008), Communication Technology and Development, *The International Encyclopedia of Communication*, Blackwell.
4. https://www.nationsreportcard.gov/highlights/ltt/2023/.
5. Hampton, K., Fernandez, L., Robertson, C., & Bauer, J. (2021, February) Repercussions of Poor Broadband Connectivity for Students in Rural and Small Town Michigan, TPRC48: The 48th Research Conference on Communication, Information and Internet Policy, http://dx.doi.org/10.2139/ssrn.3749644.
6. Burns, Mary & Santally, Mohammad Issack (2019, November 1), *ICT in Secondary Education in Sub-Saharan Africa: Policies, Practices, Trends and Recommendations*, Education Development Center, Washington, DC, p. 21.
7. See Hudson, Heather E. (1984), *When Telephones Reach the Village: The Role of Telecommunications in Rural Development*. Ablex.
8. Burns, Mary and Santally, Mohammad Issack (2019, November 1), *ICT in Secondary Education in Sub-Saharan Africa: Policies, Practices, Trends and Recommendations*, Education Development Center, Washington, DC, p. 24.
9. See https://www.vodacom.co.za/vodacom/shopping/v/vodacom-e-learning.

10. https://www.ideaonline.com/.
11. Burns, M. (2023). *Distance Education for Teacher Training: Modes, Models and Methods* (2nd edition), Education Development Center, Washington, DC.
12. Natividad, Josefina N. (n.d.), *Summative Evaluation of the Elsa Text-2Teach Project: Final Report.* University of the Philippines Diliman Quezon City.
13. Abecassis, David, Kende, Michael, Teo, Dion, & Hussain, Nabeel. (2021), *Economic and Social Impact of Meta's Submarine Cable Investments in APAC: Report for META*. Analysys Mason. https://www.analysysmason.com/contentassets/0c7320380f594f59885246a8918a2fce/analysys_mason_meta_submarine_cable_asia_study.pdf.
14. https://www.forbes.com/profile/ruangguru/.
15. https://www.atlassianfoundation.org/partners/ruangguru.
16. Alice Springs School of the Air. https://www.assoa.nt.edu.au/.
17. See http://kihs.knet.ca/.
18. https://kihs.knet.ca/.
19. Hudson, Heather E. (2015, June), *After Broadband: An Analysis of Organizational Use of Broadband in Southwest Alaska*, Institute of Social and Economic Research, University of Alaska Anchorage.
20. Hudson, Heather E. (2015, June), *After Broadband: An Analysis of Organizational Use of Broadband in Southwest Alaska,* Institute of Social and Economic Research, University of Alaska Anchorage.
21. First Mile Connectivity Consortium (2015), *Testimony in CRTC Telecom Notice of Consultation 2015-134: Review of Basic Telecommunications Services*, Ottawa.
22. Randazzo, Sara (2023, August 26), Welcome Back to School. Your Teacher Is 2,000 Miles Away, *Wall Street Journal*.
23. Herselman, M.E., Botha, A., Maremi, K.J., Dlamini, S.B., & Marais, M.A. (2020), *Mobile Technology Affecting Teaching and Learning in Rural Schools*. http://hdl.handle.net/10204/11736.
24. World Bank (2016), *Digital Dividends*, World Bank Development Report. https://www.worldbank.org/en/publication/wdr2016.
25. Burns, Mary & Santally, Mohammad Issack (2019, November 1), *ICT in Secondary Education in Sub-Saharan Africa: Policies, Practices, Trends and Recommendations*, Education Development Center, Washington, DC, p. 24.
26. Hudson, Heather E. (2015, June), *After Broadband: An Analysis of Organizational Use of Broadband in Southwest Alaska*, Institute of Social and Economic Research, University of Alaska Anchorage.

27. Triggs, Mariel (2018, October), Tribal DIY: Self-Deploying High-Speed Internet Networks on Remote Tribal Lands in the United States, *Northern Public Affairs*.
28. Author, personal observations from fieldwork.
29. World Bank (2016) *Digital Dividends*, World Bank Development Report, p. 112. https://www.worldbank.org/en/publication/wdr2016.
30. Burns, Mary & Santally, Mohammad Issack (2019, November 1), ICT in Secondary Education in Sub-Saharan Africa: Policies, Practices, Trends and Recommendations, Education Development Center, Washington, DC.
31. Èlia Borràs (2023, October 29), "'Good morning, children': Burkina Faso Radio Station Aids Learning Amid Jihadist Disruption." *Guardian*.
32. Èlia Borràs (2023, October 29) "'Good morning, children': Burkina Faso radio station aids learning amid jihadist disruption." *Guardian*.
33. World Economic Forum (2023, June) *Global Gender Gap Report 2023*. https://www3.weforum.org/docs/WEF_GGGR_2023.pdf.
34. https://www.sola-afghanistan.org/introducing-solax.
35. https://www.afghanistaneducationaction.org/heratonlineschool.html.
36. Housman, Patty (2024, January 17), Afghan Scholars-in-Exile Providing Online Education for Girls Living under Taliban. https://www.american.edu/cas/news/afghan-scholars-providing-education-for-girls-under-taliban.cfm.
37. Laidlaw, Katherine (2017, September 18), This Startup is Teaching Coding to Canada's Most Isolated Kids, *Wired*. http://www.wired.co.uk/article/pinnguaq-nunavut-computer-science-education-canada.
38. https://pinnguaq.com.
39. ITU (2022), *Global Connectivity Report 2022*, International Telecommunication Union, p. 51. https://www.itu.int/itu-d/reports/statistics/global-connectivity-report-2022/.
40. https:/skilsoft.com/technology-skills.
41. https://teachonline.ca/tools-trends/universities.
42. https://about.open.ac.uk/strategy-and-policies/facts-and-figures.
43. https://www.open.edu/openlearn/.
44. https://www.unisa.ac.za/sites/corporate/default/About/Facts-&-figures/Student-enrolments?lang=01.
45. https://www.unisa.ac.za/sites/corporate/default/Unisa-150-year-celebration.
46. https://www.athabascau.ca/about-au/history.html.
47. https://www.athabascau.ca/au-advantage/indigenous-studies-support.html.

48. Edwards-Henry, A & Thurab-Nkhosi, D. (n.d.), *The Evolution of Policy to Meet the Challenges of Distance: The Case of UWI Open Campus.* https://wikieducator.org/images/0/08/PID_252.pdf.
49. Marrett, Christine (1989), Interactive Distance Teaching in the Caribbean, *Journal of Distance Education*, 4(2).
50. https://www.usp.ac.fj/why-usp/our-impact/.
51. Hudson, Heather E. (1990), *Communications Satellites: Their Development and Impact*. Free Press.
52. See the experience of the University of the South Pacific and the University of the West Indies discussed in Heather E. Hudson (2006), *From Rural Village to Global Village: Telecommunications and Development in the Information Age.* Routledge.
53. Personal experience of the author.
54. https://cgoe.stanford.edu/.
55. https://cgoe.stanford.edu/.
56. https://www.khanmigo.ai/.
57. Khan Academy Annual Report SY22-23. https://s3.amazonaws.com/KA-share/annualreport/SY22-23+Annual+Report_Final.pdf#finances.
58. https://www.khanacademy.org/about.
59. Ruiz, F.A.Z., Lovatón, R.M., Rivera, W.F.R., Mayhua, J.A.C., & Dávila, V.L.A. (2023). Khan Academy Platform for Mathematics Teaching and Learning, *Migration Letters*, 20(11), 767–78.
60. Ferman, Bruno, Finamor, Lucas, & Lima, Lycia (2019, June 27), Are Public Schools Ready to Integrate Math Classes with Khan Academy? https://mpra.ub.uni-muenchen.de/94736/1/MPRA_paper_94736.pdf.
61. Buchela, Konstantin, Jakobb, Martina, Kuhnhanss, Christoph, Steena, Daniel, & Brunettia, Aymo (2019), Expanding School Time and the Value of Computer-Assisted Learning: Evidence from a Randomized Controlled Trial in El Salvador. https://www.consciente.ch/wp-content/uploads/2019/05/CALImpact_Evaluation_Report_April19.pdf.
62. World Bank (2016) *Digital Dividends*, World Bank Development Report. https://www.worldbank.org/en/publication/wdr2016.
63. https://blog.khanacademy.org/why-khan-academy-will-be-using-skills-to-proficient-to-measure-learning-outcomes/.
64. Coursera Investor Presentation Q3 2023. (2023, October 26). https://s27.q4cdn.com/928340662/files/doc_financials/2023/q3/COUR_Presentation_Q3-2023.pdf.
65. https://www.udacity.com/about-us.
66. Udemy (2023, November 28), *ChatGPT's First Year: Udemy Data Highlights Unprecedented Global Demand for Generative AI Skills.* https://investors.udemy.com/node/9141/pdf.

67. Burns, Mary & Santally, Mohammad Issack. (2019) *ICT in Secondary Education in Sub-Saharan Africa: Policies, Practices, Trends and Recommendations*, Education Development Center, Washington, DC, p. 59.
68. https://laptop.org/aboutolpc/.
69. Arias Ortiz, Elena & Julián Cristia (2014), *The IDB and Technology in Education: How to Promote Effective Programs?*, Inter-American Development Bank. https://publications.iadb.org/en/publications/english/viewer/The-IDB-and-Technology-in-Education-How-to-Promote-Effective-Programs.pdf.
70. https:/laptop.org/aboutolpc/.
71. EINPresswire (2023, August 1), Micro-Credential Market to Witness Massive Growth by 2028 | Coursera, edX, Udacity. https://www.einpresswire.com/article/647552567/micro-credential-market-to-witness-massive-growth-by-2028-coursera-edx-udacity.

4

TELEMEDICINE AND E-HEALTH

> "Whether healthcare enterprises are ready or not, the new reality is that virtual care has arrived."
>
> – Wosik et al.[1]

Digital technologies are increasingly involved in health care delivery. Telemedicine refers to the use of communications technologies for patient diagnosis and treatment. Telehealth or e-health is a broader term that may include health education and public health applications of ICTs. The World Health Organization (WHO) defines e-health as "the cost-effective and secure use of information and communications technologies in support of health and health-related fields, including health-care services, health surveillance, health literature, and health education, knowledge and research."[2] E-Health is frequently used interchangeably with "digital health," although WHO has adopted an expanded definition:

> digital health is understood to mean "the field of knowledge and practice associated with the development and use of digital technologies to improve health." Digital health expands the concept of eHealth to include digital consumers, with a wider range of smart and connected devices. It also encompasses other uses of digital technologies for health such as the Internet of Things, advanced

DOI: 10.4324/9781003431602-4

computing, big data analytics, artificial intelligence including machine learning, and robotics.[3]

Digital technologies including the internet can be used to support a range of health services for rural communities, including the following:

- **Emergencies**: to summon immediate medical assistance both locally and from emergency responders in distant locations (such as medical evacuations by plane);
- **Consultation**: between primary health care providers and regional physicians, or between regional physicians and distant specialists;
- **Remote diagnosis**: for example, transmission of medical data and images; interpretation of data by distant specialists;
- **Patient monitoring**: for example, transmission of patient data from home or rural clinic, often coupled with follow-up by local medical staff;
- **Training and continuing education**: of health care workers, paraprofessionals, physicians, etc.;
- **Public health education**: of particular populations, such as expectant mothers, mothers of young children, groups susceptible to contagious diseases, etc.;
- **Administration**: ordering and delivery of medications and supplies; coordination of logistics such as field visits of medical staff; transmission of billing data, etc.;
- **Electronic medical records**: accessible to health care providers and patients to coordinate care and share information;
- **Data collection**: collection of public health information such as epidemiological data on outbreaks of diseases;
- **Research and information sharing**: such as access to medical databases and libraries, and consultation with distant experts and peers.[4]

Other applications may include:

- **Tele-triage**, such as fast-tracking emergency decisions by transmission of health parameters and remote consultation;

- **Guided self-help**, such as for the delivery of psychological interventions in mental health (for example, provided through a smartphone, website or book), with brief support delivered by a person over the telephone or online.[5]

There has been considerable research on the impacts of telemedicine in rural and isolated contexts. In emergencies, or in remote areas where it is impossible to get a critically ill patient to a hospital, telemedicine consultations may save lives. Teleconsultations may also make it possible to get advice from distant specialists. In addition to improving health outcomes, telemedicine may save money by facilitating treatment of patients in their communities without evacuation to hospitals, or by enabling them to return home sooner for follow-up monitoring. Connectivity also allows health care providers to share knowledge and advice, such as through grand rounds online, and to access training remotely, saving travel costs and time away from their workplace.

Impacts of the COVID-19 Pandemic

As discussed in some of the examples below, telemedicine and digital health usage increased dramatically during the COVID-19 pandemic. The ITU points out:

> Globally, the COVID-19 pandemic added immense pressure to health systems and their ability to deliver health-care services, revealing gaps and weaknesses even in countries with robust health systems. While digital tools have been emerging over recent decades, the overwhelming public health challenges of the pandemic catalysed their use as an essential mechanism for not only strengthening pandemic response but also for ensuring the continuity of health-care services. In particular, the periods of restricted mobility underscored the need for telemedicine – the delivery of health-related services and information using information and communications technologies (ICTs) – as a critical driver for expanding access to services and promoting continuity of care.[6]

The pandemic accelerated the adoption of telemedicine, which had previously been slow because of institutional resistance to change among providers and administrators in the health care sector as well as significant barriers in some countries (such as resistance of insurance providers to covering telemedicine consultations). As an analysis of the impact of the COVID-19 pandemic in the United States concludes: "Whether healthcare enterprises are ready or not, the new reality is that virtual care has arrived."[7]

Telemedicine and Telehealth

The following are examples of telemedicine programs and projects in remote and developing regions. Evaluation and other research findings are included where available.

Alaska

Some of the most detailed research on quantifiable benefits of connectivity comes from telemedicine evaluation, for example in rural Alaska. Like many developing regions, Alaska has a shortage of physicians and medical paraprofessionals; its primarily Indigenous villages are typically isolated without road access. At the village level, health care is delivered by community health aides who are usually local residents (primarily women) and who receive basic medical training and provide first-line care for the villagers. Health aides are supervised by medical staff at regional hospitals. More than 575 health aides in 200 villages provide nearly a half million patient encounters per year.[8] Some physicians practice in regional hospitals, but the majority of physicians are located in the city of Anchorage. Alaska also faces shortages in many medical specialties, as 49 percent of its physicians are primary care physicians, compared to a U.S. average of 28 percent.

Described as "a marriage between necessity and innovation," the Community Health Aide Program (CHAP) was established in 1954, when a U.S. government report stated that "the Indigenous peoples of Native Alaska are the victims of sickness, crippling conditions, and premature death in a degree exceeded in few parts of the world."[9]

In 1972, villages in central Alaska began to communicate with a regional hospital and the Alaska Native Medical Center (ANMC) in Anchorage using a single audio channel on NASA's ATS-1 satellite. The experiment showed that reliable communications could save time and even lives, and that health aides also learned from each other's experiences (heard in consultations over the shared audio channel).[10] As a result, the State of Alaska authorized an expenditure of $5 million for the purchase of satellite earth stations for 200 villages, so that both health workers and village residents could communicate through the nation's first commercial satellite.

Today, community health aides are still the frontline providers of village health care. A program known as AFHCAN (Alaska Federal Health Care Access Network) has extended telemedicine throughout rural Alaska, using equipment designed to be simple and cost effective, consisting of a personal computer and peripherals, including EKG (electrocardiogram, for heart monitoring), electronic otoscope for observing otitis media (ear infections are common in village children), and a digital camera to send still images of patient wounds, lesions, etc.[11]

The Alaska Native Tribal Health Consortium (ANTHC) and its partners at regional Native hospitals have collected data on several applications of telemedicine and their impact on patient care and savings in costs of health care delivery. A review of 125,000 cases over an 11-year period showed that telemedicine saved both time and money. Some 80 percent of all telemedicine consultations prevented patient travel from villages to regional hospitals, or regional hospitals to Anchorage, although a few cases "caused" travel, as patients with conditions requiring treatment by physicians were identified that would otherwise have been missed.[12] These findings are remarkably similar to data from the ATS-1 satellite telemedicine experiment 40 years earlier.[13]

Preventing patient travel results in significant cost savings in Alaska because medical evacuations are very expensive – bush flights from villages to regional hospitals typically cost several hundred dollars. In addition, evacuated patients under 18 years of age must be accompanied by an escort such as a parent or guardian. A review of teleconsultations for government-funded Medicaid cases over six years found that travel was avoided for 75 percent of cases, resulting in net savings to Medicaid of more than $2.8 million. These savings were dramatic; for every dollar spent by Medicaid on reimbursement, $10.54 was saved on travel costs. In addition, the teleconsultations that resulted in avoiding travel prevented an estimated 4,777 lost days at work and 1,444 lost days at school for the patients in this study.[14]

Audiology consultations are particularly prevalent in rural Alaska because of the high incidence of middle ear infections that can impair hearing. The Norton Sound Health Corporation in Nome has completed more than 3,000 audiology consultations with the Ear, Nose, and Throat (ENT) Department at ANMC in Anchorage. Using 16 years of data, they conducted a retrospective analysis of ENT specialty clinic wait times on all new patient referrals made by the Nome providers. Prior to the use of telemedicine, 47 percent of new patient referrals had to wait five months or longer for an in-person ENT appointment. Using telemedicine, only 3 percent had to wait that long, with the rest able to receive specialist consultations over the AFHCAN network.[15] By eliminating the need for a face-to-face encounter with the specialist, the use of telemedicine reduced the number of referrals from the ENT specialty clinics by more than 95 percent. The cost savings were significant as round-trip airfare between Nome and surrounding villages cost $300 to $400 per patient. Annual cost savings alone in one year from the prevention of in-person appointments reached $250,000.[16]

Also in rural Alaska, an interactive telehealth feasibility project introduced counseling on breast cancer risk-reducing strategies for underserved, high-risk Alaska Native women. The project included a navigator to facilitate patient encounters (referrals, electronic records, and scheduling). A survey of a sample of women demonstrated overall patient satisfaction of 98 percent concerning the experience, technology, and medical consultation. The referring physicians survey found 99 percent satisfaction with the service. Researchers found that the pilot project successfully demonstrated the feasibility of establishing a sustainable telehealth service to the underserved rural population in Alaska. They concluded that elements critical to its success were the interinstitutional collaboration, the availability of dependable technology, and someone to help patients navigate the system.[17]

Several lessons from Alaska's telemedicine experience are relevant for other rural and isolated regions:[18]

- **Saving time**: Telemedicine links between a community health worker and doctor at a regional hospital can enable patients to be seen locally – they would otherwise have to wait for a visiting doctor or to be sent to the hospital. Such timely consultations may also result in faster diagnosis and treatment that can, in turn, result in improved medical outcomes (reductions in morbidity and mortality).
- **Saving money**: The telemedicine system saves money as well as time. These savings have been dramatic; over six years, for every dollar spent by Medicaid on reimbursement, more than $10 were saved on travel costs.[19]
- **Improving quality**: Diagnosing and treating patient problems early may prevent deterioration of patients' illnesses and injuries; patients may also receive follow-up care at home with family rather than in a distant hospital.
- **Designing for sustainability**: The telemedicine planners selected or adapted equipment that is rugged enough to withstand field conditions such as power and temperature fluctuations and cramped space, and that is easy to use. Concerning equipment design, the director stated:

> I believe it is our job to build systems that make providers want to use telehealth. A lot of systems out there may be attractive and glamorous, but I wanted to build a system that would make a provider say, "I can't live without this." And that is very difficult. You really have to listen to the providers and understand how they do their job … You have to build a system that providers not only can use, but also that they want to use. A big part of this for us was to make the system extremely simple … we look at the whole product solution (WPS), in which we develop a product, we provide training, and we offer support. Although we continue to improve the product, we do not begin to deploy new versions until we put in place the curriculum for training, 'the knowledge base for support, and all related services in a healthcare environment.[20]

Northern Canada

There are many examples of telehealth projects serving Indigenous communities in Canada, although none with as extensive an evaluation of benefits as in Alaska. The cost of health care per capita in northern Canada, with its significant Indigenous population, is double the cost in the rest of Canada.[21] The use of telemedicine in Indigenous communities of the northern territories and isolated northern regions of the provinces increased substantially during the COVID-19 pandemic. Use of broadband, where available, increased dramatically, with providers often unable to meet demand.

The Ontario Telemedicine Network (OTN) is one of the largest virtual care networks in the world, with more than 1,600 sites across the province. OTN partners with Indigenous provider Keewaytinook Okimakanak (KO e-Health) to facilitate care to 28 First Nation communities in northern Ontario. For example, in Fort Severn First Nation, a remote Cree community near the Hudson Bay coast, health center workers use information technology for health administration, clinical health services, professional development, and community wellness activities. The internet has become an essential tool for the health staff. Locally, they use email daily for health administration, IP (Internet Protocol) telephones, and Facebook to contact community members and schedule appointments. Health staff use videoconferencing for monthly meetings with staff in other communities as well as for professional development courses and information sessions for health professionals and community members.[22] In addition to clinical care, the regional health center in the town of Sioux Lookout uses OTN to facilitate the delivery of distance education and administrative meetings for health care professionals and patients.[23]

A study found positive reviews of the KO telehealth service by the remote Indigenous community members.[24] Another report states that the key to this success is building First Nations ownership and control of both the network and service and addressing cross-cultural barriers to implementing Western-based clinical service into a First Nation community.[25]

Nunavut is a territory in the Canadian Arctic with a population that is 80 percent Indigenous. Health system decision makers have been concerned about the sustainability of expenditures, as more than 40 percent of the territory's annual health budget is spent on medical travel and accommodation. Telehealth appears to be part of the solution. A study found that in 50 percent of telehealth patient care sessions in Nunavut, either a patient or a professional or both would have had to travel if telehealth services had not been used.[26]

Memorial University in Newfoundland has been a pioneer in telemedicine for Newfoundland outports and communities on the Labrador coast. A 2017 survey found that physician users of telemedicine consistently reported that telehealth in Newfoundland and Labrador resulted in improved patient care, reduced transfers, and collaboration and support for the patients and remote health providers. The researchers found that provision of mental health assessments for patients in a remote community in Labrador by videoconference was shown to save money without compromising patient care, and noted that telepsychiatry is now routine in Labrador.[27]

Norway

Norway's sparsely populated northern region is similar to Alaska and northern Canada. A study of the challenges and effectiveness of telemedicine in northern Norway found that it was "a useful supplemental tool to support primary health care providers at local hospitals and remote communities in their effort to offer efficient and high-quality cancer care." Telemedicine allowed patients in remote regions to interact with specialists residing in urban areas. The study found that using telemedicine, cancer patients could be seen on average in less than two days, while the mean time to receive equivalent care without telemedicine was more than ten days.[28]

Australia

Australia has a long history of providing health care at a distance, initially using two-way radio combined with aircraft to serve patients on remote sheep and cattle stations (ranches). The Royal Flying Doctor Service contacts remote families to provide advice, and dispatches small planes with healthcare teams to assist and evacuate patients when necessary. In 2023, more than 71,000 patients in rural and remote areas used their telehealth services. Remote consultations are conducted over phone, radio, and video call.[29]

Researchers who examined telemedicine-delivered telepsychiatry services in remote regions of South Australia found that community-based telepsychiatry could be effective for many elderly and patients for whom travel was difficult. Also, in many cases, patients preferred communicating over videoconferencing links from a local clinic to face-to-face consultations. They noted that patients who suffered from psychotic illnesses or who suffered from sensory disabilities tended to be less satisfied with psychiatric care via telemedicine. Other groups were either equally or more satisfied with care using telemedicine. The study concluded that telepsychiatry services were beneficial for assessment and input from specialists in certain conditions, and that they were an important tool in closing the gap in care available between rural and urban regions.[30]

However, a survey on telehealth in remote Australia identified a number of barriers, the most frequently mentioned being lack of adequate internet access. More than 95,000 Aboriginal people live in very remote Australia, with 40,000 living in the Northern Territory (NT). In Central Australia, Indigenous households are 76 percent less likely to have access to the internet than non-Indigenous metropolitan households. Other barriers hindering telehealth included consultations not being billable to Medicare, some clinicians (including specialists) not providing services via telehealth, regulatory requirements (concerning training required to deliver telehealth), and the lack of funding for patient-end connectivity.

The study noted that many remote Aboriginal people have only prepaid mobile phones and can spend a significant amount of their limited income on data. When their credit runs out, they are not able to access essential services such as health or emergency services. It concluded that access to basic and affordable internet is urgently needed for Australians in rural, regional, and remote areas.[31]

Telemedicine and telehealth services are also being introduced in many developing regions, where they often face similar challenges to those found in Outback Australia and the far North.

Cape Verde

The Ministry of Health of Cabo Verde (Cape Verde) has been implementing a national telemedicine program since 2012, with the aim of linking all the islands on a joint platform, providing more timely care and diagnoses, and reducing referrals to central hospitals for specialty care. The telemedicine program operates through hubs on the nine inhabited islands. The hubs include a multipoint videoconferencing system; peripheral sites are equipped with heart and lung auscultation and electrocardiogram equipment as well as a high-resolution camera. General practitioners and other non-specialized health workers conduct teleconsultations with specialized medical practitioners, such as neurologists, cardiologists, surgeons, endocrinologists, urologists, and dermatologists.

Health workers initially resisted these changes, primarily due to lack of knowledge about telemedicine and concerns about using the technology. The program then emphasized raising awareness among health workers and provided continuous support to help with ICT literacy and adapting clinical services to the telemedicine context. In addition, the program found that it was critical to identify local leaders or representatives of professional organizations for discussion and feedback.[32]

Indonesia

After the government of West Java in Indonesia closed clinics in response to a rising number of COVID-19 cases, residents were in danger of losing access to health care services. With Indonesia's high penetration of mobile phones, the Indonesia Planned Parenthood Association (IPPA) had previously used WhatsApp successfully to provide psychosocial counseling services to people living with HIV. During the pandemic, IPPA expanded its use of WhatsApp to offer patients counseling services, such as on adolescent health, sexually transmitted infections, and safe abortion. IPPA also used WhatsApp to communicate with patients who needed supplies such as contraceptives or antiretrovirals. The supplies were then sent via courier or in person through community health workers.[33]

After considering numerous options besides WhatsApp for connecting with patients during the pandemic, IPPA decided to use WhatsApp because of its widespread popularity. WhatsApp also offers a combination of video, audio, and text options. However, IPPA had to direct clinics to stop using individual or private WhatsApp accounts, explaining that such accounts are not secure or confidential for patients.[34]

India

The government of India's Ministry of Health and Family Welfare is rolling out nationwide telemedicine, known as eSanjeevani, a cloud-based telemedicine technology of the Centre for Development of Advanced Computing (C-DAC) in Mohali, India. The system was customized as eSanjeevaniHWC for implementation in the 155,000 Health & Wellness Centres (HWCs) of the Ayushman Bharat Scheme, the world's largest government-owned health insurance initiative.

The objectives of eSanjeevaniHWC were:

- To address the shortage of doctors/specialists;
- To reduce the burden on district hospital and tertiary care facilities due to limited primary care services;
- To initiate creation of electronic health records at primary- and secondary-level health facilities, thereby facilitating continuing care.

The project was later modified to cope with COVID-19, placing more emphasis on connecting health care workers to patients at home. As of mid-2022, eSanjeevaniHWC had served more than 42.3 million patients at more than 98,000 HCWs served by more than 11,000 hubs. As expected, telemedicine utilization was greater in the regions with higher internet penetration. However, telemedicine utilization was higher than anticipated (despite low internet penetration) in regions where locations of health care facilities were scattered or with difficult terrain. Strong local technical support was also an important factor in uptake.[35]

Vanuatu

On the remote island of Maewo in Vanuatu in the South Pacific, a telemedicine network has helped enhance health outcomes for the isolated residents. With satellite backhaul and last mile wireless connectivity, the network links two primary health centers staffed by local nurses and community health workers with doctors in referral hospitals that are a six-hour mountain trek plus a $300 flight away. The messaging platform used for telemedicine required low levels of digital skills training. Nurses and healthcare workers on Maewo indicated that they had gained trust through their use of the network and felt supported at times of need.

Research on the project indicated that the telemedicine platform has been critical to helping community health workers triage critical cases vs. non-critical ones; escalating critical cases to appropriate care centers, thereby easing the economic burden of transportation and logistics; and sensitizing community members concerned about health care procedures with effective socioculturally appropriate messaging. The researchers concluded that, in a region with among the lowest physician densities in the world, the online telemedicine platform helped marshal limited resources effectively for health care delivery.[36]

mHealth for Maternal and Child Health

Health messages delivered to the population via mobile phone, known as mHealth, are being used to reach expectant and new mothers in some developing regions. The World Bank reported that initial results from pilot projects in Bangladesh, India, South Africa, and Tanzania suggest that regular SMS communication can induce behavior changes in expectant mothers by providing information on neonatal health.[37] Below are examples from South Africa and Vietnam.

South Africa

In 2012, the government of South Africa created a National e-Health Strategy intended to serve as a roadmap for the achievement of an effective and patient-centered national health information system.

As part of its broader objective to decrease maternal and infant mortality in South Africa, the government established MomConnect, a digital health initiative designed to register approximately 1 million pregnant women in the public health system, provide them with stage-based health messaging and a feedback facility. Through MomConnect, pregnant women and new mothers receive free maternal health messaging via SMS or WhatsApp and can access a text-based helpdesk. Since its launch in 2014, almost 5 million mothers have registered on the MomConnect platforms. Mothers receive health- and pregnancy-related information until their baby is two years old. They can use the platform to seek health care guidance through an automated chatbot or a human-operated text-based helpdesk.[38]

Studies have found that MomConnect has positively impacted health behaviors, contributing to reducing the maternal mortality ratio and ending preventable deaths of newborns and children under five years of age, objectives of the UN's sustainable development goals.[39] Results included a high number of prenatal health care visits,[40] high vaccine coverage, increased breast feeding and breastfeeding knowledge, and increased family planning use among mothers with previous pregnancies.[41] MomConnect users reported that it was user-friendly and interactive, which made it easy to access, use, share, or opt out of receiving health information. However, poor access to an internet connection and a smartphone posed challenges and excluded those who could not read, write, or interact with the tool.[42] Researchers also noted that cheaper mobile data costs would facilitate an extension of MomConnect to the partners and families of pregnant women, as well as to similar programs targeting health behaviors such as HIV antiretroviral therapy adherence.[43]

Lessons from evaluation of MomConnect that are relevant for other digital health initiatives include:

- A scaled digital health implementation requires complex multi-stakeholder partnerships.
- Formal integration with the public health system – this allows MomConnect to generate demand for health services while also collecting data to strengthen delivery of services.

- It is possible to write evidence-based messages that address the most important identified perinatal and child health problems in language that women can understand.
- Large-scale mobile health programs require long-term commitment and earmarked funding for core functions and innovation.
- mHealth programs should consider evaluation from the outset, including collection of baseline data prior to implementation.[44]

Vietnam: Reducing Infant Mortality

Vietnamese ethnic minorities, who represent 15 percent of the Vietnamese population, have fertility rates and infant mortality rates that are much higher than the ethnic majority population. Ethnic minority women typically live in lower-income, more remote, mountainous communities and are much less likely to receive prenatal or postnatal care or to deliver their babies in a health facility.

To address these problems, an mHealth pilot intervention called mMOM using SMS text messaging to improve health outcomes among ethnic minority women in northern Vietnam was implemented from 2013 to 2016 with promising results. A research team from Vietnam's Institute of Population, Health, and Development (PHAD) established a Maternal and Child health information center, reaching out to pregnant women and recent mothers via mobile messages containing crucial information about pregnancy, prenatal care, birth, and postnatal care. About 900 pregnant women were reached in the pilot project in Thai Nguyen province, with 90,000 messages sent, which helped increase health knowledge and attitudes in the community.[45]

The mMOM project was expanded qualitatively (through adding COVID-19-related guidance and new technological components, including a mobile app and artificial intelligence chatbots) and quantitatively (through broadening the geographical area). Expanded as dMOM, the program is to be implemented across 71 project communes, with an evaluation planned to assess whether dMOM's SMS text messaging or mobile app delivery contributes to better maternal and child health outcomes among ethnic minority women.[46]

Electronic Medical Records

Transmission of electronic medical records (EMRs) can improve the efficiency of the medical system; instead of compiling paper records that cannot follow the patient or be accessible to other providers, records can be entered in databases accessible throughout the health care system.[47] In Alaska, Indigenous patients may be seen at clinics in various communities, or be transferred to regional hospitals or a tertiary health care center. Electronic medical records may now be accessed at any point in the system, avoiding duplication of tests and expediting treatment.[48]

Developing regions are beginning to implement electronic record keeping and access, but face many challenges. The most common challenges include technical ability, cost, poor functionality, data safety issues, logistics, and interference with patient-physician and physician-physician relationships.[49] For example, there must be sufficiently reliable and affordable connectivity to transmit the records. Software and networks must provide adequate security to protect patient confidentiality and ensure accuracy. Staff must be trained in how to code and enter the records and how to maintain patient privacy. Also, systems must be designed to avoid problems such as inability to share data because of interoperability issues or a lack of standards.

As noted in the examples above, health care providers must be involved in adoption of the system so that they can understand its benefits and can propose any modifications to make it user-friendly, and patients must be educated about how their data are protected.

Commentary

The projects discussed above offer several lessons relevant not only for digital health but for applications in other sectors as well.

- **Connectivity**: Adequate bandwidth and quality of service are critical for many telemedicine and other e-health applications, especially now that video is increasing used for consultations.
- **Privacy and security**: Electronic medical records that can be accessed by patients and shared by providers must be secured to ensure privacy of patients and to ensure that only approved entities have access.

- **Engagement**: Health workers and patients should be involved in the planning and implementation of digital health technologies so that their concerns are addressed and modifications may be made in response to their feedback.
- **Training and support**: Health workers will require training on digital technologies and applications and support to help with adoption and usage.
- **Evaluation**: Evaluation should be budgeted in project funding so that data can be collected on key indicators, preferably before and after the innovation is introduced, and lessons learned can be incorporated when e-health services are incorporated in the health care system.

Also, as discussed in Chapter 12, "The Era of Artificial Intelligence," AI may soon enhance digital health with abilities to provide diagnoses in rural settings, as well as to save time and effort by taking on administrative tasks and to extend access to global medical resources by scanning large databases in search of diagnoses and treatment options.

References

1. Wosik, J., Fudim, M., Cameron, B., Gellad, Z.F., Cho, A., Phinney, D., Curtis, S., Roman, M., Poon, E.G., Ferranti, J., Katz, J.N., & Tcheng, J. (2020), Telehealth Transformation: COVID-19 and the Rise of Virtual Care. *Journal of the American Medical Informatics Association*, 27(6), 957–62. doi: 10.1093/jamia/ocaa067. PMID: 32311034; PMCID: PMC7188147.
2. WHO (n.d.), E-Health. https://www.emro.who.int/health-topics/ehealth/.
3. WHO (2021), Global Strategy on Digital Health 2020–2025, p. 17. https://www.who.int/docs/default-source/documents/gs4dhdaa2a9f352b0445bafbc79ca799dce4d.pdf.
4. Hudson, Heather E. (2016), *Connecting Alaskans: Telecommunications in Alaska from Telegraph to Broadband*, University of Alaska Press.
5. WHO (2022), *Consolidated Telemedicine Implementation Guide, 2022*. https://www.who.int/publications/i/item/9789240059184.
6. WHO (2022), *Consolidated Telemedicine Implementation Guide, 2022*, p. iv. https://www.who.int/publications/i/item/9789240059184.

7. Wosik, J., Fudim, M., Cameron, B., Gellad, Z.F., Cho, A., Phinney, D., Curtis, S., Roman, M., Poon, E.G., Ferranti, J., Katz, J.N., & Tcheng, J. (2020), Telehealth Transformation: COVID-19 and the Rise of Virtual Care. *Journal of the American Medical Informatics Association*, 27(6), 957–62. doi: 10.1093/jamia/ocaa067. PMID: 32311034; PMCID: PMC7188147.
8. Ferguson, Stewart (2011, May). What Works: Outcomes Data from AFHCAN and ANTHC Telehealth: An 8 Year Retrospective, Alaska Native Tribal Health Consortium, Anchorage.
9. Quoted in Nice, Philip & Johnson, Walter (1999), *The Alaska Health Aide Program: A Tradition of Helping Ourselves*. University of Alaska Anchorage, Center for Circumpolar Health Studies.
10. See Hudson, Heather E. & Parker, Edwin B. (1973) Medical Communication in Alaska by Satellite, *New England Journal of Medicine*, December 20.
11. Alaska Native Tribal Health Consortium. See https://anthc.org/education-training/provider-telehealth/.
12. Ferguson, Stewart (2011, May), What Works: Outcomes Data from AFHCAN and ANTHC Telehealth: An 8 Year Retrospective, Alaska Native Tribal Health Consortium, Anchorage.
13. See Hudson, Heather E. & Parker, Edwin B. (1973), Medical Communication in Alaska by Satellite, *New England Journal of Medicine*, December 20.
14. Hays, Howard, Carroll, Mark, Ferguson, Stewart, Fore, Christopher, & Horton, Mark (2014), The Success of Telehealth Care in the Indian Health Service, *Virtual Mentor*, 16(12): 986–96. doi: 10.1001/virtualmentor.2014.16.12.stas1-1412.
15. Hofstetter, Philip J., Kokesh, John, Ferguson, A. Stewart, & Hood, Linda J. (2010), The Impact of Telehealth on Wait Time for ENT Specialty Care, *Telemedicine and E-Health*, 16(5), 551.
16. Hofstetter, Philip J., Kokesh, John, Ferguson, A. Stewart, & Hood, Linda J. (2010), The Impact of Telehealth on Wait Time for ENT Specialty Care, *Telemedicine and E-Health*, 16(5), 555.
17. Pruthi, Sandhya, Stange, Kevin J., Malagrino, Gerald D. Jr., LaRusso, Nicholas F., Chawla, Kashmira S., & Kaur, Judith S. (2013), Successful Implementation of a Telemedicine-Based Counseling Program for High-Risk Patients with Breast Cancer, *Mayo Clinic Proceedings*, 88(1), 68–73.
18. Hudson, Heather E. (2007), Rural Telemedicine: Lessons from Alaska for Developing Regions, *Journal of eHealth Technology and Application*, 5(3), 460–7.

19. Ferguson, Stewart (2011, May), What Works: Outcomes Data from AFHCAN and ANTHC Telehealth: An 8 Year Retrospective, Alaska Native Tribal Health Consortium, Anchorage.
20. Ferguson, A. Stewart (2005) Telethinking, *Telemedicine Journal & e-Health*, 11(4), 422–9. https://doi.org/10.1089/tmj.2005.11.422.
21. Canadian Institute for Health Information (2017), *National Health Expenditure Trends, 1975 to 2017.* https://www.cihi.ca/sites/default/files/document/nhex-trends-narrative-report-2019-en.pdf.
22. Kakekaspan, Matthew, O'Donnell, Susan, Beaton, Brian, Walmark, Brian, & Gibson, Kerri (2014), The First Mile Approach to Community Services in Fort Severn First Nation, *Journal of Community Informatics*, 10(2). https://doi.org/10.15353/joci.v10i2.2647.
23. Sioux Lookout Meno Ya Win Health Centre. https://slmhc.on.ca/departments-and-services/telemedicine/.
24. McKenzie, O., Kakekaspan, C., Gibson, K., O'Donnell, S., Kakepetum-Schultz, T. (2012, October), Perspectives of Rural and Remote First Nation Community Members Toward Telehealth Services: The Case of KeewaytinookOkimakanak Telemedicine (KOTM), Report presented at the Canadian Rural Health Research Society – Rural and Remote Health Research Conference – Creative Approaches, Levis, Quebec.
25. O'Donnell, S., Beaton, B., McMahon, R., Hudson, H.E., Williams, D., & Whiteduck, T. (2016, June), Digital Technology Adoption in Remote and Northern Indigenous Communities in Canada, Canadian Sociological Association 2016 Annual Conference, University of Calgary, Calgary, Alberta. http://firstmile.ca/wp-content/uploads/2016-CSA-Digital-Technology-Adoption.pdf.
26. Infotelmed Communications (2003, September 26). *Nunavut Telehealth Project Impact Evaluation Report*. Infotelmed Communications Inc., Montreal, Quebec.
27. Jong, Michael, Ivar Mendez, & Robert Jong (2019), Enhancing Access to Care in Northern Rural Communities via Telehealth, *International Journal of Circumpolar Health*, 78(2).
28. Donnem, T., Ervik, B., Magnussen, K., Andersen, S., Pastow, D., Andreassen, S., Nørstad, T., Helbekkmo, N., Bremnes, R.M., & Nordoy, T. (2012), Bridging the Distance: A Prospective Tele-Oncology Study in Northern Norway, *Support Care Cancer*, 20(9), 2097–2103. doi: 10.1007/s00520-011-1319-1. Epub 2011 Nov 11. PMID: 22076621.
29. https://www.flyingdoctor.org.au/what-we-do/tele-health/. Also see the Australian television drama series *RFDS,* now also available in several countries.

30. Dham, P., Gupta, N., Alexander, J., Black, W., Rajji, T., & Skinner, E. (2018), Community-Based Telepsychiatry Service for Older Adults Residing in a Rural and Remote Region – Utilization Pattern and Satisfaction Among Stakeholders, *BMC Psychiatry*, 18(1), 316. doi: 10.1186/s12888-018-1896-3. PMID: 30261845; PMCID: PMC6161443.
31. St Clair, Marianne & Murtagh, David (2019), Barriers to Telehealth Uptake in Rural, Regional, Remote Australia: What Can Be Done to Expand Telehealth Access in Remote Areas? In: E. Cummings et al. (Eds.), *Digital Health: Changing the Way Healthcare is Conceptualised and Delivered*, IOS Press.
32. WHO (2022), *Consolidated Telemedicine Implementation Guide, 2022*, p. 49. https://www.who.int/publications/i/item/9789240059184
33. WHO. Consolidated Telemedicine Implementation Guide, 2022. (2022), p. 52. https://www.who.int/publications/i/item/9789240059184
34. World Health Organization. Regional Office for South-East Asia. (2021). Leveraging telehealth for efficient delivery of primary health care in the WHO South-East Asia Region. World Health Organization. Regional Office for South-East Asia. https://iris.who.int/handle/10665/350199
35. WHO (2022), *Consolidated Telemedicine Implementation Guide, 2022*, p. 48. https://www.who.int/publications/i/item/9789240059184.
36. Srinivasan, Sharada & Yoo, Christopher S. (2021, January 11), Deploying Telemedicine in Capacity Constrained Contexts: Lessons from the Vanuatu Inter-Island Telemedicine and Learning Project, TPRC48: The 48th Research Conference on Communication, Information and Internet Policy, available at SSRN https://ssrn.com/abstract=3763578.
37. World Bank (2016), *Digital Dividends*, World Development Report, p. 156. https://www.worldbank.org/en/publication/wdr2016.
38. https://www.health.gov.za/momconnect/.
39. https://www.health.gov.za/momconnect/.
40. Kastrau, Philipp, Symington, Lorry, Balu, Anjani, Lusava, Rachel, & Connor, Alison (2024, April), *MomConnect – Quality-Based Messaging RCT Final Study Report*, IDinsight. https://static1.squarespace.com/static/63638a147ff81261a0319bc3/t/66b362b076a63e27d3aa50ff/1723032319748/MQR_Final+Report_19Apr2024+%5BSHARED%5D.pdf.
41. Christofides, N., Weiner, R., & Malatji, H. (2022, September), Evaluation Report – Impact Evaluation of MomConnect, WITS School of Public Health, South Africa. https://static1.squarespace.com/static/63638a147ff81261a0319bc3/t/66b362b076a63e27d3aa50ff/1723032319748/MQR_Final+Report_19Apr2024+%5BSHARED%5D.pdf

42. Mehl, G.L., Tamrat, T., Bhardwaj, S., Blaschke, S., & Labrique, A. (2018), Digital Health Vision: Could MomConnect Provide a Pragmatic Starting Point for Achieving Universal Health Coverage in South Africa and Elsewhere? *BMJ Global Health*, 3(Suppl 2), e000626. doi: 10.1136/ bmjgh-2017-000626. PMID: 29713512; PMCID: PMC5922498.
43. Barron, P., Peter, J., LeFevre, A.E., et al. (2018), Mobile Health Messaging Service and Helpdesk for South African Mothers (MomConnect): History, Successes and Challenges, *BMJ Global Health*, 3, e000559. doi:10.1136/ bmjgh-2017-000559.
44. Peter, J., Benjamin, P., LeFevre, A.E., et al. (2018), Taking Digital Health Innovation to Scale in South Africa: Ten Lessons from MomConnect, *BMJ Global Health*, 3, e000592.
45. International Development Research Centre (2018), Connecting Vietnam's Isolated Communities to Improve Healthcare. https:// idrc-crdi.ca/en/research-in-action/connecting-vietnams-isolated-communities-improve-healthcare.
46. McBride B, O'Neil J., Nguyen, P.C., Linh, D.T., Trinh, H.T., Vu, N.C. & Nguyen, L..T. (2023), Adapting and Scaling a Digital Health Intervention to Improve Maternal and Child Health Among Ethnic Minority Women in Vietnam Amid the COVID-19 Context: Protocol for the dMOM Project, *JMIR Research Protocols*, 12, e44720. doi: 10.2196/44720.
47. WHO |(n.d.), *Electronic Health Records*" http://www.who.int/gho/goe/ electronic_health_records/en/.
48. Hudson, Heather E. (2015), *Connecting Alaskans: Telecommunications in Alaska from Telegraph to Broadband*. University of Alaska Press.
49. Odekunle, F.F., Odekunle, R.O., & Shankar, S. (2017), Why Sub-Saharan Africa Lags in Electronic Health Record Adoption and Possible Strategies to Increase its Adoption in this Region, *International Journal of Health Sciences*, 11(4), 59–64. PMID: 29085270; PMCID: PMC5654179.

5

AGRICULTURE, NATURAL RESOURCES, AND THE ENVIRONMENT

"I have to define myself as an agricultural entrepreneur that is bringing new solutions and new ways."

– Young farmer in Ivory Coast (Côte d'Ivoire)[1]

This chapter examines applications of digital technologies in agriculture, fisheries, environmental monitoring, and sustainable energy. Digital connectivity can contribute to efficiency, productivity, and innovation in agriculture and fisheries as well as in the management of environmental resources and sustainable energy. ICT technologies in rural and developing regions can help to improve yield; farmers can now use GPS (Global Positioning System) mapping and agricultural data from extension services and other sources to determine where and when to fertilize and irrigate their fields. Connectivity can also be important for farmers, who now consider themselves agricultural entrepreneurs, to learn how to introduce new crops and to obtain the best prices from urban markets. ICTs are also increasingly used in fisheries to monitor and report fish harvests, as well as for marketing and logistics. Digital technologies have also become valuable tools for environmental monitoring, such as for ocean temperatures, ice depths, and wildfires, and for managing sustainable energy sources.

DOI: 10.4324/9781003431602-5

Agriculture

As the World Bank points out:

> Agriculture is location-specific, and farmers need accurate local weather forecasts, advice on agricultural practices and input use, and real-time information about prices and market logistics. Harnessing the rapid growth of the internet and associated digital technologies such as mobile phones is critical to helping farmers obtain the information they need and to promoting transformative agricultural development.[2]

In the 1960s, Everett Rogers defined diffusion as the means by which an innovation is communicated through certain channels over time to members of a social system. He identified various steps in the process of adopting an innovation, the role of information at various steps in the process, and channels that included both mass media and interpersonal communication.[3] Numerous communication researchers have applied diffusion theory in analysis of the adoption of innovations in developing regions.[4] The impact of ICTs in agriculture builds on the theory of diffusion of innovations to reach farmers, first through mass media such as broadcast radio, which extended the reach of extension agents, and then through mobile phones to add interactivity and access to additional information.

Adoption of New Farming Practices

For behavior change to occur, for example in farming practices, *awareness* must be coupled with *adoption*. Interactivity, through in-person discussion or mobile phones, can be critical to the adoption of new practices. For more than 20 years from the 1940s to the 1960s, Canadian farmers gathered to listen to and discuss agricultural programs as part of a rural listening group project called the Farm Radio Forum. The Forum also included a feedback system to collect farmers' comments and experiences for future broadcasts and to share with government agencies.[5]

In many developing regions, extension agents visit rural communities to share expertise and answer questions on farming practices.

However, that knowledge can be shared much more widely through mass media. A UNESCO report on the Farm Radio Forum encouraged India, Ghana, and other countries to adopt its technique of combining agricultural radio broadcasts with listening groups.

The rural radio forums in Canada operated on the principles of "Listen, discuss, act." In Africa, Farm Radio International (FRI) has been one of the pioneers both in introducing this model and in innovating with ICTs to increase *interaction*, and, thereby, *adoption* of agricultural practices presented in radio broadcasts. FRI's efforts to integrate interactive ICTs in the radio campaigns are based on lessons from research on the role of communication in development: first, that modern technology can be used for the production of more compelling and entertaining content that can build and hold an audience's attention over time, and, second, that modern technology can facilitate more substantive interaction from the listening audience. In turn, engaging content and audience interactivity could result in increased knowledge acquisition and the adoption of agricultural practices presented in the radio programs. The use of ICTs, particularly mobile phones, has become an important component of FRI's strategy.[6]

For several decades, FRI has developed agricultural content for use by African radio stations, and in recent years it has trained African broadcasters to produce and deliver development programs for farmers. The second step of "discussion" can potentially benefit greatly from the two-way nature of interactive radio programming incorporating mobile phone technology. The community listening groups share a wind-up, solar-powered, radio set with an MP3 recording and playback built in to facilitate group listening. They can also record the programs for later listening and record their discussion or comments. The radios also have SD (secure digital) card slots so that the cards may be swapped out by radio staff, providing access to programs in areas where reception is poor. FRI has added interactivity via mobile phones, so that farmers listening to the programs can call the radio station with their comments and questions, which are then answered on the air. These innovations enable FRI programs to expand from a one-way information delivery medium to a platform for knowledge exchange and discussion among farmers.

FRI's Participatory Radio Campaign (PRC) is a planned series of radio programs broadcast to a targeted farming population over a specified period of time (usually about four months), intended to help farmers adopt a particular farming practice or improvement. PRCs are designed to engage farmers in the selection of topics and to engage farmers at every step. Farmers are involved in:

- selecting the improvement or innovation to be featured;
- discussing the pros and cons of adopting it;
- making an informed decision about whether or not to take up the improvement;
- providing practical advice during the adoption process.[7]

A key component is a Community Listening Group (CLG), which listens to the programs, discusses them, and provides regular feedback. The CLG provides interactivity through discussion along the lines of the original farm radio forum, but it also uses ICTs to provide feedback and interact with the radio programmers and resource people interviewed, such as extension officers.

Across Africa, fees apply to the person who places a phone call, but not the one who answers it. To save money, rather than paying for text messages or voice calls, people may call and let the phone ring once and hang up (known as "beeping"), to signal a message to someone they know or to ask them to call back. FRI has adapted this technique as a means for farmers to provide feedback about radio programs, without paying for mobile calls, such as answering a poll question, receiving information through an interactive voice response system, or recording a question for experts. An example is Beep-2-Vote, in which a broadcaster might ask listeners to vote on which topic they want to hear about the following week by beeping a different telephone number for each choice. The broadcaster can tally the votes and announce the winning selection on the air.[8]

Using low-cost software to build a database of mobile phone numbers, FRI-affiliated stations can build a contact list of members of the community listening groups so that they can be reminded to listen to the program, for example by sending automatic callouts 30 minutes before a program starts. The software can also aggregate beeped responses and display them in real time.

More advanced Interactive Voice Response (IVR) systems can be used to provide several forms of interactivity with listeners. Listeners can call a number, hang up, and be called back by the system so that they do not have to pay to opt-in for future information. IVR systems can also be designed with menus for polls or quizzes. The listener can call the IVR number, hang up, and receive a return call offering prompts to select choices from menus. These IVR call-back systems are free for callers and also do not require literacy.

An example of this participatory approach was a project in Burkina Faso, Ghana, Tanzania, and Uganda designed to reduce widespread Vitamin A deficiency by cultivating orange-fleshed sweet potatoes rich in beta-carotene rather than the more common pale yellow African sweet potatoes. Strategies to involve target audience members in project design, listening groups, and interactive ICTs were designed to improve cultivation, marketing, preparation, consumption, and nutrition. Research indicated that participatory activities including the use of interactive ICTs helped to engage audiences, increased knowledge of agricultural improvements and innovations, and contributed to higher levels of adoption than result from listening alone. Results from the listening groups also highlighted the potential of this approach to enhance women's participation and access to information.[9]

Productivity and Income

Some 90 percent of Africa's domestic rice is produced by smallholder farmers. As noted by FRI, African farmers may have poor knowledge of good agronomic and management practices and limited access to markets, both for inputs and for sales. RiceAdvice is an Android-based application developed by AfricaRice in consultation with end-users, designed to provide farmers with personalized advice on rice management practices for increasing rice yields and grower incomes. Recommendations are validated in field trials and continuously updated through further research.

RiceAdvice has reached more than 19,000 rice farmers, either on their own smartphones or through a third party if they do not own a smartphone or tablet. More than 300 service providers from the public and private sectors have received training on how to use RiceAdvice to support rice farmers. Research cited by the German Development Agency found that farmers using the app can increase their yields by around 0.6 to 1.8 tonnes per hectare, reduce fertilizer inputs by up to 50 percent and thus increase their income by $100 to $250 per hectare.[10] They also point out that some farmers have indicated a willingness to pay for the service, indicating the potential for a sustainable business model.

In Ghana, researchers found that internet use in a rural region increased farm income and household income by 20.1 percent and 15.5 percent respectively. The analysis revealed that internet use was influenced by off-farm employment, education, access to credit, non-fixed assets, age, and perception variables. The estimates also indicated that internet use increased household income by 31.8 percent for farm households that engaged in off-farm employment and by 15.3 percent for those that had access to non-fixed assets. Further, internet use increased the household income for households that did not engage in off-farm activities by 24.9 percent.[11]

In rural China, Ma and colleagues found that age, education, family labor, logistic service, and improved infrastructure were the main factors that drive farmers' decision to use the internet. In turn, internet use increases the likelihood of farmers' willingness to adopt e-commerce by 20 percent. Farmers' willingness to adopt e-commerce was also affected by age, risk preference, remittance status, and e-commerce training.[12]

Ma and colleagues also investigated the effects of internet use on household income and expenditure in rural China. The results show that internet use increases household income and expenditure significantly, but that internet use has a larger impact at the upper distributions of household income and expenditure. Household size and off-farm work participation were the two most important factors that affected household income, while the household expenditure of rural households was mainly determined by the level of education of household heads, household size, and rural credit access.[13]

Another study in China considered the intermediary transmission effect of entrepreneurship and non-agricultural employment on the impact of internet use on Chinese farmers' income growth.

The results showed that internet use has a direct effect on rural residents' income growth, but also that rural residents' entrepreneurial or non-agricultural employment affects internet use and their income growth. However, the direct promotion effect of internet use was stronger than the indirect promotion effect of entrepreneurship and non-agricultural employment.[14]

Research in China also suggests that improving the availability of broadband access in a rural area, promoting internet-related training and education, and increasing government investment in rural ICTs infrastructure can contribute to the reduction of chemical fertilizer use.[15] Similarly, research in Vietnam found that internet access was associated with a 6–7 percent higher value of agricultural output. This result was apparently realized through more efficient use of chemical fertilizer. Researchers found that results were stronger for younger households. Geographically, the results were strongest in the least-developed northern provinces, indicating that marginal productivity is greater in areas where agricultural productivity is initially lower.[16]

In India, the agricultural market is characterized by small land holdings, weak infrastructure and the involvement of numerous intermediaries. Without viable alternatives, farmers may end up selling their products at exploitative prices to the intermediaries. Established in 2000, e-Choupal is a nation-wide e-procurement network founded by ITC Limited, one of India's largest companies. E-Choupal info-kiosks enabled farmers to sell their produce at ITC shops at competitive market rates. Through an information dissemination channel accessible through the information kiosks, e-Choupal was able to provide farmers with better prices for their products. In turn, the company benefitted by buying high-demand farm produce such as soy, coffee, and prawns, directly from the producers.

Entrepreneurial farmers managed the "click and mortar" enterprise as *sanchalaks* (kiosk operators). By 2018, there were about 6,100 installations covering over 35,000 villages and serving over 4 million farmers. Around 2020, with the proliferation of mobile phones, ITC began to transition from a desktop-based interface at the village level to a mobile platform base. Mobile-based Choupal 4.0 will retain the basic features of ITC's approach to increasing farmer income; it intends to continue to focus on four elements of farmer profitability:

"improve farm productivity, improve product quality and integrity, reduce cost of cultivation, and risk mitigation."[17]

In the Mekong region of Myanmar, Greenovator is an agritech organization with the mission to empower farming communities to improve their livelihoods and to help build a more resilient and sustainable agricultural sector. Its first mobile app, named Green Way, was developed to connect farmers with technicians for timely answers to farmers' questions as well as to access information on best farming practices. Greenway was founded as a social enterprise by young alumni from Yezin, Myanmar's agriculture university.[18] Subsequently based in Singapore, it evolved to also offer a tool to connect smallholder farmers with agricultural and livestock businesses.

Free to download, Green Way generates revenue from providing agricultural services such as consultancy, research, and translations to NGOs and enterprises. It also includes an e-commerce marketplace (Zay Tan Gyi) platform that enables farmers to buy agricultural supplies and sell their produce directly to traders and consumers.[19] As of late 2021, the Green Way app had 30,000 active monthly users and had been downloaded by over 280,000 farmers.

An additional feature of the Green Way app was Asein Yone Mat Tan (Asein meaning "green" and Mat Tan meaning "data"), the first digital farm management solution in Myanmar to provide solutions for contract farming businesses. With Asein Yone Mat Tan, farmers can plan timelines, record activities, and track yields. A participating farmer commented "We used to just farm the way our parents showed us. But after getting the app, I now see how we should be doing it … it's better to use proper techniques rather than just working blindly."[20] The development team also created a group function for users to start group discussions about agricultural topics. The purpose is to strengthen existing networks and create new networks of farmers with similar interests and goals.[21]

Smart Agriculture

North American farmers can now monitor machinery remotely in their fields, troubleshoot problems without hauling equipment to repair shops, and receive real-time data on soil, seeds, and planting.

Many farmers rely on mobile cellular signals to use digital services. However, about 30 percent of land farmed in the United States lacks adequate communications coverage, and in the developing world most agricultural land may lack coverage. A major farm machinery manufacturer is collaborating with Space-X's Starlink, which operates LEO satellites, to connect tractors, seed planters, crop sprayers, and other equipment in areas that lack adequate internet service, enabling them to use its digital services. The satellite antennas are customized for dusty, rugged conditions.[22]

A wheat farmer on the Canadian prairies uses Starlink for connectivity to his home and 120,000-acre farm. He also uses GPS coordinates to guide his tractor in spraying pesticides to avoid duplicate spraying, and he is testing drones to deliver pesticides in his fields. He is also able to monitor and control equipment such as a grain dryer from his mobile phone.[23]

Women farmers in India are also learning to fly drones to reduce use of pesticides and increase crop yields. Namo Drone Didi aims to empower women-led self-help groups by equipping them with drone technology (*didi* is the Hindi word for "sister"). Drone technology significantly enhances the precise application of pesticides and fertilizers. With advanced GPS and sensor technology, drones can be programmed to follow precise flight paths over fields, reducing the use of chemicals, minimizing environmental impact, and lowering costs for farmers. One Drone Didi can cover as much as five acres in the same time it would take five people to cover half an acre. This initiative is expected to generate an additional income of at least 100,000 rupees (1 lakh) per year (about $1,175) for each self-help group, contributing to the women's economic empowerment and sustainable livelihoods.[24]

In Ivory Coast, agriculture is the main source of livelihood for two-thirds of households, but erosion and crop destruction are becoming increasingly common, associated with fluctuating seasonal cycles driven by climate change. In Canada, young farmers from Ivory Coast learned how to use weather forecasts in daily planning and to annualize weather data to help adjust to climate change. They now request meteorological data from the agricultural ministry and run it through predictive models such as aWhere, a platform specializing in agricultural intelligence. Some Ivorian agritech startups also use drone technology to monitor crop conditions and gather field data.[25]

Smart agriculture on a smaller scale involves computer-managed inputs for high value vegetables. In China, sensors control water, temperature, and humidity in a "smart tent" to grow mushrooms. In Iceland, greenhouses with computer-controlled light, heat, water, and nutrients produces tomatoes year-round so that fresh tomatoes can be supplied every day to grocery stores in Reykjavik and other towns.[26] Some young Africans are also introducing "smart" hydroponic farming of vegetables including on rooftops of urban buildings.[27]

Fisheries

Like the agricultural examples above, access to timely and relevant information may also benefit the fisheries sector. After mobile phone service was introduced in Kerala, India, mobile phone usage among sardine fishermen and wholesalers was shown to benefit both producers and consumers through improved information and better functioning markets.[28] A frequently cited study by Robert Jensen found that the introduction of mobile phone service dramatically reduced price dispersion and waste in the sardine catch, increasing economic welfare for producers and consumers.[29]

In southwest Alaska, seafood processors rely heavily on connectivity with their head offices for administrative services, such as payroll, other human resources functions, accounting, shipping and receiving, purchasing, and ERP (enterprise resource planning). Monitoring of systems by IT staff for maintenance and security can also be carried out remotely.[30] These businesses also provide internet access for their employees, most of whom are seasonal and from other states or countries. Some provide Wi-Fi for seasonal employees to use their own devices, and some provide internet kiosks.

Seafood processors also use database software to track fish tickets, which are required by the Alaska Department of Fish and Game to document commercial harvest from a public resource. Some fish processors now use the state's online eLandings system, which generates printable tickets.[31] A woman who runs a small commercial salmon operation out of Bristol Bay, Alaska, had internet access there for the first time after mounting a LEO satellite terminal to an old freezer, drawing power from a generator. It was "fantastic for my daily reports to Fish and Game, business calls and texts, and personal staying in touch with family," she said. She added that the connection allowed her to better market her catch online as well.[32]

Satellite terminals on fishing boats have also improved connectivity significantly, providing much more bandwidth and reliability than available from mobile coverage offshore. Fishers can access updated weather reports, repair manuals, and possibly life-saving medical information. Other uses of digital technologies in fisheries include sonar for locating fish as well as GPS for navigation and location finding, and Web-based information and networking resources. Digital technologies such as high-speed 5G and mesh networks connecting sensor platforms can also enable managers to better monitor fish stocks and catches, track individual fishing boats, and spot illegal fishing, a significant problem off the coasts of many developing regions and islands.

The Environment

Digital technologies can also contribute to environmental protection, ranging from reducing the need for transportation to contributing to monitoring environmental indicators, managing alternative energy systems, and contributing to green rural jobs. For example, Indigenous governments in both Alaska and Canada use online tools for land management and mapping. In northwestern Ontario, Poplar Hill First Nation operates a comprehensive lands and resource mapping system for its traditional lands. This tool has also been used to digitize all aspects of the community infrastructure including buildings, roads, electrical, cable, water, wastewater, and housing.[33]

Managing Renewable Energy

In rural Alaska, the internet is being used to manage electrical power for energy conservation. Alaska has abundant wind resources, primarily in the western and coastal portions of the state. There are at least 28 wind installations operating in rural communities. The availability of wind resources in combination with the high cost of diesel electricity generation in rural Alaska makes wind power an economical and clean alternative to traditional fossil fuels. Researchers estimate that a typical 1,000-kW wind turbine can displace about 17,800 gallons of diesel fuel per year, a saving of nearly $55,000 to an electric utility paying $3.10 per gallon for diesel fuel.[34] Remotely located software developed at the University of Alaska Fairbanks is being used to manage some of these wind/diesel operations.

In the Alaska village of Kongiginak, the cheapest source of energy is excess wind power which occurs most often during the winter months, when heating demand is also high. Maximizing use of available wind power is both cheaper and cleaner than relying on diesel-powered village generators The local tribally-owned utility implemented an innovative strategy to manage their wind power by storing excess power in the form of heat, rather than in chemical batteries, by installing thermal electric stoves in individual residences. The stoves are lined with ceramic fire bricks with a high heat capacity and density as well as an electric heating element that warms when there is cheap power available. The homeowners can then use that heat by turning on a fan that blows air through channels in the hot ceramic bricks.

The stoves are continually monitored to respond nearly instantaneously to changes in supply or demand.

> In other words, the stoves can automatically "see" when there is excess wind power and turn on to suck it up. They are also in constant communication with each other, programmed to turn on and off sequentially so they don't all run at the same time, ensuring every household gets a fair share.[35]

Smart Grids

"Smart grids" may be defined as a range of sensors, meters, and controls enabled by information technology, as well as large-scale and real-time data collection that can enhance the operational efficiency of the electricity system by optimizing energy transactions.[36] The integration of digital technologies into the grid can improve system security through more rapid analysis of service interruptions and prediction of outages. Connected devices and software offer customers access to real-time data to help them manage their energy usage more effectively. Sensors attached to energy systems such as solar panels and batteries can capture remote real-time data about the equipment, enabling the provider to monitor performance and offer maintenance support.[37] Low-cost sensors that can be factory-installed in electrical appliances such as televisions, refrigerators, and air conditioners allow both the monitoring and control of electricity use by consumers and electricity suppliers.

In India, a pilot project installed devices in volunteers' homes to measure the availability and quality of electricity on a continuous basis. The results provide a potentially powerful, crowd-sourced flow of information that could help consumers understand the causes and impacts of power shortages, and help policymakers and electric utilities prioritize power system investments.[38]

Environmental Monitoring

In the near future, digital connectivity has the potential to reduce carbon emissions in many sectors of the economy. The ITU reports that the Global e-Sustainability Initiative found that an increased use of ICT solutions such as travel substitution and environmental monitoring could deliver a 20 per cent reduction of global CO_2 emissions by 2030, a reduction of almost ten times that of the ICT sector footprint during the same period.[39] New tools are now available to monitor the concentration of ambient pollutants; however, barriers to introducing air monitoring systems include the high cost of installing and maintaining the networks and a shortage of professionals and technicians with specialized skills.

Satellite-based sensors that measure pollution concentrations from space can supplement information provided by sparse terrestrial monitors to produce estimates of pollution concentrations over larger areas. Remote sensing data could be particularly useful for developing regions with limited terrestrial monitoring. Also, lower-cost sensors and information technologies can reduce the cost to regulators of enforcing limits on emissions from sources such as factories, farms, and energy producers. Sensors can be placed within facilities, at fence lines, or in downwind communities to continuously monitor emissions and transmit data to regulators. These devices make it possible to gauge actual pollution over time, instead of through occasional sampling. Personal mobile technologies could also improve pollution monitoring, with sensing apps downloaded to mobile phones or on individual mobile sensing devices.[40]

Cloud-based computing and mapping, combined with new mobile platforms, make local air quality reports and forecasts publicly accessible and reduce the costs of data collection and dissemination. The World Bank reported that ratings programs in India and Indonesia have had a significant measurable impact in reducing pollution by the worst performing industries.[41]

In the Caribbean, Grenada has launched an innovative project to address climate change. The Blue Bot project uses artificial intelligence to analyze images captured by underwater reef robots and monitor species and climate change patterns to aid conservation efforts and sustainable fisheries management. On land, the Climate Smart Agriculture and Rural Enterprise Program monitors changes in climate, soil conditions, and market prices; this information helps to promote more climate-resilient and sustainable agriculture.[42]

Grenada and many other countries have launched apps with real-time information via mobile alerts on how to respond during natural disasters.

Energy Demand and e-Waste

A potential symbiotic relationship exists between the development of ICTs and increasing energy access in Africa and other low-access areas. For example, when energy utilities extend power for cell towers, they may also upgrade the energy generation unit of the tower to provide local consumers with access to electricity. Electric utilities may also install optical fiber or microwave links to monitor their grid. They may add excess broadband capacity that could be used to extend connectivity to rural communities.

Although they may contribute to sustainable energy, digital technologies may also create increased demand for energy as well as generate e-waste. The World Bank notes that efforts to meet the Agenda

2030 Sustainable Development Goal to "ensure access to affordable, reliable, sustainable, and modern energy for all" will require the effective use of information and communication technologies, including data and advanced analytics, requiring power for data centers and communications facilities. Data centers and transmission networks used around 2 percent of global electricity in 2020. Data centers are proliferating worldwide, while telecommunication network upgrades are improving efficiency. For example, fiber-optic cable is more energy-efficient than copper wire, and each generation of wireless technology uses less energy than previous generations.[43] Smartphone and computer manufacturers are supporting device return and recycling collection programs.

However, despite recycling in many countries, global e-waste continues to increase. Tackling connectivity-related environmental challenges is essential to minimize the environmental impact of ICTs, from discarded equipment that contains dangerous materials (such as mercury, cadmium, and lead), to telecommunication network carbon emissions and the significant power needed to run data centers. The ITU Connect 2030 Agenda has set global targets of a 30 percent e-waste recycling rate, increasing the number of countries with e-waste legislation to half of all countries, and reducing the volume of redundant e-waste by 50 per cent before the end of the decade.

In the mobile industry, the GSMA is working with mobile network operators to transition the industry to net zero emissions. The GSMA states that operators representing more than 60 percent of the industry by revenue have committed to rapidly cut their direct and indirect emissions by 2030, and almost half the industry have committed to reach net zero by 2050.[44]

Green Rural Jobs

Many of these digital technology-supported environment initiatives could generate a significant increase in rural jobs. About 65 percent of the total population of Africa is below the age of 35 years; 10 million young Africans enter the continent's workforce each year. Research by the development agency FSD Africa and an impact advisory firm predicts that 3.3 million jobs could be generated across the

Africa by 2030. The report predicts that about 70 percent of the jobs will be in the renewable energy sector, and that agriculture should employ "hundreds of thousands," with more than half of those jobs in climate-smart technology.[45]

Commentary

As shown in the cases above, access to marketing information and agricultural expertise can increase farmers' productivity and income. Digital tools are increasingly applied in crop management as well as energy management and environmental monitoring. Also, as shown by FRI, changing behavior of farmers (or other groups such as expectant mothers) requires both *awareness* of the proposed innovation and its *adoption*. Interactivity, whether through discussion groups, mobile phones, or online chats can increase both awareness of new practices and their adoption.

Yet in research reported in 2014, Nakasone and colleagues stated:

> We find that access to mobile phones has generally improved agricultural market performance at the macro level; however, impacts at the micro level are mixed. Evidence regarding the impact of market information systems (MIS) delivered through mobile phones on farm prices and income is limited, but the evidence points to strong, heterogeneous impacts.[46]

While access to mobile phones in rural developing regions has increased dramatically since 2014, and there are many examples of the importance of contributions of ICTs to agricultural and environmental management discussed above, the evidence on impacts is still "mixed."

Part of the explanation is that it is necessary to consider the rural context including factors such as access to markets and availability of credit to purchase recommended inputs. As Deichmann et al. point out:

> … even when farmers are seemingly better informed, they may not necessarily be able to act on that information because of the inaccessibility of alternative markets and the complex interlinked

> relationships between buyers and sellers in low-income developing economies. Rather than assuming that an information and communication technology (ICT) approach will always be cost-effective and yield a better outcome, a more nuanced understanding of the underlying institutional environment and constraints is warranted.[47]

Digital connectivity shows considerable promise for environmental monitoring and energy management, although ICTs, particularly data centers, also require energy to operate.

References

1. Quoted in Abebe, Abyssinia (2025, July 18), In West Africa, young agribusiness leaders apply climate solutions learned in Quebec, *The Globe and Mail*. https://www.theglobeandmail.com/world/article-in-west-africa-young-agribusiness-leaders-apply-climate-solutions/.
2. World Bank (2016), *Digital Dividends*, World Development Report. https://www.worldbank.org/en/publication/wdr2016.
3. Rogers, Everett M. (2003), *Diffusion of Innovations* (5th edition), Free Press.
4. Zanello, Giacomo, Fu, Xiaolan, Mohnen, Pierre, & Ventresca, Marc (2016), The Creation and Diffusion of Innovation in Developing Countries: A Systematic Literature Review, *Journal of Economic Surveys*, 30(5), 884–912.
5. https://farmradio.org/our-history/.
6. Hudson, Heather E., Leclair, Mark, Pelletier, Bernard, & Sullivan, Bartholomew (2017). Using Radio and Interactive ICTs to Improve Food Security Among Smallholder Farmers in Sub-Saharan Africa, *Telecommunications Policy*, 41(7), 670–84.
7. FRI (2015), *Final Report: Developing Ongoing Demand-Led Interactive Farm Radio Services*, Farm Radio International, Ottawa.
8. Farm Radio International. (2015). *How to Use Information and Communication Technologies (ICTs) to Interact with Your Listeners: Three Methods*, Farm Radio International, Ottawa. https://farmradio.org/?s=How+to+use+information+and+communication+technologies+%28ICTs%29+to+interact+with+your+listeners%3A+Three+methods.
9. Hudson, Heather E., Leclair, Mark, Pelletier, Bernard, & Sullivan, Bartholomew (2017). Using Radio and Interactive ICTs to Improve Food Security Among Smallholder Farmers in Sub-Saharan Africa, *Telecommunications Policy*, 41(7), 670–84.

10. *Harnessing the Chances of Digitalization for Rural Development: Lessons-Learnt in German-Funded Rural Development Projects* (2018), Deutsche Gesellschaft für Internationale Zusammenarbeit (GIZ) GmbH, Bonn, p. 31. https://www.bmz-digital.global/wp-content/uploads/2022/08/180807_Harnessing-A4-1.pdf.
11. Siaw, A., Jiang, Y., Twumasi, M., & Agbenyo, W. (2020) The Impact of Internet Use on Income: The Case of Rural Ghana, *Sustainability*,17 April.
12. Ma, W., Zhou, X., & Liu, M. (2019), What Drives Farmers' Willingness to Adopt e-Commerce in Rural China? The Role of Internet Use, *Agribusiness*, July.
13. Ma, W., Nie, P., Zhang, P., & Renwick, A. (2019), Impact of Internet Use on Economic Well-Being of Rural Households: Evidence from China, *Review of Development Economics*, December. DOI: 10.1111/rode.12645.
14. Zhou, X., Cui, Y., & Zhang, S. (2020). Internet Use and Rural Residents' Income Growth, *China Agricultural Economic Review*, 12(2), 315–27.
15. Yuan, F., Tang, K., & Shi, Q. (2021), Does Internet Use Reduce Chemical Fertilizer Use? Evidence from Rural Households in China, *Environmental Science and Pollution Research*, 28(5), 6005–17.
16. Kaila, H., & Tarp, F. (2019). Can the Internet Improve Agricultural Production? Evidence from Viet Nam, *Agricultural Economics*, 50(6), 675–91.
17. Mathew, Joe (2018), ITC e-Choupal 4.0 by Mid-2019; Shift to Mobile Platform, Handholding of Agri-Startups Key. *Business Today*. https://www.businesstoday.in/sectors/agriculture/itc-e-choupal-4.o-mid-2019-shift-mobile-platform-handholding-agri-startups-key/story/303861.html.
18. *Greenway: Myanmar's First Digital Farming App*. https://www.greenovator.co/products/green-way.
19. https://www.zaytangyi.com/info/about-us.
20. Agence France Press (2018), Myanmar Farmers Going Against the Grain with Apps, February 18. Quoted in https://www.nationthailand.com/Startup_and_IT/30339171.
21. https://directory.growasia.org/green-way/.
22. Tita, Bob & Maidenberg, Micah (2024), John Deere, Meet Elon Musk: SpaceX Satellites to LinkFarm Giant's Equipment, *Wall Street Journal*, January 15.
23. Personal communication, July 2024.
24. https://www.india.gov.in/spotlight/namo-drone-didi.
25. Quoted in Abebe, Abyssinia (2025, July 18), In West Africa, young agribusiness leaders apply climate solutions learned in Quebec, *The Globe and Mail*. https://www.theglobeandmail.com/world/article-in-west-africa-young-agribusiness-leaders-apply-climate-solutions/.

26. Personal interviews by the author, 2023.
27. Quoted in Abebe, Abyssinia (2025, July 18), In West Africa, young agribusiness leaders apply climate solutions learned in Quebec, *The Globe and Mail*. https://www.theglobeandmail.com/world/article-in-west-africa-young-agribusiness-leaders-apply-climate-solutions/.
28. Jensen, R. (2007), The Digital Provide: Information (Technology), Market Performance, and Welfare in the South Indian Fisheries Sector, *Quarterly Journal of Economics*, 122(3), 879–924. https://doi.org/10.1162/qjec.122.3.879.
29. Jensen, R. (2007), The Digital Provide: Information (Technology), Market Performance, and Welfare in the South Indian Fisheries Sector, *Quarterly Journal of Economics*, 122(3), 879–924. https://doi.org/10.1162/qjec.122.3.879.
30. Hudson, Heather E., Sharp, Suzanne, & Hill, Alexandra (2015), After Broadband: A Study of Organizational Use of Broadband in Southwest Alaska. https://scholarworks.alaska.edu/handle/11122/5959.
31. See http://www.adfg.alaska.gov/index.cfm?adfg=fishlicense.fishtickets.
32. Hughes, Zachariah, DeMarban, Alex, and Naiden, Alena. (2023, August 20), In Just A Few Months, Satellite Internet Has Reshaped Web Access in Rural Alaska, *Anchorage Daily News*.
33. O'Donnell, S., Beaton, B., McMahon, R., Hudson, H.E., Williams, D., & Whiteduck, T. (2016, June), Digital Technology Adoption in Remote and Northern Indigenous Communities in Canada, Canadian Sociological Association 2016 Annual Conference, University of Calgary, Calgary, Alberta. http://firstmile.ca/wp-content/uploads/2016-CSA-Digital-Technology-Adoption.pdf.
34. Rural Energy Alaska Project (REAP). See http://alaskarenewableenergy.org/index.php/clean-energy-in-alaska/wind/.
35. Meadows, R., Edgerly, E., Jordan, R., & Beshilas, L. (2025), *Renewable Energy Integration in Remote Alaska Communities*, Technical Report NREL/TP-5700-90685, 2522802, MainId: 9246.
36. World Bank (2016), *Digital Dividends*, World Bank Development Report. https://www.worldbank.org/en/publication/wdr2016.
37. World Bank (2016), *Digital Dividends*, World Bank Development Report. https://www.worldbank.org/en/publication/wdr2016.
38. World Bank (2016), *Digital Dividends*, World Bank Development Report. https://www.worldbank.org/en/publication/wdr2016.
39. ITU Global Connectivity Report 2022. (2022) Geneva: International Telecommunication Union, p. 59. https://www.itu.int/itu-d/reports/statistics/global-connectivity-report-2022/.

40. Nyarku, M., Mazaheri, M., Jayaratne, R., Dunbabin, M., Rahman, M.M., Uhde, E., & Morawska, L. (2018), Mobile Phones as Monitors of Personal Exposure to Air Pollution: Is This the Future? *PLoS One*, 13(2). e0193150. doi: 10.1371/journal.pone.0193150. PMID: 29474387; PMCID: PMC5825064.
41. World Bank (2016), *Digital Dividends*, World Bank Development Report. https://www.worldbank.org/en/publication/wdr2016.
42. United Nations Department of Economic and Social Affairs (2022), *The Future of Digital Government*, Survey, United Nations e-Government Survey:
43. ITU (2022), *Global Connectivity Report 2022*, International Telecommunication Union, p. 58. https://www.itu.int/itu-d/reports/statistics/global-connectivity-report-2022/.
44. ITU/UNESCO (2023, September), *The State of Broadband 2023: Digital Connectivity. A Transformative Opportunity*, ITU/UNESCO Broadband Commission for Sustainable Development. https://www.itu.int/dms_pub/itu-s/opb/pol/S-POL-BROADBAND.28-2023-PDF-E.pdf
45. Kimeu, Caroline (2024, July 26), Green Economy Could Generate 3.3m Jobs Across Africa by 2030 – Report, *The Guardian*. https://www.theguardian.com/global-development/article/2024/jul/26/green-economy-could-generate-33m-jobs-across-africa-by-2030-report.
46. Nakasone, E., Torero, M. & Minten, B. (2014), The Power of Information: The ICT Revolution in Agricultural Development, *Annual Review of Resource Economics*. Annu. Rev. Resour. Econ. 2014. 6:533–50. doi: 10.1146/annurev-resource-100913-012714.
47. Uwe Deichmann Aparajita Goyal Deepak Mishra (2016) Will Digital Technologies Transform Agriculture in Developing Countries? *Agricultural Economics*, 47(S1), 21–33. https://doi.org/10.1111/agec.12300.

6

E-COMMERCE

> "I do everything with my phone; it's an extension of my arm."[1]
>
> – Indigenous resident, Outback Australia

From the Telegraph to e-Commerce

Rural residents increasingly rely on mobile phones for economic activities. This chapter examines the role of digital technologies in rural e-commerce, facilitating rural business activities. It also examines the growing adoption of mobile money and the opportunities and challenges for online and gig workers, such as those relying on digital connectivity for on-demand jobs like delivery and ride-hailing services, or more skilled piecework such as translation or coding. And, increasingly, rural residents do everything with their mobile phones.

Telecommunications have facilitated financial transactions since the invention of the telegraph, which made it possible for investors to get same-day updates on stock prices and send orders to their brokers. By the 1860s, the stock market used telegraph lines to transmit transactions in close to real time, and printed them out on rolls of tape. As the telephone network expanded in the late nineteenth century, it also became a means for transmitting financial information.[2] By 1920, there were an estimated 88,000 telephones in the Wall

DOI: 10.4324/9781003431602-6

Street district of New York.[3] (Similar technological trends in finance occurred in Europe, and later in Japan and Hong Kong.) Electronic terminals began to replace stock tickers in the 1960s; the introduction of NASDAQ (the National Association of Securities Dealers Automated Quotations system) led to the virtual trading floor, and then to competitive online trading platforms accessible from a personal computer or a smartphone, and the rise of e-commerce.

Major types of e-commerce are:

- business-to-business (B2B), i.e. transfers of funds and information between commercial entities, such as companies in a supply chain;
- business-to-consumer (B2C), i.e. interactions directly between commercial sellers and consumers, such as online selling to remote consumers;
- business-to-government (B2G), i.e. financial transactions between commercial businesses and government entities, such as for procurement of equipment and services;
- consumer-to-consumer (C2C), i.e. direct transactions between individuals, such as remittance payments from overseas workers to family members.

Mobile commerce (m-commerce) refers to any of the above types of transactions carried out on wireless technologies, primarily mobile phones. M-Commerce has been adopted in developing regions where households and small businesses are primarily mobile phone users. One of the most popular applications is "mobile money," whereby individuals can transfer funds, pay for, and receive payment for goods and services.

Digital technologies can provide many benefits across a wide range of business processes and transactions. ICT applications improve information and knowledge management inside the organization, and they can also reduce transaction costs and increase the speed and reliability of transactions for B2B, B2C, and B2G transactions. ICT applications can make communication within the firm faster and the management of the firm's resources more efficient.

The internet can be a facilitator for e-commerce as it allows businesses to showcase and sell their products and services online and gives potential customers and business partners access to information about their products and services.[4] Digital connectivity can reduce transaction costs and increase the speed and reliability of transactions, improving coordination and thereby efficiency between firms in the value chain. Online B2B interactions can reduce information asymmetries between buyers and suppliers and build closer relationships among trading partners, reducing transaction costs and increasing transaction speed and reliability. Seamless transfer of information through shared electronic files and digital networks increases the efficiency of business processes such as documentation, data processing, and other back-office functions such as payroll and invoicing.

Mobile Money

Digital payment systems help overcome barriers to accessing financial services. The mobile industry estimated that in 2023 more than 1.6 billion people worldwide had access to mobile money services, whereas 2 billion people did not have access to a bank account.[5] Mobile money schemes allow people who own a phone but do not have a bank account to make and receive payments. Mobile money systems store money in the national currency as credit on smart cards or with a system provider and enable payments through mobile phones. These systems can offer lower fees and easier use than traditional payment systems and can facilitate transactions for those without a bank account.

An example is M-PESA (*pesa* means money in Swahili), which was launched in Kenya in 2007 to make funds transfers for remittances as simple as sending a text. Owned by telecommunications providers Vodacom and Safaricom, M-PESA allows customers in seven additional African countries (Democratic Republic of Congo, Egypt, Ghana, Lesotho, Mozambique, Tanzania) to instantly and securely send funds, pay bills, make in-store payments, send money abroad, and access financial services such as loans and overdraft facilities. As of 2025, 51 million customers were making $314 billion in M-PESA transactions per year.[6] M-PESA was able to grow exponentially in Kenya because of the lack of regulation that protects the banking systems from disintermediation or other forms of competition in many countries. Disintermediation refers to the removal of the middle institution or process, typically banks in the financial sector, exemplified by the rise of non-traditional providers of financial services such as money transfers, savings, and lending.

South Africa-based mobile carrier MTN provides similar services in 16 countries and has also innovated in financial technology (fintech) applications. MTN Mobile Money Open APIs (application programming interfaces) provide developers with complimentary access to the MTN Mobile Money proprietary software platform to enable them to create innovative digital financial services for Africans.[7]

In 2020, Brazil's central bank launched PIX, a payment system that allows users to make and receive instant payments on their mobile phones, using a bank account and an identifying key such as a phone number or QR code. PIX has been adopted by 175 million Brazilians and accounts for almost half the country's financial transactions. Data from Brazil's central bank shows that Brazilians are relying less on cash, with cash withdrawals dropping by about a third since 2020.[8]

Before PIX, moving money was slower and more expensive, usually through expensive transfers from one bank to another, or payment vouchers known as *boletos bancários*, which could take days to clear. Analysts state that the system has played a key role in making Brazil's financial system more inclusive. Many low-income and informal workers who formerly dealt only in cash can now use digital payments, building a track record with financial institutions.[9]

In Pakistan, government-owned institutions have also introduced digital financial services in collaboration with the private sector. For example, Pakistan launched the Asaan Mobile Account (AMA) platform, a joint initiative by the State Bank of Pakistan (SBP) and Pakistan Telecommunication Authority (PTA) in collaboration with branchless banking providers, telecommunications operators, and other development partners. This platform enables citizens to open digital accounts and access financial services quickly.[10]

Digital payments can reduce costs to recipients in obtaining payments, thereby saving them money. Farmers in Niger realized time savings for each digital payment equivalent to an amount that would feed a family of five for a week. Digital payment systems can also increase security compared to traveling with large amounts of cash, which is common in many developing countries. Speed in delivering cash can also be especially important in emergencies such as natural disasters, as discussed below. Digital finance can increase the incentive to save, through automatic deposits, text reminders, or default options. For example, texted reminders increased savings in Bolivia, Peru, and the Philippines by up to 16 percent.[11]

Digital Financing

Many small businesses face difficulties obtaining loans in the traditional financial system. Lenders typically have little information about a potential borrower's ability to repay a loan, and are therefore unlikely to risk making a loan. In China, Alifinance (now part of Ant Financial, a subsidiary of the Chinese e-commerce giant Alibaba) estimates credit scores from digital footprints. Alifinance's credit scoring model is based on at least three months of a vendor's online activity; it makes loan decisions automatically and almost instantly, authorizing loans up to about $5,000 with flexible repayment terms.[12]

Microlenders in African serving small farmers or small businesses may use mobile phone payment records to assess credit risk. Ghanaian start-up Cignifi uses borrowers' mobile phone records to judge their creditworthiness.[13] M-Shwari, operated by the Commercial Bank of Africa and Safaricom, is a bank account linked to Kenya's M-PESA payment system. M-Shwari pays interest on deposits and provides short-term loans with approval decisions made almost instantly based on M-PESA usage history. Loan amounts might be as small as $15.

Digital financing not only eliminates the need for traditional banks but can also enable peer-to-peer lending. Part of the Alibaba Group, Yu'E Ba ("leftover treasure" in Mandarin) is a fixed-income investment fund into which customers can transfer balances from their Alipay digital payment accounts to peer-lending platforms. Users can then make loans to others on the platform without traditional financial intermediaries, instead matching potential lenders and borrowers directly.[14]

Remittances

Remittances sent from citizens working abroad are an important source of income for many developing economies. Using a data set composed of 71 developing countries, World Bank researchers found that a 10 percent increase in per capita official international remittances can lead to a 3.5 percent decline in the share of people living in poverty.[15] In more than 60 countries, remittances account for 3 percent or more of the GDP. Since 2015, remittances have been the largest source of external finance flows to low- and middle-income countries other than China. In 2023, remittances to low- and middle-income countries were estimated at $656 billion. The top five recipient countries for remittance inflows among LMICs were: India ($120 billion), Mexico ($66 billion), China ($50 billion), the Philippines ($39 billion), and Pakistan (27 billion).[16] As a percentage of GDP, small/fragile states are more heavily dependent on remittances, with the top five being Tonga (remittances 41 percent of GDP), Tajikistan (39 percent), Lebanon (31 percent), Samoa (28 percent), and Nicaragua (27 percent).[17]

The World Bank states: "it is critical that both remittance senders and receivers have access to a multitude of payment methods and channels in order to deliver and receive remittances in an affordable and fast manner."[18] Digital technologies and competition make remittances cheaper. For example, the prices for international transactions such as sending remittances from overseas workers to relatives in countries such as Mexico, the Philippines, and Bangladesh have fallen dramatically with the availability of competitive digital service providers.

M-PESA is the destination for over $1.5 billion remittances annually, including 60 percent of formal remittances into Kenya and 20 percent into Tanzania.[19] In Kenya, in 2008 shortly after M-PESA entered the market, the cost of sending $100 domestically was $12 by MoneyGram, $20 by bank wire, $6 by postal money order, and

$3 by bus, compared to $2.50 by M-Pesa.[20] Currently, to transfer about $100 domestically via M-PESA costs about $0.77, or less than 1 percent of the transaction.

Extending Rural Markets

Mobile phone connectivity to digital commerce sites has extended rural access to domestic and international markets. In Borneo, an artist was able to return from urban Malaysia to his remote village where he established a gallery with global online sales.[21] In Africa, Jiji is an online marketplace launched in 2014 that grew rapidly to more than 10 million unique visits per month. It hosts 2 million active ads worth a total of $10 billion. Joji is present in Ethiopia, Ghana, Kenya, Nigeria, Tanzania, and Uganda; its growth strategy is primarily mobile phone-based.

In Arctic Canada, entrepreneurs in Nunavut promote their goods and services on websites. Inuit artists and carvers sell their work online to collectors around the world. In the settlement of Arviat, Kiluk Ltd. produces fine fur and leather clothing, with much of their product sold online to buyers across Canada.[22] Kivalliq Arctic Foods in the settlement of Rankin Inlet on Hudson Bay processes Arctic char, caribou, and musk ox, and ships these traditional foods to other Nunavut communities, generating sales primarily through Facebook. Over the past six years, they have hired more employees and purchased increased quantities of fish and meat from local harvesters, contributing to the local economy.[23]

The following are more detailed examples of rural e-commerce, primarily consisting of m-commerce, i.e. using mobile phones.

e-Commerce

China: Taobao Villages

There are now more than 1.1 billion mobile internet users in China. The internet penetration rate is 85.3 percent in urban regions while lower but very substantial at 67.4 percent in rural areas.[24] China's Taobao Villages are perhaps the most dramatic example of efforts to use digital services to increase rural incomes. The Taobao Villages, named for the e-commerce platform Taobao owned by Alibaba, are rural e-commerce hubs that use Alibaba's logistics, service, and training to encourage farmers to engage in online sales of farm produce and local specialties. To be nominated as a Taobao Village, Alibaba requires total annual e-commerce transactions of over 10 million yuan (about $1.5 million) and more than 100 online stores located in the village. Participants use Alipay, owned by a subsidiary of Alibaba, for e-payment, online banking, and a peer-to-peer payment system that functions like an escrow account. The buyer sends their payment to Alipay, which releases it when the buyer says they have received the goods. Alipay China states that it delivers payment services to over 1 billion users and 80 million merchants.[25]

The World Bank refers to Taobao as "e-commerce with Chinese characteristics," contributing to inclusion, efficiency, and innovation. Online commerce has allowed producers in towns and villages to participate in the national and even global economy. Alibaba and other Chinese firms operate business-to-business platforms that facilitate intra- and interindustry trade as well as exports. Online trade has not only helped raise rural incomes but also made shopping more efficient. Taobao and other e-commerce platforms are examples of innovation generated by the economies of scale when transaction costs drop drastically, such as by use of highly automated platforms.[26]

Research by Li found that e-commerce adopters obtained significantly higher income than non-adopters, and such a large income gain was mainly due to increases in sales income. He notes that the Taobao Villages are mostly concentrated in relatively developed provinces with a track record of high-level private entrepreneurship.[27] Li also highlights the role of the state as well as of the e-commerce giant Alibaba:

> The development of Taobao Villages indicates the complex state–business relationship in China, where capable e-commerce giants are required to provide public goods in return for business opportunities, while the party-state not only provides supervision, but also participates in organising e-commerce business at the grassroots level to achieve state objectives such as poverty reduction and economic growth in the rural areas, arguably for greater political legitimacy.[28]

Proponents of Taobao villages and Alipay point out: "Alipay has become a pivotal part of rural economic infrastructure where traditional physical banking has been inconvenient for many villagers."[29] Concerning inclusion, Taobao enables people in rural towns and villages to participate in the national or even global economy. Most of the businesses are small, with an average of 2.5 employees. About one-third of owners are female, and one-fifth were previously unemployed. About 1 percent are persons with disabilities.[30] Innovation can be stimulated by the economies of scale made possible when transaction costs drop drastically, while automation can keep fees low.

One of the most valuable assets Alibaba and other e-commerce operators accumulate is data. Each transaction contributes to better knowledge about the economy and consumer behavior. The data generated from transactions have also enabled the Ant Group to innovate in offering other products such as consumer finance, wealth management, and insurance.[31] This information can also advance financial inclusion; for instance, Alibaba's Ant Financial teamed up with the International Finance Corporation to expand credit to female entrepreneurs in China.[32] Yet there appears to be no privacy protection in China for personal data that can be traced to individual mobile phone users.

Some Taobao villagers point out difficulties:

> Alibaba sucks us dry. It sucks the blood out of us, and it will suck the blood out of this village. As sellers, all our money is kept in Alipay because that's how buyers send money. At the drop of a pin they can demand a refund, and because of the escrow service, the money gets sent back to them, even if I've shipped the order already. Or maybe they don't like the material, they think it's cheap. But we have to keep on making worse quality stuff. How are we supposed to keep prices low and compete with others? The government … keeps building roads, putting in broadband. And Alibaba uses all this infrastructure for free, relies on us to make decisions on lowering the quality of goods. There's only so much cutting corners we can do … What happens when this system fails?[33]

Vietnam

Vietnam has a growing digital economy, driven by its rapidly expanding e-commerce sector and one of the highest internet penetration rates worldwide. There are approximately 80 million internet users in Vietnam, out of a total population of 100 million, with digital use driven by widespread smartphone adoption.

Once among the most cash-dependent nations in Asia, Vietnam is embracing cashless transactions at an unprecedented pace. The value of digital payment transactions in Vietnam is projected to reach $45 billion in 2028, surpassing Singapore and Malaysia.[34] By 2024, more than 60 percent of Vietnamese consumers regularly used QR codes for transactions – more than traditional card payments. This shift is fueled by mobile banking apps, digital wallets, and increasing merchant acceptance, even in smaller cities and rural areas, enabling seamless transactions with neighboring countries such as Laos. E-wallet operators are among the key players driving this transformation. However, fierce competition coupled with high customer acquisition costs and low transaction fees are challenging their profitability. In response, e-wallet providers are diversifying their business models, expanding into areas such as partnerships, lending services, and the use of embedded financial solutions to generate new sources of revenue.

Another e-commerce activity is online recruitment. VietnamWorks is one of Vietnam's leading online recruitment platforms; it posts new jobs for 5.5 million candidates, providing recruitment solutions for more than 60,000 companies. It also offers guidance on preparing CVs, professional education, and a "numerology analysis" – "a reference tool to help you suggest suitable careers based on the strengths and weaknesses of the numbers related to you."[35]

Laos

Access to Finance for the Poor (AFP) aimed to enhance financial inclusion in Laos with a focus on the rural poor. Its objective was to increase the numbers of rural people using financial services provided by network-supported village banks. In its first 8 years, the project helped to provide more than 115,000 members with access to financial services through more than 600 village banks. Women represent more than 50 percent of members, have access to 77 percent of all accounts, and fill more than a third of the village banks' leadership positions.[36]

Gig Work

Outsourcing

Electronic outsourcing of work to developing regions began with editing and translation of documents that did not require real-time connectivity,[37] followed by real-time voice services such as telephone directory assistance.[38] The rise of outsourcing has been made possible by investment in telecommunications infrastructure and competition in digital international connectivity services that have dramatically lowered the price of international connection with a skilled, relatively low-income workforce. For example, educated workers with fluency in English plus international submarine fiber connectivity have enabled the Philippines and India to develop an IT-based outsourcing sector with call centers and other "back-office" functions for technical support, customer services, and administrative support businesses based in the United States and Canada. Call centers also operate from several Caribbean countries, while francophone workers in northern and western Africa provide similar services for businesses based in France.

The Philippines' offshore outsourcing industry, with a valuation of approximately $34 billion in 2024, contributes approximately 8 percent to the country's GDP, employing more than 1.8 million workers.[39] While originally based around metro Manila, back-office services are now also located in regional hubs such as Cebu, Clark, Davao, and Iloilo. The growth of the sector has been stimulated by several factors, including government initiatives that created special economic zones with tax incentives, substantial private sector investments in telecommunications infrastructure, and educational reforms designed to provide training to meet industry requirements.

In India, in 2025, the projected revenue in Business Process Outsourcing (BPO) market was $7.75 billion.[40] Outsourced work ranges from call center functions to human resources and other administrative support to high-skilled, higher-paid occupations such as software maintenance and testing, engineering design and digital mapping, production and support of digital games, and other applications. India has a vast population of young English-speaking college-educated professionals, and labor costs significantly lower than in North America and Europe. The liberalization of the Indian economy in the 1990s opened the Indian economy to foreign investment, leading to the growth of several industries, including the BPO industry. The Indian government has also supported the BPO industry through various incentives and tax breaks to BPO companies. In addition to outsourced services, India's tech sector includes major technology manufacturing, software development, IT research, and applications in numerous fields. This broader digital economy now contributes an estimated 12 percent to GDP. IT sector revenues for fiscal year 2024 were $268.8 billion with 5.7 million employees.[41]

Many smaller outsourcing ventures are found in rural India and other developing regions, where people may work from home or at digitally connected businesses or community centers. The government of Kerala, India, outsources information technology services to cooperatives of women from poor families through the Kudumbashree ("Prosperity of the Family") project. Women in more than 230,000 Neighborhood Groups are engaged in income-generating activities. Nine in ten of the women had previously not worked outside the home. To strengthen the marketing capabilities of women entrepreneurs, Kudumbashree has listed more than 140 products on the Open Network for Digital Commerce (ONDC) platform.[42]

Ride Hailing and Deliveries

Indonesians spent over $53 billion online in 2023, almost as much as the rest of Southeast Asia combined. The growing popularity of e-commerce on social media apps like TikTok allows Indonesian businesses to reach distant customers. Mobile digital payment systems are very popular in Indonesia. GoJek, which began as a small business, disrupted the taxi industry with its ride-hailing app. Other ride-hailing apps and new entrepreneurial services drove demand for always-on connectivity and location-tracking services. GoJek has since merged with Tokopedia to form GoTo, a company that provides on-demand, e-commerce, and digital payments services; it accounts for almost 2 percent of Indonesia's GDP.

OVO, a stand-alone digital payments app backed by another ride-hailing app, Grab, and local conglomerate Lippo Group, is the top e-wallet application in Indonesia, including more than 300,000 retailers, and leading Indonesia digital service providers such as Tokopedia. OVO is a smart application that can be used for electronic money services such as payment transactions at online merchants and offline merchants. More than 110 million Indonesians use OVO for more than 1 billion annual transactions; its management states that OVO is a major contributor to financial inclusion in Indonesia.[43]

During the COVID-19 pandemic, ordering for delivery became very popular in Indonesia, supporting a growing number of delivery gig workers:

> Iksan knows the roads around his hometown on the Indonesian island of Sumatra like the back of his hand. He runs a package sorting center from his garage, a small but essential piece of a sprawling network delivering goods bought on Tokopedia, the country's biggest homegrown e-commerce company.
>
> His team of three motorcycle riders slog through rice fields and palm oil plantations to bring their neighbors boxes and padded envelopes that were purchased online just days before …
>
> Tokopedia and other companies have developed software to help dispatchers and drivers monitor traffic on tiny side streets in out-of-the-way places and the perpetually clogged highways of the capital, Jakarta …
>
> The packages leaving the warehouse can take every imaginable form of transportation – truck, boat, motorcycle, even ox cart – to reach their destination.[44]

In other regions, online delivery services are used both within countries and by the diaspora to send food and gifts to family members at home. Members of the Ugandan diaspora combine the transfer of online funds and online food delivery services to send in-kind remittances to family members. Ethiopians living abroad can order goats to be delivered to family members for important occasions.[45]

In a study of location-based platform workers in Cape Town and Johannesburg, Ahmed and colleagues found that location-based platforms offer workers some positive features such as gainful employment and income, which were the top two motivating factors for many workers. Other key motivating factors included the lack of alternative employment opportunities and better work flexibility. However, almost all the workers in all the focus groups were making "survivalists choices within a very constrained set of options." They also faced challenges from the precarious nature of the work and lack of high-quality jobs.[46]

Obstacles facing gig workers, in addition to the need for internet connectivity, typically via a smartphone, include:

- *Gender divisions*: Men are more likely to work in ride-hailing or e-delivery, which require owning or renting a vehicle, while domestic work sites typically recruit women, perpetuating gender stereotypes and lower pay for women.
- *Working conditions*: There is typically no regulation of "gig work" and benefits that might be provided by traditional employers such as guaranteed minimum wages and health insurance are not offered.
- *Lack of privacy*: Workers have limited privacy and do not control their own data, which can be used for surveillance of their location and activity. Gig workers in the South Africa study said they had no possibilities to access or dispute their customer service ratings, or to receive information used to justify removal from a platform, or to transfer their data to other platforms.[47]

Tourism and Digital Nomads

Digital connectivity has become an important asset to encourage travelers, including ecotourists, to visit developing regions. Guest houses and tourist lodges in Alaska, northern Canada, the Caribbean, and other rural regions market their facilities online and are increasingly expected to provide reliable online connections for their guests. Rural residents may also advertise their homes for short-term rentals. While generating additional revenue for the owners and the visitors they attract, these rentals can increase local living costs by reducing the housing availability for local residents. For example, residents of Maui in Hawai'i were divided on whether to eliminate short-term rentals on the island to provide more housing for residents who had lost their homes when a wildfire destroyed the town of Lahaina, or whether it was more important to preserve accommodation to generate tourist revenue.[48]

"Location independent" workers or digital nomads may be freelancers, consultants, entrepreneurs, and employees who may work from home or choose to work from other cities or countries in temporary accommodation or co-working spaces. The availability of reliable and affordable broadband in some developing regions contributed to the growing number of "digital nomads" during the COVID-19 pandemic. Urban professionals who could work remotely left their homes in industrialized countries for pleasant lower-cost surroundings. Tourism destinations with lower living costs than cities in the Global North, such as Chiang Mai in Thailand, Bali in Indonesia, and Medellín in Colombia, became highly attractive digital nomad centers. More than 50 countries now offer work visas to attract nomadic professionals.[49] Most of these countries are located in Europe, Latin America, and the Caribbean. Countries in the Global South ranked in the top 50 for such travelers include Thailand, Brazil, Argentina, Costa Rica, Uruguay, Vietnam, and Colombia. Amenities that are rated highest include broadband speed and cost, mobile network speed, average monthly rent, and availability of a "working holiday visa."[50]

Commentary

The benefits of connectivity for small businesses can be more valuable in remote than in urban regions.[51] The digital economy could potentially provide alternative forms of work and opportunities for those facing barriers to enter traditional labor markets in developing regions. However, both providers and users of online services face challenges. For example, connectivity often is not sufficient for rural e-commerce. The survival of small businesses depends on digital skills: "To survive, rural businesses need to develop a strong online identity to reach a wider market, be a party to opportunities and important developments within their sector, and find potential areas of collaboration."[52]

The availability of funds transfer as a service on mobile phones has brought large numbers of "unbanked" people in developing regions into the financial system for the first time. However, as the World Bank points out, this innovation requires – or should require – consumer education and consumer protection, including promoting financial literacy and fraud prevention, dispute resolution mechanisms, and data privacy.

Gig workers also face challenges and risks. Souza argues that "the platformisation of delivery services has resulted in the further casualisation of work, as jobs previously governed by employment contracts and paid on the basis of time worked, are replaced by a task-based system under the guise of self-employment."[53] Castel-Branco and Dawson refer to "Digital Taylorism," referring to the scientific management theory originated by Frederick Taylor a century ago, and now applied in algorithmic management of worker tasks, such as task assignment, time allocated, and performance evaluation.[54]

These challenges may also apply to workers hired to perform tasks such as removing inappropriate content from social media or labeling objects for AI recognition for major multinational tech firms. Not only can the work be tedious or emotionally disturbing, but the workers may be hired by contractors that pay lower wages compared to employees of the tech firms themselves and do not offer benefits.[55]

References

1. Forde, S. et al. (2024), *Radio, Television and Digital Media in 21st Century Indigenous Broadcasting: A Place of Old and New Ways*, Griffith Centre for Social and Cultural Research, Griffith University, Queensland, Australia.

2. Sobel, Robert (1965), *The Big Board: A History of the New York Stock Market*. Free Press.
3. *History of Technology Impacts on the Stock Market Prior to World War II* (n.d.). https://www.laits.utexas.edu/~anorman/long.extra/Projects.F97/Stock_Tech/page1.htm#:~:text=The%20telephone%20made%20its%20first,to%20buy%20and%20sell%20securities.
4. UNECA, ICT, Science & Technology Division (2008), *E-Trade and Economic Growth in Africa: Opportunities and Challenges*, October, pp. 10–12.
5. GSMA-SOTIR-2023_Web.pdf.
6. https://www.vodafone.com/about-vodafone/what-we-do/m-pesa.
7. https://www.mtn.com/digital-services/.
8. https://www.bcb.gov.br/detalhenoticia/20673/noticia.
9. Ionova, Ana (2025, September 29), Brazil Has a New Digital Spending Habit, *New York Times*. https://www.nytimes.com/2025/09/29/world/americas/brazil-digital-payments.html.
10. ITU/UNESCO (2023, September), The State of Broadband 2023: Digital Connectivity, A Transformative Opportunity. ITU/UNESCO Broadband Commission for Sustainable Development. https://www.itu.int/dms_pub/itu-s/opb/pol/S-POL-BROADBAND.28-2023-PDF-E.pdf
11. World Bank (2016), *Digital Dividends*, World Bank Development Report. https://www.worldbank.org/en/publication/wdr2016.
12. World Economic Forum (2018, September), *The Digital Enterprise: Moving from Experimentation to Transformation*. Geneva.
13. World Bank (2016), *Digital Dividends*, World Bank Development Report. https://www.worldbank.org/en/publication/wdr2016.
14. Li, J. (2015), An Empirical Study on the Effect of Yu'ebao to the Deposits in Chinese Commercial Banks, *Open Journal of Social Sciences*, 3, 142–8.
15. Adams, H. Jr. & Page, John (2005), Do International Migration and Remittances Reduce Poverty in Developing Countries? *World Development*, 33(10), 1645–69. ISSN 0305-750X. https://doi.org/10.1016/j.worlddev.2005.05.004. https://www.sciencedirect.com/science/article/pii/S0305750X05001270.
16. World Bank (2024, September 18), *Brief: Remittances*. https://www.worldbank.org/en/topic/migration/brief/remittances-knomad.
17. World Bank (2024, September 18), *Brief: Remittances*. https://www.worldbank.org/en/topic/migration/brief/remittances-knomad.
18. World Bank (2024, September 18), *Brief: Remittances*. https://www.worldbank.org/en/topic/migration/brief/remittances-knomad.
19. https://www.vodafone.com/about-vodafone/what-we-do/m-pesa#how-it-works.

20. World Bank (2016), *Digital Dividends*, World Bank Development Report. https://www.worldbank.org/en/publication/wdr2016.
21. Fieldwork conducted by the author.
22. https://ndcorp.nu.ca/we-invest/subsidiaries/kiluk/.
23. See https://ndcorp.nu.ca/kivalliq-arctic-foods/.
24. https://www.statista.com/statistics/1062706/china-Internet-penetration-rate-rural-areas/.
25. https://www.antgroup.com/en/business-development (2025).
26. World Bank (2016), *Digital Dividends*, World Bank Development Report. https://www.worldbank.org/en/publication/wdr2016.
27. Li, A.H.F. (2017), e-Commerce and Taobao Villages. A Promise for China's Rural Development? *China Perspectives*.
28. Li, A.H.F. (2017), e-Commerce and Taobao Villages. A Promise for China's Rural Development? *China Perspectives*.
29. Wang, Xiaowei (2020), *Blockchain Chicken Farm*, FSG Originals, Farrar, Straus, Giroux, p. 194.
30. World Bank (2016), *Digital Dividends*, World Bank Development Report. https://www.worldbank.org/en/publication/wdr2016.
31. https://www.antgroup.com/en/business-development?tab=finance.
32. World Bank (2016), *Digital Dividends*, World Bank Development Report. https://www.worldbank.org/en/publication/wdr2016.
33. Wang, Xiaowei (2020) *Blockchain Chicken Farm*, FSG Originals, Farrar, Straus, Giroux, pp. 199–200.
34. https://www.statista.com/topics/9797/digital-payments-in-vietnam/#topicOverview.
35. https://www.vietnamworks.com/intech?utm_source_navi=footer.
36. *Harnessing the Chances of Digitalization for Rural Development: Lessons-Learnt in German-Funded Rural Development Projects* (2018), Deutsche Gesellschaft für Internationale Zusammenarbeit (GIZ) GmbH, Bonn, p. 38.
37. See Hudson, Heather E. (2013), *From Rural Village to Global Village: Telecommunications and Development in the Information Age.* Routledge.
38. For example, operator assistance for a major Alaska telecommunications company was moved from Alaska to the Philippines. Alaskans complained not only about loss of jobs but about the Filipinos' lack of knowledge of Alaska's geography. Personal research by author.
39. https://www.piton-global.com/blog/back-office-outsourcing-philippines-the-essential-guide/.
40. https://www.statista.com/outlook/tmo/it-services/business-process-outsourcing/india.

41. https://www.nasscom.in/sites/default/files/media_pdf/Nasscom%20SR%20Press%20release.pdf.
42. https://lsgd.kerala.gov.in/en/waste-management/supporting-institutions/kud umbashree/.
43. Economic and social impact of Meta's submarine cable investments in APAC | B–3. Ref: 706675498-385.
44. Tobin, Meaghan & Nindita, Hasya (2024, October 30), Delivering a Package in a Country with 17,000 Islands, *New York Times*. https://www.nytimes.com/2024/10/30/business/tiktok-indonesia-tokopedia-ecommerce-logistics.html.
45. https://minenetazez.com/product/a-goat-gift-for-holiday-and-occasional-days/.
46. Ahmed, Shamira, Chinembiri, Tapiwa, Moyo, Mpho, & Gillwald, Alison (2021), Future of Work in the Global South (FOWIGS): Digital Labour, New Opportunities and Challenges (Working paper), Research ICT Africa. https://africaportal.org/wp-content/uploads/2023/05/Future-of-Work-in-the-global-South-FOWIGS-Working-Paper-1.pdf.
47. Ahmed, Shamira, Chinembiri, Tapiwa, Moyo, Mpho, & Gillwald, Alison (2021), Future of Work in the Global South (FOWIGS): Digital Labour, New Opportunities and Challenges (Working paper), Research ICT Africa. https://africaportal.org/wp-content/uploads/2023/05/Future-of-Work-in-the-global-South-FOWIGS-Working-Paper-1.pdf.
48. https://www.hawaiipublicradio.org/local-news/2025-06-23/maui-short-term-rental-bill-sparks-debate-over-free-speech-and-threatening-language.
49. World Youth Student & Educational (WYSE) Travel Confederation (n.d.), *Growth and Development in the Digital Nomad Market Since Covid-19*. https://www.wysetc.org/2023/01/growth-and-developments-in-the-digital-nomad-market-since-covid-19/.
50. https://www.circleloop.com/nomadindex/
51. Townsend, L., Wallace, C., & Fairhurst, G. (2015). "Stuck out here": The critical role of broadband for remote rural places. *Scottish Geographical Journal*, 131(3-4), 171–180. https://doi.org/10.1080/14702541.2014.978807
52. Townsend, L., Wallace, C., & Fairhurst, G. (2015). "Stuck out here": The critical role of broadband for remote rural places. *Scottish Geographical Journal*, 131(3-4), 171–180. https://doi.org/10.1080/14702541.2014.978807
53. Souza, L. (2023) The work of food couriers in Rio de Janeiro and digital labour platforms: the paths of precarisation, *Work in the Global Economy*, *3*(2): 161–80. doi: 10.1332/27324176Y2023D000000004 In

Castel-Branco, R., & Dawson, H. J. (2023). The remaking of working classes: digital labour platforms and workers' struggles in the Global South. *Work in the Global Economy*, *3*(2), 109-115. https://doi.org/10.1332/27324176Y2023D000000008

54. Castel-Branco, R., & Dawson, H. J. (2023). The remaking of working classes: digital labour platforms and workers' struggles in the Global South. *Work in the Global Economy*, *3*(2), 109-115. https://doi.org/10.1332/27324176Y2023D000000008
55. "Humans in the Loop" CBS *60 Minutes*, June 29, 2025. https://www.cbsnews.com/video/ai-workers-kenya-60-minutes-video-2025-06-29/.

7

E-GOVERNMENT AND NON-PROFIT SERVICES

> "Enabling access is not sufficient for e-government inclusion; meaningful engagement among vulnerable segments of the population is possible only if relevant content and services are made available."
>
> – International Telecommunication Union[1]

Governments, non-profit organizations, and development agencies are also incorporating digital technologies for delivering services, administration, and other functions. The United Nations Department of Economic and Social Affairs (UNDESA) states:

> The development of digital government has seen a significant upward trend worldwide, with all regions leveraging technology to enhance government services and improve people's engagement. This shift has accelerated during the post-pandemic recovery period, with increased investment in resilient infrastructure and cutting-edge solutions such as cloud computing and broadband. The rapid digitalization of services, the shift towards remote work, the integration of artificial intelligence (AI), the emphasis on digital identity and data management, and the increased use of data and emerging technologies for policymaking are key global megatrends.[2]

DOI: 10.4324/9781003431602-7

But as the ITU points out, relevant content and services must be made available to vulnerable populations.

Humanitarian Aid

Digital finance for social protection provided by governments was accelerated during the COVID-19 pandemic, with almost 60 governments in LMICs using digital payments for COVID-19 assistance. For example, in Paraguay, some 300,000 people received emergency assistance through transfers from the government using telecommunication providers' mobile money platforms. Nearly half of the adults in Argentina who received government transfers received them digitally for the first time during the pandemic. In Latin America as a whole, 11 percent of the population (almost 50 million individuals age 15 years and older) started using digital payments for the first time in 2020 during the pandemic.[3]

In Africa, the government of Togo's Novissi cash transfer scheme used existing data and machine-learning systems to identify the most vulnerable households eligible for government social protection schemes and executed quick and cost-effective social payment transfers in partnership with mobile network providers. It filled gaps in household-level economic data using machine-learning predictions that pulled data from open geospatial and mobile usage sources. Novissi propelled financial accessibility by enabling anyone with a SIM card to register for the scheme. During the COVID-19 pandemic, Novissi distributed $22 million (in three monthly mobile phone payments of $20 for men and $22 for women) to 600,000 residents. The project was made possible through a multi-stakeholder partnership involving the government of Togo, a philanthropic organization, and academia. The Novissi scheme was designed to last beyond the pandemic, through future-proofing to adjust to the changing needs of the population through real-time tracking of cash transfer registrations, stages of disbursement, and allocations.[4]

Digital money is also being adopted to accelerate delivery of funds to refugees and those suffering from natural disasters. For example, in Bétou, a frontier town in the Republic of the Congo, refugees who had fled from violence in the Central African Republic built shacks on an undeveloped patch of land. Since refugees were not allowed to acquire land where they could grow their own crops, they relied on food from the World Food Program (WFP). The WFP transitioned from providing bags of food to giving "digital food" in the form of mobile money transfers that people could use to buy food.

> With mobile money, we could load cash on to the refugees' phones within days of it arriving in our own account. We could instruct the mobile money operator to "push" credit to their numbers; as soon as the credit hit their phones, refugees could pick out and buy the foods they needed from local retailers.[5]

WFP's introduction of cash transfers in this remote area was part of a global trend among humanitarian organizations to provide assistance through cash or vouchers. They hoped that people would have more choice in the items they could buy with cash, and that local economies would benefit from the cash injection. Humanitarian cash transfers were virtually nonexistent in the early 2000s, but had reached \$5.6 billion by 2020.[6] However, in Bétou, initially the refugees did not trust using phones to receive cash instead of food; WFP then hired and trained local fieldworkers to help with the transfers. A larger problem remained – the refugees still could not feed themselves without aid. Eventually, an agreement allowed refugees to lease farmland from local owners for three to five years, enough time for them to plant food crops for themselves and sell the surplus. The refugees soon began to grow cabbage and tomatoes that they consumed but also sold at Bétou's riverside market. The reporter pointed out: "Technology had streamlined one aspect of food delivery, but the larger issue of access to land, and a sustainable future for the refugees, could only be resolved through negotiations between human beings."[7]

Access to Government Services

The Indian government launched Aadhaar in 2010 to create a national biometric database for all Indian citizens, providing everyone with an Aadhaar number. The system generates a 12-digit random number as a unique personal ID; its architecture is open and scalable, and built to process 100 million Aadhaar authentications per day.[8] During COVID-19, using this authentication system, the Indian government facilitated disbursements to more than 200 million women, and to more than 18 million vulnerable building and construction workers. The world's largest digital identity system had generated more than 1.42 billion Aadhaar numbers by mid-2025.

This digital biometric ID is ubiquitous in daily life as "Indians now need an Aadhaar number to buy a house, get a job, open a bank account, pay their tax, receive benefits, buy a car, get a sim card, book priority train tickets and admit children into school."[9] Many banks and payment facilities in India now use Aadhaar. For example, the Reserve Bank of India's National Payments Corporation of India allows citizens to use Aadhaar to transfer money via its Bharat Interface for Money application by entering the recipient's Aadhaar number.

While Aadhaar has streamlined these tasks, some of the poorest and least educated in India have been unable to get an Aadhaar number because they are illiterate or lack sufficient education or required documents. Consumer researchers state that the scheme has been highly exclusionary and therefore punitive, depriving some of those who need it most from being able to receive welfare or work. "We have seen those in tribal, hilly or remote areas being unable to get an Aadhaar … Ultimately, it's a system that undermines access to essential social security and welfare for those that need it most."[10]

Also in India, e-Seva has established local digital kiosks or Kendras as a vehicle for the delivery of government, private, and social sector services to rural, semi-urban, and urban citizens. Begun as a single center in 2013, e-Seva has grown into a nationwide network of over 25,000 online centers. The e-Seva Kendras are designed to be one-stop shops where individuals can access a wide range of products and services. These centers are common platforms that integrate social and commercial goods and services.[11] Basic government documents like birth, income, and caste certificates are also made available through the centers for a nominal amount, as all such records are now available digitally. Citizens can also make requests for copies of land records online.[12] In addition, users can pay telephone and utility bills and local government taxes through the centers.

In Thailand, the Digital Government Development Agency (DGA) was founded in 2018 under the Thai Office of the Prime Minister to provide services and support to all government agencies regarding digital government transformation. Its initiatives include an e-government portal that serves as a central information hub to help people obtain public services provided by different Thai agencies.[13] The government portal receives around 400,000 visits per month on desktop and mobile web applications. The DGA also introduced the CITIZENinfo app in 2019 to provide information on the location of state agencies nationwide and the documents required for applications for public services.

Improved connectivity has also facilitated the transition to digital services by the government of Malaysia, which has digitized many services including online applications for vehicle insurance and road tax and benefit payments to citizens. By 2020, Malaysia placed nineteenth among 73 countries in government e-payments adoption, ranking first in the B2G transaction category and eighth in the C2G (citizen-to-government) and G2C (government-to-citizen) transaction categories, whereby citizens can access a range of C2G and G2C transactions through an interoperable platform.[14]

In 2006, Bangladesh initiated a project called "Access to Information" intended to create an inclusive society free from discrimination through the use of information technology. In 2020, the project's name was changed from "Access to Information" to "Aspire to Innovate."[15] The Bangladesh National Portal Framework is a special initiative of the a2i program; the National Portal is an e-architecture where a citizen-friendly framework has been implemented. One of the objectives of this initiative is to create a common website for all government organizations and to reduce time, cost, and number of office visits in providing e-services to citizens.[16]

A collaborative initiative involving the Ministry of Social Welfare, Ministry of Finance, and Bangladesh Bank developed the "Citizen's Choice Architecture" for digital payments of social safety net programs such as elderly allowance, allowance for widowed, deserted, and destitute women, and allowance for financially insolvent disabled people. They use the "AIM Principle" (Account + Identity = Mobility) as a framework for the disbursement of allowances at accessible cash-out points or at the homes of the elderly or disabled persons. More than 12 million citizen-beneficiaries can now simply walk a short distance to the nearest digital center or agent banking booth where they use biometrics to cash out their allowance from their own bank account that is tied to their unique national ID number.

The government of Brazil has established the Strategy for Digital Transformation ("E-Digital"), which has driven digital transformation of its public sector services, digitizing 68 public services, thereby saving more than 90 percent of service costs.[17] Its Portal de Serviços is a single website through which more than 1,750 citizen services can be accessed with citizen identification and login authentication. This portal allows citizens to access a variety of government services online, such as renewing their driver's licenses, paying taxes, and applying for social benefits.[18] Electronic payment cards also reduced costs of social transfers in Bolsa Família, Brazil's cash transfer program for low-income families, from almost 15 percent to under 3 percent of total payments.[19]

In some rural Alaska communities, residents can come to the Tribal government office to do job searches and fill out forms online. Staff may also help to provide access to social services for clients. Some Tribal governments access training webinars for workforce development. Tribal councils and local governments use digital connectivity for online banking, checking the status of their bank accounts, and monitoring spending through use of credit cards rather than cash, as well as administrative functions including employee payroll direct deposits, bookkeeping and use of QuickBooks®, applying for grants, submitting reports, and paying federal taxes. Indigenous community governments in Canada also use digital services for similar administrative functions.[20]

Serving People with Disabilities

About 15 percent of the world's population have a disability. Persons with disabilities face accessibility challenges when using smartphones, computers, apps, and websites. The United Nations Convention on the Rights of Persons with Disabilities, adopted in 2006, states that Parties are called upon to "promote access for persons with disabilities to new information and communications technologies and systems, including the Internet."[21] Article 9 of the

Convention focuses on accessibility, mandating that countries take appropriate measures to ensure accessibility within both the physical and the virtual environment. Also, ensuring public access to information is one of the focal points of Sustainable Development Goal target 16.10, stating that individuals should be able to access information without discrimination, and public information should be presented in a way that is understandable to all.

Some technological solutions are now widespread, such as speech recognition systems that can translate speech to text and vice versa, and document scanners that can be coupled with speech synthesis for the blind. Smartphones can provide captions, audio descriptions of video, text-to-speech, voice-activated controls, and other accessibility tools. For example, persons with visual impairment are using smartphone technology to scan and read documents, to get accessibility ratings for public places, and to receive audio and vibration alerts when approaching obstacles.

E-Government content may include access to public services such as disability subsidies, social welfare payments, links to employment opportunities, support for e-commerce, legal advice, and citizen participation. Thus, persons with disabilities need access to e-government platforms to fully participate in public sector activities and benefit from government services. In turn, governments need to require that commercial services such as online banking and e-commerce are available to the disabled.

Many leading technology companies have adapted products to be more disability-friendly through features such as enabling large fonts and screen readers, and many adhere to the W3C (World Wide Web Consortium) global standard for web accessibility.[22] Yet e-government is far from being accessible for everyone with disabilities. Lack of access to both physical services and e-services continues to leave the disabled at a significant disadvantage.

Voting

With the expansion of digital connectivity, e-voting from community polling stations or kiosks or from personal or home devices became possible. Estonia was the first country to adopt e-voting in 2005, with both electronic voting as well as paper ballot options.[23] In 2023, Estonia held "the world's first mostly digital elections," with more electronic votes cast (51 percent) than paper votes (49 percent).[24] Some other countries such as France, Norway, Mexico, and the Philippines allow online voting for citizens abroad; others, such as Switzerland, allow e-voting in some regions. Some states in the United States allow online voting by the military and citizens living abroad and by disabled voters.[25] e-Voting has been adopted for municipal and other local elections in some other industrialized countries. However, concerns over access to connectivity and security of ballots have limited adoption of e-voting in rural regions and most of the Global South.

Some First Nations in Canada have experimented with online voting. Community-engaged surveys in three First Nations (Tsuut'ina Nation, Wasauksing First Nation, and Whitefish River First Nation) found broad support for online voting and satisfaction from Indigenous voters. Though online voters tended to be older, educated, wealthier and live off reserve, survey results indicate online ballots could engage some Indigenous electors to vote more frequently. Researchers concluded that online voting could be a critical tool to reach and engage off-reserve citizens.[26]

In India, the world's most populous country with nearly 970 million voters or more than 10 percent of the world's population, voters elected 543 members to the lower house of parliament for five years during staggered elections.[27] Citizens could not vote online in the 2024 national elections, but officials used helicopters, buses, trucks, boats, donkeys, and mules to carry electronic voting machines to remote voters to provide a sort of "portable" e-voting. Election officials set up polling stations in tents, shipping containers, and school buildings in remote areas. The machines, which recorded the votes, were then carried back to administrative centers to count the votes.

In Kenya, a digital initiative called Uchaguzi was launched to monitor Kenya's 2010 constitutional referendum. The effort combined citizen crowdsourcing with analysis by specialized civil society organizations with experience in monitoring elections to provide actionable information to local and national government officials. This partnership was a success, with the government responding to a majority of the reports. Developers of Ushahidi, a previous digital initiative that was not successful, had an implicit belief that the platform would by itself be the agent of change. The organizers learned that the platform could work only if it amplified rather than replaced existing institutions. A case study of Uchaguzi concluded: "The main lesson is that governments may be dysfunctional, but can only rarely be bypassed."[28]

Commentary

To provide a performance rating on e-government development of its member states, the UN has created an e-Government Development Index (EGDI). The EGDI is a composite measure of three important dimensions of e-government, namely: provision of online services, telecommunication connectivity, and human capacity.* As these are national-level data, they do not take into account urban-rural disparities. Unsurprisingly, the highest ranked are industrialized countries and other high-income countries, while the lowest are low-income countries, primarily in sub-Saharan Africa. However, most countries in Latin America, as well several in South and Southeast Asia are ranked in the top 50 percent, including those discussed in the examples above.

The UN indicators compare some important requirements for e-government, but other factors may also limit adoption and effectiveness. Roman argues that "[i]n order for e-government to deliver on its original promises it needs to fulfil expectations along three broad dimensions: security, functionality and transformation," and that major failures on any of these dimensions can seriously jeopardize digital transformation. If citizens do not feel that digital solutions are secure, that digital solutions provide valuable functionality, or

* The EGDI is the weighted average of normalized scores on three important dimensions of e-government, namely: (i) the scope and quality of online services quantified as the Online Service Index (OSI); (ii) the status of the development of telecommunication infrastructure or the Telecommunication Infrastructure Index (TII); and (iii) the inherent human capital or the Human Capital Index (HCI). e-Government Development Index. https://publicadministration.un.org/egovkb/en-us/About/Overview/-E-Government-Development-Index.

that the public sector is improved through the use of digital solutions, then digital transformation will lose legitimacy and potentially fail.[29]

Reasons for lack of adoption include lack of awareness of the services, lack of access to digital technologies or skills to access the services, lack of perceived relevance of services offered, and/or lack of citizens' trust in the technology or the government. For example, e-government services may not be utilized because people are unaware of the concept, although they could benefit from government information and services. Researchers in Tanzania concluded:

> From the demand side, on the one hand, we see that people … do not know about e-government; they do not know the concept, and they are not aware of what services governmental agencies can offer. On the other hand, we have found a demand among people [for other services]. Farmers find useful agricultural information and services through the internet, and pupils and students as well as teachers, doctors, and lawyers find relevant information and services when they need it.[30]

Another study in Tanzania concluded:

> As a general experience … it seems like the G-side in the G2C context has focused very little on how the citizens may achieve access to the services. They offer it and that is it. It seems to be the citizens' own responsibility, or up to "intermediaries" like telecentre staff, to arrange the access and to make efforts to use the information and services.[31]

Sustainability of such e-government services depends largely on citizens' participation and reliable ICT infrastructure. In Ghana, a study explored the factors contributing to low citizen usage of e-government services. The main findings included lack of awareness, lack of publicity, lack of internet access, economic factors, and lack of trust as some of the main barriers to citizens' adoption and use of e-government service.[32]

The COVID-19 pandemic forced many governments to develop digital solutions to ensure the continuity of public services. Yet despite the increasingly widespread reliance on digital technologies for service delivery, comprehensive digital transformation in the public sector trails innovation in the private sector. The acceleration of digitalization in the private sector has raised people's expectations for more effective public services delivery.

Part of the problem is that generally the public sector lags the private sector in attracting talent and updating employee skills to develop and maintain digital services. Also, high costs of broadband access may hinder citizen adoption. Human support in terms of digital literacy training and personal help from public service staff or community "infomediaries" may also be required. In addition, as the ITU points out: "Enabling access is not sufficient for e-government inclusion; meaningful engagement among vulnerable segments of the population is possible only if relevant content and services are made available."[33]

References

1. ITU (2021), Access to Telecommunication/ICT Services by Persons with Disabilities and Other Persons with Specific Needs, *Output Report on ITU-D Question 7/1 for the Study Period 2018–2021*, International Telecommunication Union. https://www.itu.int/hub/publication/d-stg-sg01-07-5-2021/.
2. UNDESA (2024), *United Nations e-Government Survey 2024: Accelerating Digital Transformation for Sustainable Development*, United Nations Department of Economic and Social Affairs, New York. https://publicadministration.un.org/egovkb/en-us/.
3. ITU/UNESCO (2023, September), *The State of Broadband 2023: Digital Connectivity. A Transformative Opportunity*. ITU/UNESCO Broadband Commission for Sustainable Development. https://www.itu.int/dms_pub/itu-s/opb/pol/S-POL-BROADBAND.28-2023-PDF-E.pdf
4. ITU/UNESCO (2023, September), *The State of Broadband 2023: Digital Connectivity. A Transformative Opportunity*, ITU/UNESCO Broadband Commission for Sustainable Development. https://www.itu.int/dms_pub/itu-s/opb/pol/S-POL-BROADBAND.28-2023-PDF-E.pdf
5. Bauer, Jean-Martin (2024, July 18), Food, Water, Wifi: Is this the Future of Humanitarian Aid? *Guardian*. https://www.theguardian.com/news/article/2024/jul/18/food-water-wifi-is-this-the-future-of-humanitarian-aid.
6. CALP Network (2020), The State of the World's Cash. https://www.calpnetwork.org/resources/collections/state-of-the-worlds-cash-2020/.

7. Bauer, Jean-Martin. (2024, July 18), Food, Water, Wifi: Is this the Future of Humanitarian Aid? *Guardian.* https://www.theguardian.com/news/article/2024/jul/18/food-water-wifi-is-this-the-future-of-humanitarian-aid.
8. https://uidai.gov.in/en/my-aadhaar/about-your-aadhaar/features-of-aadhaar.html.
9. Ellis-Petersen, Hannah (2025, 14 October), Your Basis to Live Is Checked at Each and Every Step: India's ID System Divides Opinion, *Guardian.* https://www.theguardian.com/world/2025/oct/14/india-id-system-divide-opinion.
10. Chakradhar Buddha, Libtech India, quoted in Ellis-Petersen, Hannah (2025, 14 October), Your Basis to Live is Checked at Each and Every Step: India's ID System Divides Opinion." *Guardian.* https://www.theguardian.com/world/2025/oct/14/india-id-system-divide-opinion.
11. https://e-seva.in/services.php.
12. Garai, Atanu & Shadrach, B. (2006), *Taking ICT to Every Indian Village: Opportunities and Challenges*, One World South Asia.
13. www.egov.go.th.
14. Malaysia Ranked 19th in Government Payment Adoption. https://www.malaysiakini.com/news/471812
15. https://a2i.portal.gov.bd/site/page/3721c3cf-bf6b-4c5b-bf5e-9d8cd64ff9d1/-.
16. https://a2i.portal.gov.bd/site/page/d9b89541-b633-4b88-9568-d1caeb54113d/-.
17. Filgueiras Fernando, Flávio, Cireno, & Palotti, Pedro (2019, 12 November), Digital Transformation and Public Service Delivery in Brazil, *Latin American Policy*. https://doi.org/10.1111/lamp.12169.
18. https://www.gov.br/acessoainformacao/pt-br.
19. Bolsa Família. https://www.worldbank.org/en/news/feature/2010/05/27/br-bolsa-familia.
20. O'Donnell, S., Beaton, B., McMahon, R., Hudson, H.E., Williams, D., & Whiteduck, T. (2016, June), Digital Technology Adoption in Remote and Northern Indigenous Communities in Canada, Canadian Sociological Association 2016 Annual Conference, University of Calgary, Calgary, Alberta, June. http://firstmile.ca/wp-content/uploads/2016-CSA-Digital-Technology-Adoption.pdf.
21. United Nations Convention on the Rights of Persons with Disabilities, Article 9(2)(h). https://social.desa.un.org/issues/disability/crpd/article-9-accessibility.
22. Web Accessibility Initiative. https://www.w3.org/WAI/.
23. https://www.weforum.org/stories/2024/04/what-is-electronic-voting/.

24. https://e-estonia.com/how-did-estonia-carry-out-the-worlds-first-mostly-online-national-elections/.
25. https://www.simplyvoting.com/countries-and-us-states-using-online-voting/.
26. Goodman, Nicole, Gabel, Chelsea & Budd, Brian (2018, September 6), Online Voting in Indigenous Communities: Lessons from Canada. https://link.springer.com/chapter/10.1007/978-3-030-00419-4_5.
27. Associated Press (2024, April 25), Ferrying Voting Machines to Mountains and Tropical Areas in Indian Elections Is a Herculean Task. https://apnews.com/article/india-election-electronic-voting-machines-photos-2bb38afcb450e145431b10b077997c73?utm_source=copy&utm_medium=share.
28. World Bank (2016), *Digital Dividends*, World Bank Development Report. https://www.worldbank.org/en/publication/wdr2016
29. Roman, Alexandru (2013), *Realizing e-Government: Delineating Implementation Challenges and Defining Success.* https://www.researchgate.net/publication/264273654_Realizing_e-government_Delineating_implementation_challenges_and_defining_success.
30. Furuholt, B. & Matotay, M. (2017), Supply and Demand of e-Government Services in Developing Countries: Cases from Tanzania. In: R. Pooley, J. Coady, C. Schneider, H. Unger, C. Barry, & M. Lang (Eds.), *Information Systems Development*. Springer.
31. Furuholt, B. & Sæbø, Ø. (2018), The Role Telecentres Play in Providing e-Government Services in Rural Areas: A Longitudinal Study of Internet Access and e-Government Services in Tanzania. *The Electronic Journal of Information Systems in Developing Countries.* https://doi.org/10.1002/isd2.12006
32. Tahiru,F., TeiAsare, B., Asante, G., & Agbesi, S. (2021), Internet Access and Cost and Its Impact on Citizens Engagement on e-Government Services, Paper presented at the Telecommunications Policy Research Conference, Washington, DC.
33. ITU (2021), Access to Telecommunication/ICT Services by Persons with Disabilities and Other Persons with Specific Needs, *Output Report on ITU-D Question 7/1 for the Study Period 2018–2021*, International Telecommunication Union. https://www.itu.int/hub/publication/d-stg-sg01-07-5-2021/.

8

LANGUAGES, CULTURES, AND GENDER

"We fear, not that we will be left behind, but that we will be run over."[1]
– Rosemarie Kuptana, Canadian Inuvialuit broadcaster and politician

From Passive Consumption to Content Production

Inuvialiut broadcaster and activist Rosemarie Kuptana told Canadian regulators in the 1980s that she was concerned that the coming "information society" would leave Indigenous people behind, because she had seen the early impact of the introduction of television in Canada's North. At that time, there was little Indigenous language content on television, and it was broadcast after normal viewing hours. She said that the Arctic land of the midnight sun had become the land of midnight television.

She cautioned that new technologies could destroy Indigenous cultures:

> We might liken the onslaught of Southern television, and the absence of Native television, to the neutron bomb. This is the bomb that kills the people but leaves the buildings standing. Neutron-bomb television is the kind of television that destroys the soul of a people but leaves the shell of a people walking around. This

DOI: 10.4324/9781003431602-8

> is television in which the traditions, the skills, the culture, the language – count for nothing. The pressure, especially on our children, to join the invading culture and language and leave behind the language and culture that count for nothing is explosively powerful.[2]

Indigenous and minority populations around the world remain concerned about the potential cultural consequences of global digitalization. They recognize that the major content producers and platforms are controlled by large entities and include primarily Western culture and dominant languages. Yet they also recognize that these are interactive technologies, with the capacity to enable users to share their knowledge and distribute their own content. Burton points out: "It takes a conceptual shift to move from 80 years of passively consuming radio and television content into being a content producer. When given a chance, youth and elders can lead the way."[3]

Indigenous Initiatives in the Far North

Indigenous Content and Games

Indigenous people in the North are using the internet to preserve their culture and history. The Inuit Circumpolar Conference includes Inuit in Alaska, the Canadian Arctic, and Siberia, and uses a variety of digital media to share cultural materials and to address shared issues such as climate change, ocean resources, and natural resource exploitation.[4]

In 2014, a bill passed by the Alaska Legislature declared the 20 Alaska Native languages as official state languages.[5] Indigenous Alaskans are using technology to help preserve and revitalize these languages. Two Inupiat brothers have developed the "Chert" app, which consolidates characters from all 20 Alaska Native languages on an iPhone keyboard. They explained that the name Chert comes from a stone "traditionally used … to fashion spear points, arrowheads, and other tools" – and they wanted a name that symbolized a connection between the past and present.[6] Also in Alaska, the Alaska Commercial Company is using labels in Yup'ik (Yugtun) on products in its general stores in conjunction with a smartphone app that reads the label aloud.[7]

A Native language map first produced at the University of Alaska Fairbanks in the 1970s has now been updated to include both traditional and modern place names, with links to a GIS database. The map data is intended to be available online so that others may add demographic, scientific, or historical information about locations on the map.[8]

Recognizing the need for an updated Iñupiat textbook, the University of Alaska Fairbanks created a website to provide an alternative and updated textbook-like resource for the Iñupiat language. The authors state: "it is our hope that Iñupiat language teachers and language learners from across the state (and farther) will use this site for their instruction and learning."[9] The Alaska Native Cultural Center also provides historical and cultural materials on its website.[10]

Interactive games can also teach about Indigenous cultures. Alaska's Cook Inlet Tribal Council wanted to find new ways to share the heritage of its 34 villages representing about 19,000 Indigenous residents. It worked with computer game developers to create "Never Alone," featuring the Inupiaq tribes of Alaska. The game includes striking artwork and adventure game activities that incorporate legends and stories of the Indigenous people of Arctic Alaska.[11] Also, to encourage use of the Yugtun language in southwestern Alaska, the Yugtun language app has games and lessons, accompanied by pictures of local people acting out words and phrases.[12] Other Indigenous language digital innovators include Yuarcuun, a Yup'ik-led group with a mission to revitalize Inuit languages using computer science tools.[13]

In Canada, software and keyboards were first developed for computer composition with the syllabic writing system used for Ojibwe/Cree and Inuktitut languages. Now the government of Nunavut (a predominantly Inuit territory) is developing new tools to help Inuktitut speakers work more easily on computers, as part of efforts to contribute to establishing Inuktitut as the working language of the government. Nunavut Utilities is a package of Microsoft Office tools to make working in the Inuit language easier; it contains a syllabic font converter, a transliterator to convert text from Roman orthography to syllabics, or vice versa; and orthographic rule checkers. Also, the "InuktutNaqittautit" app allows users to type in syllabics on Apple and Android devices.[14]

The video game *Otsi: Rise of the Kanien'keha:ka Legends*, developed with youth in the Skins Game Development Workshop from Kahnawake Mohawk Territory in Quebec, merges many traditional stories into a journey in which the player becomes the village hero. *Mikan*, another video game, is an adaptation of the Anishinaabe version of a traditional "moccasin game." *Mikan* players click on moccasins to find birch bark carvings of tools and belongings related to harvesting wild rice. Throughout the game, players hear Anishinaabemowin, the Anishinaabe language spoken around the Great Lakes region.[15]

Videoconferencing also provides a means for elders to communicate in Indigenous languages. Indigenous elders in the Canadian Atlantic provinces and in Ontario and Saskatchewan meet via videoconference for discussions in their own languages. In the Atlantic region, the only opportunity some elders have to speak Mi'kmaq is during these videoconferences because there are no other Native language speakers in their communities.[16] Many projects also use video to record the stories and wisdom of Indigenous elders. The resulting video documentaries may be accessed through Indigenous websites or shared through YouTube.

In New Brunswick, Canada, Indigenous students created stage plays and videos on fetal alcohol spectrum disorder and on suicide prevention to respond to challenges they were seeing in their own communities. About 160 First Nations communities connected via videoconference with another 500 webstream connections enabling people in these communities to see these videos and to discuss the topic of suicide.[17]

Social and Community Digital Activities

In northern Canada and Alaska, Indigenous residents are using digital technologies for a wide range of personal and organizational purposes, including contact with family and friends through social networking, email, online banking and bill paying, online shopping, access to online government services, and education. Tablets and smartphones are increasingly popular for personal internet access, with smartphone access via Wi-Fi where mobile data service is not available locally. Facebook is generally the most popular means of online information sharing by individuals and local organizations, including job postings and local news. Some innovative applications include local online buy-and-sell, online fundraising, and software for learning Indigenous languages. A resident of an Indigenous community in northern Canada commented: "People are 'power users' compared to people in cities. They don't have local shops – they shop online. Their whole life is online."[18]

In northern Quebec, the Eeyou Communications Network (ECN), a majority Cree-owned fiber optic network, provides broadband services to 14 communities as well as to anchor institutions such as health boards, hospitals and clinics, schools and school boards, and First Nation and municipal offices. Using ECN's broadband network, the James Bay Cree Communications Society (JBCCS) operates nine radio stations through the James Bay Eeyou Istchee territory, delivering daily news and information programming in the Cree language and a range of digital services. JBCCS offers services that facilitate participation in public and cultural life such as live-streaming chief and council meetings, general assemblies of the Cree school and health boards, funerals of important figures in the Cree communities, and consultations on a lithium mine in Cree territories. Researchers point out that these services are "an important component of both keeping Cree community members informed of what is happening in their nation and territories and allowing Cree to participate in real-time through chat, messaging, and call-in features."[19]

The communications society has also undertaken other activities to sustain and improve Cree language skills and fluency, including broadcasting radio programs entirely in Cree, repatriating Cree language audio and video materials held by non-Cree institutions, coordinating the maintenance of repositories for Cree language video and audio recordings, and recording and preserving elders' stories to create an online archive.[20] Similarly, the Wawatay Native Communications Society produces Indigenous language radio programs transmitted to community radio stations throughout northern Ontario as well as a newspaper in English and Oji-Cree (a hybrid of Ojibwe and Cree Indigenous languages). Hard copies of the newspaper are delivered with mail and freight in small planes to remote communities that do not have road access, but online versions are also available.[21] Wawatay's motto, "Blending Tradition with Technology" could apply to many of the examples in this chapter.*

In Atlantic Canada, Mi'kmaw Kina'matnewey (MK) has developed more than 20 apps designed to support and preserve the Mi'kmaw language, including a program for young children. *Antle Discovers His Voice* uses a holistic approach to learning and assessment to measure and support oral language learning for children aged 3 to 6 years old. This program combines an iPad with an engaging moose puppet named Antle to measure language usage and fluency in the home, school, and community. Teachers and parents are directed to learning activities for their children and students that promote language development.[22]

In the Canadian Arctic, the Inuvialuit Regional Corporation (IRC) was established to represent the rights and interests of Inuvialuit (Inuit of Canada's Western Arctic). One of the goals of the Inuvialuit Final Agreement (IFA) is to "preserve Inuvialuit cultural identity and values within a changing northern society." IRC's Cultural Resource Centre has developed mobile language applications in all three Inuvialuit dialects to preserve and teach future generations of Inuvialuit. As well, Inuvialuit CEDO (Community Economic Development Organization) has partnered with the Gwich'in Tribal Council and Aurora Research Institute to offer courses to introduce local Indigenous artists to computer and other technologies to enable them to increase the reach of their art.[23]

The Arviat Film Society, based in the Inuit settlement of Arviat on the west coast of Hudson Bay, uses video to preserve Inuit culture and language, to gather knowledge from elders, and to inspire youth.

* Before the Indigenous communities had internet access, the newspapers were dropped in plastic garbage bags into the villages from low-flying bush planes when freeze-up and break-up of the ice kept the planes from landing on the lakes

The film society uploads the videos to YouTube and Facebook so that they can be viewed in other Inuit communities. Its videos are also available on IsumaTV, a collaborative multimedia platform for Indigenous filmmakers and media organizations.[24]

Pinnguaq (Inuktitut for "play") is an organization that works with rural, remote, Indigenous, and other communities underrepresented in STEAM (science, technology, engineering, art, and math).[25] Through the various teaching settings, the delivery team helps students to develop and build digital skills in areas such as coding, digital art, 3D modeling, and 3D art, and digital storytelling. Students learn to use the digital tools to create stories and games.[26] (See also Chapter 3.)

Hunting and Trapping

In the Canadian sub-Arctic, a mobile app and web platform called Siku, the Inuktitut word for "sea ice," allows users to trade observations about dangerous conditions, document wildlife sightings, and trade hunting stories. The app was developed by the Arctic Eider Society, an organization based in Sanikiluaq, Nunavut, on an island in Hudson Bay where residents hunt eider ducks for food and collect their down for making clothing and duvets. It integrates weather, sea ice, and satellite imagery and allows users to add their own terms for dangerous conditions. Through the app, hunters can upload information into Siku and tag other areas of interest, such as wildlife they have tracked. Siku is available as an online platform as well as a mobile app that runs on Android and iOS. The manager of the Sanikiluaq Hunters and Trappers Association, explains: "We're copying what our parents used to do, but in modern ways."[27]

Mapping

Northern Canada

In northern Canada, digital technologies have helped Indigenous hunters; for example, a young Indigenous Cree trapper now uses GPS for trapping in the winter. At home in the village, he downloads GPS data to his mobile phone, which he takes with him when he snowshoes out to lay his trapline in the forest.[28] For several decades, Indigenous hunters used two-way high-frequency (HF) radios to stay in touch with their communities while at remote hunting and fishing camps. Today, they may use satellite phones where there is no mobile phone service. Without such communication for emergencies, they were reluctant to take children to the camps, with the result that they were deprived from learning traditional hunting and fishing skills.

Africa: The Congo Basin

In Africa's Congo Basin, forest dwellers are using GPS mapping tools to help them establish rights to land they have inhabited for generations and where they are largely excluded from decisions about the forests they depend on. Lack of reliable and transparent information on their use, ownership, and possession of forests as well as the threats facing these Indigenous people contributes to their marginalization. "Mapping For Rights" is an initiative to equip forest guardians with simple, low-cost tools to map, monitor, and protect their lands. They use an approach called participatory mapping, "a set of approaches and techniques that combines the tools of modern cartography with participatory methods to record and represent the spatial knowledge of local communities."[29] The information can contribute to bringing about greater accountability and transparency in the planning and management of forests.

Community Networks and Broadcasting

Hawai'i

In Hawai'i, Indigenous Hawai'ians, also known as Kānaka Maoli, are striving to maintain their language and to revitalize their culture. Although considered an endangered language, *'Ōlelo Hawai'i*, the Hawai'ian language is spoken by an estimated 2,000 native speakers. There are numerous internet-based resources for learning to speak the language including courses, audio and video materials, and online dictionaries as well as mobile phone apps.

Kānaka Maoli, an Indigenous Hawai'ian organization, and other residents of Hawai'i are engaged in activities to restore *ea*, that is, "the breath and sovereignty of the *lāhui* [assembly], *'āina* [land], and its people."[30] An organization called the Nation of Hawai'i has installed a community broadband network to provide connectivity to the internet.

> [T]he community network project is perceived as a means and expression of cultural revitalization tied to the legal basis of the Nation of Hawai'i's claims to sovereignty, for example, by connecting the community network project to broader efforts to restore the *Ahupua'a* communal land tenure system.[31]

The network also enables the Nation's citizens to connect with one another and to participate in political and collaborative activities. The IT manager of *Kānaka Maoli* commented:

> Right now, sovereignty for us as Hawai'ians and a lot of Indigenous people is limited to physical boundaries and limited to political jurisdictions and political obstacles, whereas the internet is free. The Internet goes through borders. To have a presence on the internet and to have our people be able to have access to that presence is a form of sovereignty that we need to not only foster but expand upon. The integrity of the connection is important for the residents who are in the Nation … It's almost like the duty of keeping the connection up and running. It's like my *kuleana* [responsibility]. It's more like it's my ancestral calling …[32]

Australia

Aboriginal broadcasting began in Outback Australia in the 1970s and 1980s. The Central Australian Aboriginal Media Association (CAAMA), based in Alice Springs, commenced Aboriginal radio programming in 1979 and later added music recording and video production. Some communities began to experiment with video production using portable video equipment and VCRs in the 1980s.[33] With the launch of the national AUSSAT satellite system in 1985, many remote Aboriginal communities were able to access national broadcast TV and radio for the first time.

As in northern Canada, many Indigenous people in the Outback feared their language and culture would be lost. As a response to the perceived threat to Indigenous languages and culture posed by AUSSAT, in 1987, the federal government funded the Broadcasting in Remote Aboriginal Communities Scheme (BRACS), equipping remote communities with technology for local video and radio production and local retransmission. Between 1987 and 1996, BRACS was launched in 103 remote communities; however, many BRACS local production projects were not sustainable, with insufficient funding and training.[34]

Today, Indigenous Australians are likely to use their smartphones to access audio and video, including social media. Smartphone ownership rose from 43 percent of remote Indigenous residents in 2013 to 72 percent in 2023, with most of this growth occurring since 2016.

Research carried out by a team from Griffith University in 2023–2024 found that social media use is widespread, including in remote areas, with the most common platforms cited being Facebook (and Facebook Messenger) for social and cultural connections, TikTok for news, and YouTube for accessing and uploading digital content associated with maintenance and repairs in remote areas, as well as music and entertainment. Indigenous broadcasting remains highly valued, particularly in remote areas where Indigenous broadcasting is often the primary media source. The researchers also noted the need to develop skills within Indigenous media organizations to meet the demands of a new and ever-changing digital and social media world. As one interviewee said: "The old mob use the old ways, but the new mob use YouTube."[35]

A literature review by Rice and colleagues on Australian Indigenous use of social media identified several major themes about how and why Indigenous young people use social media: identity, power and control, cultural compatibility, and community and family connections. They also included examples of marketing for health and health promotion approaches that utilize social media and digital technologies. They noted that strong cultural identity and community and family connections, which can be enhanced through social media, are linked to improved educational and health outcomes.[36]

Yet a gap remains in digital inclusion between Australian First Nations and non-First Nations people, with a wider gap in remote regions. Case studies have shown that digital inclusion for Indigenous people, particularly in relation to access and affordability diminishes with remoteness.[37] The Australian government's First Nations Digital Inclusion Plan (FNDIP) provides a strategic framework and a list of existing and proposed actions to improve First Nations digital inclusion in three areas: access, affordability, and digital ability. The plan's goal is that, by 2026, First Nations people will have equal levels of digital inclusion to Australians in general.[38]

Content in Local Languages

New Zealand

The Māori language is an official language along with English in New Zealand. Māori make up one-fifth of the New Zealand population, and they are a decade younger on average than the total New Zealand population. More than 80 percent of Māori have a smartphone. Social media and online video are popular; and online gaming is particularly popular with young Māori.[39] A Māori group has launched an app called "Tōku Whānau," derived from *tōku* meaning "mine," and *whānau* meaning "the whole community." It is to be an Indigenous platform with groups, connections, events, news, and other Māori content.[40]

Te Kete Ipurangi (TKI) is New Zealand's education portal, which is intended to enhance the visibility of best practices in education and to foster improvement in learning outcomes. *Te Kete Ipurangi* means "The basket of the internet" in Māori; the traditional flax basket is a recurring motif on the site. These baskets, still in everyday use in New Zealand, are associated in Māori proverbs and mythology with the concept of sharing:

> ... *nau te rourou, naku te rourou, ka ora te manuwhiri.*
> ... *with your food basket and my food basket everyone will be fed.*[41]

This notion that the portal is not a product but a process of those in education coming together and sharing for the good of learners was key for the team that developed and manages the portal. To extend access to broadband connectivity for education, the New Zealand government's Rural Broadband Initiative plans to fund infrastructure to provide 95 percent of rural schools with access to ultra-fast broadband speeds of 100 Mbps.[42]

Mali

Most students in rural Mali had never seen their Bambara language in written form before.

> Now … they were eagerly sounding out the words appearing on laptops, sometimes stumbling as they read a story written entirely in Mali's most popular language, Bambara … Sitting in the classroom in Safo, a dozen students who had dropped out of public school or never attended one were following along as their instructor led them in reading a story about the things children should not do, including wasting food, picking on their siblings and talking back to adults. At various points, the instructor called on individual students to read aloud, which they did eagerly, sometimes gently correcting each other.[43]

The story on their screens had been generated, translated, and illustrated using artificial intelligence. RobotsMali has used artificial intelligence to create more than 140 books in Bambara. Now, a Ministry of Education official said that both the government and the people "are engaged in wanting to learn and valorize local languages."[44] Instead of simply translating French classics into Bambara, RobotsMali aims to produce stories that reflect the lives and culture of regular Malians. Their team puts a prompt into ChatGPT such as: "Tell me mischievous things kids do." The team eliminates examples that would not be relevant to most children in Mali, then uses Google Translate (which added Bambara in 2022 and employs AI to improve its translations) to do a first round of translation. An Education Ministry staff member then corrects any mistakes, and another staff member uses AI image creators to illustrate the stories, ensuring that the characters are relatable to Malian children. ChatGPT is then used to create reading comprehension tests.

Multilingualism and On-Demand Translation

More than 7,000 languages are spoken in the world; half do not have a "digital footprint," i.e. there are no keyboards, operating systems, or fonts available. Less than 0.5 percent of the world's living languages are considered to have attained full digital capabilities. This digital language divide particularly affects countries that are linguistically diverse or where large segments of the population do not speak an official language.[45] GSMA points out that almost 60 percent of websites are in English, followed by Russian at 5 percent and Spanish at 4 percent. Almost three-quarters of mobile apps are available in English, with the next most popular mobile languages being Spanish, Arabic, and Portuguese.[46]

The exclusion of minority languages means that speakers of these languages have no access to online services such as many of those discussed in previous chapters. App developers may have little incentive to produce apps in minority languages if they cannot reach sufficient scale to justify their investments. Also, there is limited original content available in many minority languages. Endangered languages may therefore fall out of use if they are not available online. Yet, as discussed above, many Indigenous organizations and entrepreneurs are developing content in their own languages.

However, on-demand translation, such as through Google Translate enhanced by AI, is facilitating communication of verbal and written content to speakers who do not share a common language. This instant translation can be used not only for tourism, but to enable immigrants to communicate with hosts and workers from different backgrounds to communicate with each other. Google Translate offers translation in more than 240 languages, using a large language AI model. Some recently added languages are major world languages with over 100 million speakers. Google states:

> Others are spoken by small communities of Indigenous people, and a few have almost no native speakers but active revitalization efforts. About a quarter of the new languages come from Africa,

representing our largest expansion of African languages to date, including Fon, Kikongo, Luo, Ga, Swati, Venda and Wolof.[47]

However, some countries have blocked online use of minority languages. Clothey examined interactive Uyghur language websites as a vehicle for informal education, concluding that an understanding of cultural context, illuminated by an analysis of the content of social media messages, may contribute to more appropriate and successful educational policies for minority populations.[48] However, suppression of the Uyghur language has forced Uyghurs within China to use Chinese in public communication. Also, Google Translate is not available in Mainland China.

Gender Empowerment

The United Nations' Sustainable Development Goal 5 is "to achieve gender equality and empower all women and girls."[49] As research and examples in previous chapters have shown, the ability to communicate, including access to the internet, is important to empowerment. Women in Afghanistan have shown how they can challenge their government by publicizing its restrictions online. Afghan women, both inside and outside the country, have posted videos of themselves singing in protest against the Taliban's laws banning women's voices in public. After the Taliban published new restrictions on women, including that women must not sing or read aloud in public, nor let their voices carry beyond the walls of their homes, defiant women began uploading videos of themselves singing. "No command, system or man can close the mouth of an Afghan woman," a young woman said after posting her own video showing her singing outdoors: "I am not that weak willow that trembles in every wind. I am from Afghanistan."[50] She has been joined online by Afghan women from around the world.

Yet women in rural areas of developing countries remain significantly disadvantaged and continue to lag behind men in their access to mobile phones, especially smartphones, and their use of digital technologies. The ITU reports that, globally, 70 percent of men use the internet, compared to 65 percent of women, resulting in 189 million more men online than women. However, although the global digital gender gap has decreased since 2021, it has actually widened in the least developed countries (LDCs). In 2024, only 29 percent of women in LDCs were using the internet, compared to 41 percent of men and compared to 93 percent of women in high-income countries.[51] The UN points out that there is an inverse relationship between the e-Government Development Index and the Gender Inequality Index (GII), indicating that there is more gender inequality in countries with low EGDI values.[52] It is important to note that the EGDI index is strongly correlated with national economic indicators; most nations with low EGDI scores are low-income or least developed countries.[53]

Affordability is generally more of a barrier for women than men because of their typically lower incomes, reduced financial independence, and limited access to lending sources. Women are also less likely to own a smartphone. GSMA reported that women in LMICs were 19 percent less likely than men to use mobile internet in 2023, although the divide was declining from 25 percent in 2017. Affordability, particularly of handsets, remains the primary barrier to mobile ownership, although relatively inexpensive Chinese smartphones are becoming widely available in developing regions. Bandwidth-related usage charges also make mobile internet expensive for prepaid (or pay-as-you-go) customers. The countries with the highest internet costs have the lowest numbers of women online and the largest gender gaps in internet use.

As discussed in Chapter 6, digital finance can increase women's participation in the economy. Women can control access to their own revenue and finances through mobile commerce and banking apps. They may also qualify anonymously for microloans based on their online transactions. Access to savings instruments can also increase female empowerment and the consumption and productive investment of female entrepreneurs. Women's confidence regarding their digital abilities generally rises dramatically with increased education. In addition to formal education, as pointed out in earlier chapters, digital literacy training and assistance from mentors such as field staff from government agencies or community members can help to provide women with the skills and confidence to go online.

While the gender gap is narrowing in digital technology use, a significant employment gap remains between men and women in technology occupations. Cultural norms and gender stereotypes contribute to girls being less likely than boys to be educated in STEM topics or to be employed in technology-related fields. Some NGOs are combating gender stereotypes through mentoring and training. Girls Who Code offers summer programs and online courses as well as materials for teachers; it has trained more than 760,000 girls and women since 2012.[54] Girls Who Code, which is based in the United States, also has operations in India, where women account for just 26 percent of engineers in the tech workforce.[55] Evaluation of two virtual summer GWC programs in the United States found that the participants were significantly more likely to major in a computer science-related field than comparison students, and that the summer programs consistently demonstrated positive effects on majoring in a computer science-related field across most minority and underrepresented groups.[56]

Other organizations such as foundations and tech companies as well as the ITU offer training and activities for girls to help them to prepare for tech careers. For example the EQUALS Global Partnership (supported by the ITU, the UN University (UNU), UN Women, the International Trade Centre (ITC), and the mobile industry association (GSMA) brings together more than 100 public and private sector actors to provide women and girls with opportunities for collaboration, education, and networking. Among other ITU initiatives are regional coding camps and workshops, such as the African Girls Can Code Initiative (AGCCI) and Americas Girls Can Code (AGCC), which train young women and girls to become computer programmers, tech creators, and designers.[57] While these activities show promise in enhancing both skills and confidence, there remains little research on their impact in terms of women entering tech careers, especially among girls and young women in rural and developing regions.

Commentary

While fears of Indigenous languages and cultures being left behind or "run over" remain legitimate, interactive digital services, as opposed to one-way mass media, and the ability to create relevant content in minority languages are promising for cultural preservation. AI may facilitate translation and content development in minority and Indigenous languages. Also, women may have more opportunities for employment, entrepreneurship, and access to government services, as more women in developing regions have access to digital services. Yet once more, as with adoption of other digital services discussed in previous chapters, awareness of context, control of content, and barriers such as affordability and digital literacy need to be addressed if women and those with diverse cultural and linguistic backgrounds are to benefit from digital applications and services.

References

1. Kuptana, Rosemarie (1982), Inuit Broadcasting Corporation Presentation to the CRTC on Cable Tiering and Universal Pay TV. https://inuitbroadcasting.ca/neutron-bomb-speech/.
2. Kuptana, Rosemarie (1982), Inuit Broadcasting Corporation Presentation to the CRTC on Cable Tiering and Universal Pay TV. https://inuitbroadcasting.ca/neutron-bomb-speech/.
3. Burton, Kevin (2018), First Nation Networks Help Protect Indigenous Languages and Culture, *Northern Public Affairs*, October.
4. See www.inuit.org and www.iccalaska.org.
5. HB 216 (2014), An Act adding the Inupiaq, Siberian Yupik, Central Alaskan Yup'ik, Alutiiq, Unangax, Dena'ina, DegXinag, Holikachuk, Koyukon, Upper Kuskokwim, Gwich'in, Tanana, Upper Tanana, Tanacross, Hän, Ahtna, Eyak, Tlingit, Haida, and Tsimshian languages as official languages of the state, Alaska State Legislature, Juneau.
6. Hughes, Zachariah (2016, Noember 17), Kotzebue Brothers Make First App for All 20 Alaska Native Languages, Alaska Public Media. https://www.alaskapublic.org/2016/11/17/kotzebue-brothers-make-first-app-for-all-20-alaska-native-languages/.
7. KTUU TV (2017. November 9), Alaska Company Introduces Yupik Translation App at Stores. https://www.ktuu.com/content/news/Alaska-company-introduces-Yupik-translation-app-at-stores-456392863.html.
8. See http://www.uaf.edu/anlc/.
9. See https://inupiatlanguage.community.uaf.edu/.
10. See www.alaskanative.net.
11. See http://neveralonegame.com/.

12. Ross, Isabelle (2019, October 15), Learning Yup'ik on the Go: A New Language App for Bristol Bay, Alaska. https://www.alaskapublic.org/2019/10/15/learning-yupik-on-the-go-a-new-language-app-for-bristol-bay/.
13. Liu, Christopher (n.d.), *Egalaaq*. See www.yugtun.com.
14. See https://www.gov.nu.ca/culture-and-heritage/information/computer-tools.
15. Video Games Encourage Indigenous Cultural Expression (2017, March 2). http://theconversation.com/video-games-encourage-indigenous-cultural-expression-74138.
16. O'Donnell, S., Beaton, B., McMahon, R., Hudson, H.E., Williams, D., & Whiteduck, T. (2016), Digital Technology Adoption in Northern and Remote Indigenous Communities in Canada, First Mile Connectivity Consortium, Report to Innovation, Science and Economic Development Canada (ISED).
17. Burton, Kevin (2018, October), First Nation Networks Help Protect Indigenous Languages and Culture, *Northern Public Affairs*.
18. O'Donnell, S., Beaton, B., McMahon, R., Hudson, H.E., Williams, D., & Whiteduck, T. (2016), Digital Technology Adoption in Northern and Remote Indigenous Communities in Canada, First Mile Connectivity Consortium, Report to Innovation, Science and Economic Development Canada (ISED).
19. Toso, Tricia & Forward, Scott (2023), Dispatches from Eeyou Istchee: Cree Networks, Digital, and Social Inclusion, *Social Inclusion*, 11(3), 298–308.
20. Toso, Tricia & Forward, Scott (2023), Dispatches from Eeyou Istchee: Cree Networks, Digital, and Social Inclusion, *Social Inclusion*, 11(3), 298–308.
21. https://www.wawataynews.ca/.
22. Burton, Kevin (2018, October), First Nation Networks Help Protect Indigenous Languages and Culture, *Northern Public Affairs*.
23. Smith, Duane Ningaqsiq (2018, October), Inuvialuit in the Digital Age, *Northern Public Affairs*.
24. https://www.isuma.tv/producers/arviat-film-society?page=8.
25. See https://pinnguaq.com/ and https://amp.ca/.
26. https://pinnguaq.com/partner-with-us/digital-skills-training/.
27. See https://www.cbc.ca/news/canada/north/inuit-app-land-siku-1.5384727.
28. Hudson, personal communication, 2020.
29. https://www.mappingforrights.org/.
30. Aikau, Hōkūlani K. & Gonzalez, Vicuña (Eds.) (2019), *Detours: A decolonial guide to Hawai'i*, Duke University Press.

31. McMahon, Rob, Buente, Wayne, Hudson Heather E., Maka'awa'awa, Brandon, Garcia, John Kealoha, & Kanahele, Dennis "Bumpy" (2023), Indigenous Community Networking in Hawai'i: A Case Study, *Social Inclusion*, 11(3), 286–97.
32. McMahon, Rob, Buente, Wayne, Hudson Heather E., Maka'awa'awa, Brandon, Garcia, John Kealoha, & Kanahele, Dennis "Bumpy" (2023), Indigenous Community Networking in Hawai'i: A Case Study, *Social Inclusion*, 11(3), 286–97.
33. Michaels, E. 1986. *The Aboriginal Invention of Television: Central Australia 1982–1986*, Australian Institute of Aboriginal Studies, Canberra.
34. Kral, I. (2010), Plugged In: Remote Australian Indigenous Youth and Digital Culture,Centre for Aboriginal Economic Policy Research, CAEPR Working Paper No. 69/2010.
35. Forde, S. et al. (2024), Radio, Television and Digital Media in 21st Century Indigenous Broadcasting: A Place of Old and New Ways, Griffith Centre for Social and Cultural Research, Griffith University, Queensland, Australia.
36. Rice, Emma S., Haynes, Emma, Royce, Paul, & Thompson, Sandra C. (2016), Social Media and Digital Technology Use Among Indigenous Young People in Australia: A Literature Review, *International Journal for Equity in Health*, 15, 81. doi 10.1186/s12939-016-0366-0.
37. Australian Digital Inclusion Index. https://digitalinclusionindex.org.au/digital-inclusion-the-australian-context-in-2023/.
38. Commonwealth of Australia (2023), National Indigenous Australians Agency, First Nations Digital Inclusion Plan – July 2023.
39. NZ on Air (2024), *Where Are The Māori Audiences?* https://www.nzonair.govt.nz/news/make-them-laugh-the-wants-and-needs-of-the-growing-maori-media-audience/.
40. Andrews, Emma (2025, August 12), New Social Media Platform: A "Digital Marae" for Māori, Radio New Zealand. https://www.rnz.co.nz/news/te-manu-korihi/569664/new-social-media-platform-a-digital-marae-for-maori.
41. Tāhūrangi curriculum hub. https://tahurangi.education.govt.nz/.
42. https://www.mbie.govt.nz/science-and-technology/it-communications-and-broadband/digital-connectivity-programmes/policy-and-regulation.
43. Chason, Rachel (2024, April 13), With French Under Fire, Mali Uses AI to Bring Local Language to Students, *Washington Post*.
44. Chason, Rachel (2024, April 13), With French Under Fire, Mali Uses AI to Bring Local Language to Students, *Washington Post*.
45. GSMA (2023), *The State of Mobile Connectivity Report 2023*. https://www.gsma.com/r/somic-2023/.

46. GSMA (2023), *The State of Mobile Connectivity Report 2023*. https://www.gsma.com/r/somic-2023/.
47. https://blog.google/products/translate/google-translate-new-languages-2024/.
48. Clothey, Rebecca A. (2017), The Internet as a Tool for Informal Education: A Case of Uyghur Language Websites, *Compare: A Journal of Comparative and International Education*, 47(3), 344–58.
49. *Transforming Our World: The 2030 Agenda for Sustainable Development*. https://sdgs.un.org/2030agenda.
50. Kassam, Ashifa (2024, September 1), Afghan Women Sing in Defiance of Taliban Laws Silencing Their Voices. *Guardian*. https://www.theguardian.com/world/article/2024/sep/01/afghan-women-sing-in-defiance-of-taliban-laws-silencing-their-voices.
51. ITU (2025, May), *WTISD-25: Gender Equality in Digital Transformation*. https://www.itu.int/hub/2025/05/wtisd-25-gender-equality-in-digital-transformation/.
52. United Nations (2024) *UN e-Government Survey 2024: The Future of Digital Government*. https://publicadministration.un.org/egovkb/en-us/Reports/UN-E-Government-Survey-2024.
53. e-Government Development Index. https://publicadministration.un.org/egovkb/en-us/About/Overview/-E-Government-Development-Index.
54. https://girlswhocode.com/about-us/research.
55. https://girlswhocode.com/en-in.
56. American Institutes for Research (2024, March), *Girls Who Code Program Evaluation Final Report*. https://girlswhocode.com/assets/downloads/craft-prod/downloads/GWC_Impact_Evaluation_Study_Final_Report.pdf.
57. ITU (2025, May), *WTISD-25: Gender Equality in Digital Transformation*. https://www.itu.int/hub/2025/05/wtisd-25-gender-equality-in-digital-transformation/.

9

FIELD RESEARCH AND EVALUATION

"I learned from reviewing the data collected that few women were using the telecenter, so I worked on getting more women involved."
– New manager of a community telecenter in rural Uganda[1]

The Need for Evaluation

The previous chapters have included many examples of applications of digital technologies for rural development, but few carefully designed studies on the impact of these projects and innovations. Where documentation does exist, evidence is often based on case studies or simply anecdotes that offer valuable insights, but do not produce findings that can be generalized or replicated. For example, a United Nations report presented findings from a systematic review of evaluations of the local economic impact of broadband. The review considered more than 1,000 policy evaluations and evidence reviews from OECD countries. Of those identified, it found only 16 impact evaluations that met its minimum standards for research rigor, with methodologies designed to ensure that evaluations could establish causality.[2]

Case studies may provide evidence of usage, but few attempt to find quantifiable benefits or to link them to specific uses or demographic characteristics of users such as age, gender, or education level. Also, narrowly focused studies may miss externalities such as economic benefits resulting from residents organizing to provide connectivity

DOI: 10.4324/9781003431602-9

for their communities or region; these locally operated networks may not only provide access to services but may also result in jobs for local residents.

Macro-level studies on broadband attempt to address economic impacts, but leave many questions unanswered. Bertschek and colleagues conclude from their review of studies on economic impact of broadband that "almost all adoption-related broadband studies find positive effects on economic outcomes whereas this finding is clearly less evident in availability-related broadband studies,"[3] i.e. where broadband was available but there was no specific information on its adoption. Without knowing whether and how people used the internet, we cannot conclude that the usage made a difference – such as adopting new farming techniques, or finding jobs, or getting better prices for their products. And it is unclear in the macro-studies whether the relationship between digital connectivity and income is correlational or causal. Does use of the internet lead to higher income? Or does higher income enable people to pay for digital devices and online services? Or both?

This chapter presents techniques and methodologies for evaluation of digital applications for rural development, particularly in field settings, as guidance for those reviewing field research reports or planning evaluations of digital applications in rural and developing regions. It also shows how evaluation research can involve and provide insights for community members, as the telecenter manager in rural Uganda learned about the need to involve more women.

Purposes of Evaluation

Evaluation may serve several purposes. *Formative* evaluation relates to process. It can provide feedback in early stages – for example, to identify strengths and weaknesses in projects such as how well innovations are working, what changes or improvements should be made, and what was learned that could be applied in other similar projects.

Summative evaluation relates to outcome and impact: what difference did it make? For example, did the project achieve its goals? What was learned about the contributions of the digital technologies and services to rural development? These are usually the most important questions for funding agencies concerned about whether their investments have made a difference, and for decision makers responsible for budgeting for communications facilities and services or establishing policies and regulations to support development goals.

The purposes of formative and summative evaluation are related in that the feedback or process information collected may help to improve projects so that they are more likely to accomplish their goals. Demographic data collected about who is using the facilities and for what purposes can be useful both for feedback to the project and for tracing the impacts of projects, as shown below.

Information and the Development Process

In designing the evaluation of projects requiring digital connectivity, it is necessary to consider the role of information in the development process. Digital technologies and the services they provide contribute more than a connection between people; they serve as a link in the chain of the development process itself. As discussed in earlier chapters, the ability to access and share information can contribute to the development process by improving effectiveness, equity, efficiency, and reach. However, none of these benefits occurs in isolation. Those who need to access or share information must have the necessary skills or have access to a resource person ("infomediary") to help them. Other factors may also need to be considered, for example, access to credit for inventory or spare parts, a reliable transportation system to get goods to market, or a curriculum that can be adapted to new teaching methods and information sources. Thus, in order to learn how connectivity may contribute to development, we must also understand what information users need, and what other factors may influence impacts of activities that can be considered developmental from economic, social, and/or cultural perspectives.

In considering users and potential benefits, concepts from diffusion theory and economics are helpful:

- **The early adopter**: Some people may be more likely to use online services sooner than others: for example, those with more

education and those with clearly defined information needs such as teachers, community leaders, artisans who need to find markets, and business managers who need to contact suppliers and do payroll and taxes. An analysis of adoption data may also identify those who are later adopters as well as the characteristics of those who may be laggards or resist adoption of new services and practices.
- **Indirect benefits or externalities**: An analysis of benefits must recognize that the user may not be the actual beneficiary. For example, the user may be the health aide or nurse, the librarian, or the tribal administrator, while the beneficiaries are patients, students, and community members in general.
- **Institutional incentives and barriers**: The evaluation must include an analysis of the institutional context, such as whether employees are given time or incentives for training to use new technologies, or whether there are barriers to adoption such as lack of funding for equipment and technical support.

Short-term benefits of access to information may include saving lives as a result of health workers receiving advice using telemedicine or successful grant applications for local governments whose staff are able to find and apply successfully for grants online. But much of the impact is likely to take longer and be much more indirect. Timely information about prices and markets for local products may result in more income, and students with access to the internet may be more likely to qualify for jobs or training for future employment. These benefits may result in more local people being employed, or fewer young people leaving. But these effects take time.

Identifying Objectives

In order to plan an evaluation, it is important to understand the objectives of the project. Although this may sound straightforward, stakeholders such as donors, partners, and various community groups may have quite different objectives. Also, the objectives may be rather vague or general, such as "empowering local people" or "creating new economic opportunities." In addition, reasonable timeframes for achieving different objectives may vary. For example, teaching digital literacy may be accomplished much more quickly than generating new jobs for the community.

One approach to identify objectives is to ask the various stakeholders: "What would make this a successful project?" Their answers might include:

- Majority of community residents trained in digital literacy;
- Adoption of digital services by specific groups: for example, women, young people, entrepreneurs;
- Sustainability: the ability of the project to continue to operate past the pilot phase;
- Economic development in the community: for example, job creation, better prices for products, new outlets for products from the community;
- Social development in the community: for example, the adoption of better health practices, improvements in school completion rates, and new job skills.

Having made these goals explicit, the evaluators must then devise methods and tools to determine to what extent the project achieved them. Questions they need to consider include:

- How do we define access to digital services?
- How should we define sustainability?
- How can we isolate the effects of the project from other factors that might influence community development such as improved transportation, a new business or a government grant?

Costs, Benefits and Sustainability

Evaluation research should include questions and analysis designed to understand what economic benefits may be derived directly or indirectly from use of digital connectivity. Is there evidence of new jobs, economic activities, markets, or savings in time or money? Are there intermediate changes such as learning new skills or exploring new techniques learned online that could be inferred to result in economic impact in the future?

Researchers should also look for evidence of internet usage that could lead to longer-term impact, such as students doing research online for school, adults taking courses online to finish high school or for continuing education, people using online services to look for jobs or information relevant to their work as farmers, tradespeople, entrepreneurs, and parents, etc.

Also, what can be learned about the demographic profiles of users, including early adopters? Is adoption widespread, or are there barriers such as costs, skills, or cultural norms? Is there evidence that the network can be sustainable – such as significant adoption, plans to cover operating expenses, or technical training to operate and maintain facilities?

The evaluation should also be designed to identify any barriers that could impede longer-term impacts – for example, lack of funds to continue the project, unaffordable usage charges, or lack of local jobs for newly trained workers.

Engagement: Evaluation as Learning

It is important that evaluation not be perceived as judgmental by the target population (such as farmers, health workers, teachers, or rural residents in general) but as an opportunity to:

- Provide feedback on what is working well in the project and what needs to be changed or improved;
- Plan for the sustainability of the project;
- Identify successful strategies and lessons learned that could be shared with other projects or networks.

Evaluation can appear threatening or a waste of time to community leaders. One way of reducing such tensions is to suggest that what they have learned would be useful to others starting a similar project, by asking them, for example: "What problems did you face and how have you solved them, or tried to solve them?" and "What advice would you have for someone else starting a project like yours?"

Another strategy is to involve the local people who have helped to implement the project in identifying what information would be useful to them, and then to train them to be interviewers and data collectors. In this way, the staff or volunteers themselves hear from the community and collect information on how people are using the digital services and what problems or barriers they face. The danger in this approach is that the data collection may be biased if the interviewers "tune out" any negative feedback or solicit responses only from close friends or colleagues. However, if they approach the data collection as a learning process, and if they are trained in asking questions consistently and coding the responses accurately, the evaluation can be a valuable resource for them as well as for external funders or service providers.

Project Design

Evaluations of outcomes and impacts of digital applications or services are often conducted after the fact by external researchers. However, particularly where initial funding is provided by government agencies, international agencies, or other donors, the projects themselves should be designed and funded to include evaluation. As the German Development Agency points out, digital projects should be data driven. Guidelines it proposes include:

- Design projects so that impact can be measured at discrete milestones with a focus on outcomes rather than outputs;
- Evaluate innovative solutions and areas where there are gaps in data and evidence;
- Use real-time information to monitor and inform management decisions at all levels.[4]

Research Design

Stories and anecdotes can yield useful insights and lessons learned from individual projects. However, while interesting, stories alone may lead to unsubstantiated conclusions or overgeneralizations. Well-designed case studies can provide greater depth and analysis, valuable in understanding the experiences and lessons learned in particular communities, but they may not address fundamental questions of causality such as, for example, whether use of digital services actually contributed to the creation of new jobs or new sources of revenue.

Where there are several project sites or opportunities to track sites over time, it may be possible to gauge longer-term impacts and issues of causality through research designs that are known as "quasi-experimental" because, in field settings, they cannot control for all the extraneous factors that may influence outcomes, unlike in a laboratory experiment. The following designs are not perfect, but are superior to stand-alone case studies in controlling for some of the variables that could influence outcomes:

- **Before-after**: Surveys are administered and other sources are identified to collect data on specified indicators before and after the introduction of digital connectivity.
- **After only**: Where no baseline information is available, it is difficult to isolate and quantify impacts. However, strategies that can be used here include: *retrospection*, i.e. asking the users to remember how they got the information or carried out the task before they could go online, and *contrary-to-fact questions* such as: 'If you did not have online access, how would you do this, or could you do this?"

The limitation in both these designs is that they can lead to false conclusions, such as "using the internet created more jobs," because they do not control for extraneous factors that might have had this effect anyway, such as a new funding initiative or a new road. Validity and generalizability can be improved by adding a *control group* Other design strategies include:

- **Matching**: Evaluators can gain better insights into causality if they can add a group of sites without access that are similar in population size, isolation, economic base, etc., and collect the same data at all these sites.
- **Random selection**: It may be possible to use randomly selected sites if there are many potential sites to draw from, or if the project can be designed to randomize the selection of where the facilities will be installed. However, this approach may also appear to penalize communities that are not selected for the project.

- **Multiple measurements**: Whether or not a control group of sites can be included, collecting data at several points after digital connectivity is introduced is likely to provide better insights into causality than any single "after-only" data collection. Also, later waves of data collection will help to determine whether use of digital services dropped off after initial interest, or whether demand and applications changed over time.
- **Sampling**: In collecting community data, using a systematic approach to drawing a sample (rather than interviewing the first people encountered or people known to the interviewers) strengthens the validity of the data. Examples include random selection of households, or selection of every *nth* household.

Research instruments such as questionnaires or interview protocols should be designed and pre-tested to achieve high levels of validity and reliability. Validity refers to the extent in which the true value of a variable is correctly measured by the instrument, i.e. that it measures what it intends to measure. Reliability refers to the degree to which a measure gives "consistent" or reproducible values when applied in different situations.[5]

Online surveys can be designed to collect and analyze data by asking users to answer questions on a computer or their mobile phone. Unless no other option is available, researchers should not solely rely on recruiting subjects to respond to online surveys. While such surveys may provide some information about usage and possible impacts, the danger is that only those who are able to go online, are able to complete the questions, or have heard about the survey will complete it, thus ignoring other segments of the target population who may lack digital access or skills.

The goal of engagement should also be included in research design. Otherwise, communities may feel ignored or insulted by researchers, and opportunities to learn from their experience will be lost. For example, a digital network project in the Asia/Pacific arbitrarily selected villages to receive satellite terminals matched with other villages without connectivity, sent in evaluators, and then removed satellite facilities where the service was underutilized. It did not try to engage leaders in site selection or ask for suggestions about where to move equipment – for example, to other villages that had expressed interest in participating in the project.[6]

Taking Advantage of Existing Data Collection

If a stand-alone household survey on digital usage is not feasible, one alternative is simply to insert key questions into an existing survey. Labor force surveys can be useful, since they exist in most countries and are typically conducted regularly, with adequate samples for population coverage. Some countries such as Mexico and Ghana have also included questions on internet access and use in their national census.

Data-gathering efforts by non-governmental organizations can also help to fill data gaps. Research ICT Africa has conducted household surveys in several countries for many years. The surveys, now known as "After Access," examine connectivity for households and individuals, and include questions that can explore aspects of digital inequality. Similar surveys were also conducted by LirneAsia in Asia and by DIRSI (a Spanish-language acronym for Regional Dialogue on the Information Society) in Latin America and the Caribbean.[7]

Available data on internet speed can help in making decisions on government investments in connectivity and can also aid first responders in emergencies by getting a better understanding of the type, level, and quality of network connectivity after a disaster.[8] For example, the Speedtest Global Index compares internet speed data from hundreds of millions of tests every month around the world.[9] However, such national comparisons mask rural disparities; crowdsourcing connectivity speeds in rural areas by asking residents to access and record connectivity speeds on available online tests, can be a more useful tool to identify rural disparities.

Other Considerations

In all circumstances, whether collecting data from users or analyzing data generated from user activities (such as financial transactions, education/training test scores, or medical diagnoses), strict protocols must be required to protect privacy of participants and security of the data.

- **Confidentiality**: It is important to preserve confidentiality and to respect community values. For example, respondents may not want their names used, or their ages or incomes revealed. Responses can be designed with age ranges (under 18, 18 to 30 years, 31 to 50 years, over 50 years of age, etc.) and questions that include occupation or whether the respondent is employed or self-employed, or number of people employed in a household can serve as proxies to estimate income.
- **Pre-testing**: Survey questions should be pre-tested with volunteers similar to the intended respondents to ensure that wording and terminology are clear and easily understood, and that the questions do not ask for information considered to be private or inappropriate.
- **Serendipity and unexpected outcomes**: Researchers should also be alert to anecdotes or examples of unexpected usage or outcomes. Inclusion of probes ("Can you tell me more about that?") or open-ended concluding questions ("Is there anything else you would like to add?") may elicit unexpected responses or insights. Unanticipated usage from research cited earlier in this book included a young hunter who uses online mapping to lay out a trapline, a remote artist who finds new online customers thousands of miles away, young people who develop apps for learning Indigenous languages, and elders who use videoconferencing to share stories and memories with relatives in other communities.

Disseminating Results

The principle of evaluation as learning should also be reflected in how the results are shared with the various stakeholders. Simply sending a copy of a research report to representatives of communities where research was conducted may not be sufficient. Researchers should be prepared to return to the community and to meet with the community residents and local stakeholders to explain the findings.

Results could also be shared with the users or their representatives by using less formal means and terminology such as a slide show or video presentation at a public meeting, a story for a local newspaper, or an interview on a local radio station.

Study participants may also be able to suggest changes that could be made in response to the feedback, such as providing outreach to underserved target groups, organizing more opportunities for training new users, or reviewing pricing of access. Researchers may also be able to propose other opportunities for learning and sharing information, such as workshops and exchange visits between participants in similar projects.

The evaluation results should also be made available to other entities such as funding agencies, government ministries and regulators, and providers of digital services. Presentations at conferences, papers in journals, and postings on the Web can also help to disseminate the findings globally to others, such as students, researchers, professionals, and practitioners interested in the impacts of digital connectivity in rural and developing regions.

BOX 9.1 INDICATORS: MEASURING OUTPUTS AND OUTCOMES

The following are examples of indicators that could be used in evaluation of rural digital connectivity projects and services:

Users and Usage

- Users:
  - Demographic information about digital connectivity users and non-users: age (or age categories), gender, student/non-student, education level, occupation, employed/not employed, self-employed or gig worker, etc.
  - Reasons for non-use or infrequent use: lack of equipment, lack of skills, lack of awareness, affordability, etc.

- How users connect:
  - On mobile phones, on tablets or computers at home, at school, at work, at a library, at a community or tribal center, etc.
  - Whether they use their own or shared devices.
  - Before the project, how they went online (if they did).
- Frequency of usage:
  - Several times per day, daily, several times per week, occasionally, never, etc.
- Purposes of use:
  - How people use digital connectivity: for personal/family communication, for work, for school, for buying or selling, for connecting with interest groups, for education or training, etc.
  - How users did (or did not) accomplish these tasks previously.
- Digital literacy
  - How people learned to go online: by themselves, from friends or family, at work, at school, etc.
  - Whether training was offered on digital literacy and, if so, demographic profiles of those who participated.
- Business use:
  - How local businesses use online services.
  - If business practices changed after connectivity was introduced.
  - Whether online services have contributed to saving time, saving money, generating new business, etc.
  - What problems or difficulties businesses face (if any) with online services.
- Non-profit organizations, local governments, and Indigenous governments:
  - How these organizations use online services.

- What benefits or changes online access has made in serving community residents, running their organizations, obtaining funding, etc.
- What problems or difficulties they face (if any) with online services.

- Schools:
  - How digital services are used in schools.
  - Whether students are expected to use online services to complete assignments or projects.
  - Whether the school allows students to take tablets or laptops home.
  - Whether teachers received training or support in adopting digital materials.
  - Whether technical support is available.
  - Any changes in curriculum or adoption of online courses or tutoring.
  - Number of students taking online courses; completion rates for these courses.
  - What changes (if any) teachers have observed after the school has had digital connectivity.
  - What problems or difficulties educators face (if any) with online services.
- Libraries and other public access locations (such as community centers, local government offices, or schools if the public can also use their facilities):
  - What online services are provided.
  - How patrons use these services: for connecting with family or friends, for schoolwork, for webinars or other instruction or training, etc.
  - What assistance, if any, the staff provide.
  - Whether librarians or other staff received training or support in accessing digital materials.
  - Whether technical support is available.

- What problems or difficulties public access sites face (if any) with online services.

- Adult education and training:
  - Availability of online webinars, training courses, distance education, etc.
  - Demographic information about participants in these activities.
  - Whether there is local assistance for those studying or doing training online.
  - Estimates of dropout rates or completion rates.
  - Outcomes of participation these activities: worker promotions, qualifications for local jobs, credentials for further education, etc.
  - What problems or difficulties participants face (if any) with online services

- Health care:
  - Local health care facilities available and services provided: clinic, nursing station, etc.
  - Digital connectivity available at health care facilities: bandwidth, quality of service.
  - Number and type of local health care staff: physicians, physicians' assistants, nurses, health aides, etc.
  - Distance and time to reach nearest hospital.
  - Whether local health providers use any online services for: telemedicine (consultations), telehealth (mental health or other services), electronic health records, in-service training, public health activities, etc.
  - For each application: information on types of usage, data on saving time or money or providing services not otherwise available.
  - If online services are not used, what barriers are perceived: lack of security or confidentiality, lack of training, lack of equipment, equipment/services not budgeted, etc.

- Barriers to usage of digital connectivity and services:
  - Barriers residents and organizations faced before the project: unreliable connectivity, insufficient bandwidth, lack of equipment or access to equipment (smartphones, tablets, laptops, etc.), high prices for access, overage charges, etc.
  - Barriers if any after digital connectivity installation: lack of skills, lack of equipment or access to equipment (smartphones, tablets, laptops), lack of technical support, affordability, content not relevant, etc.

Sustainability

- Costs:
  - Start-up costs: equipment, site preparation, training, etc.
  - Ongoing operating costs of the project: personnel, supplies, spare parts, rental, utilities, technical support, etc.
  - Costs for backhaul: middle mile or backbone, etc.
  - How costs (local networking and backhaul) are to be covered: from charges to users, grants, subsidies, or some combination.
  - Whether charges are considered affordable for users and sustainable for local network operators.
  - What other sources of revenue the project could develop, such as selling additional services, finding major clients as underwriters, or building operating costs into a community or institutional budget.
- Equipment:
  - Implementation problems: delays, budget overruns, etc. and their resolution.
  - Whether the equipment proved reliable in field settings.
  - Whether power supplies and backhaul networks are sufficiently reliable.

- Support:
    - Whether timely technical support and spare parts are available when needed.
    - Whether local people have been trained and hired to operate and maintain the network.

Commentary

This chapter has reviewed field research plans, methodology, and data collection techniques that could be implemented for evaluation of digital projects in a variety of settings. It emphasizes the importance of careful planning to ensure validity of the findings and potential replicability in other settings, as well as engagement with participants to ensure use of appropriate techniques for collecting information as well as guarantees of personal privacy and data security.

Research using existing data such as traffic over digital networks, volume of online financial transactions, number and purpose of telemedical consultations, and employment trends should also be carefully designed to control for other factors (besides digital connectivity) that may contribute to interpretation of results.

References

1. Presentation at a research seminar for African telecenter managers conducted by the author.
2. ITU/UNESCO (2017), *The State of Broadband Report 2017.* https://www.itu.int/pub/S-POL-BROADBAND.18-2017.
3. Bertschek, I., Briglauer, W., Hüschelrath, K,. Kauf, B., & Niebel, T. (2015), The Economic Impacts of Broadband Internet: A Survey, *Review of Network Economics*, 14(4), 201–27. https://doi.org/10.1515/rne-2016-0032.
4. *Harnessing the Chances of Digitalization for Rural Development: Lessons-Learnt in German-Funded Rural Development Projects* (2018), Deutsche Gesellschaft für Internationale Zusammenarbeit (GIZ) GmbH, Bonn, p. 74. https://www.bmz-digital.global/wp-content/uploads/2022/08/180807_Harnessing-A4-1.pdf.

5. Saw, S.M. & Ng, T.P. (2001), The Design and Assessment of Questionnaires in Clinical Research, *Singapore Medical Journal,* 42(3), 131–5
6. Personal communication, 2018.
7. ITU (2022) *Global Connectivity Report 2022*, p. 176. https://www.itu.int/itu-d/reports/statistics/global-connectivity-report-2022/.
8. ITU (2022) *Global Connectivity Report 2022*, p. 179. https://www.itu.int/itu-d/reports/statistics/global-connectivity-report-2022/.
9. See https://www.speedtest.net/global-index.

10

TECHNOLOGIES TO EXTEND DIGITAL CONNECTIVITY

"Blending tradition with technology."

– Motto of Wawatay Communications Society, an Indigenous organization that publishes a newspaper, and produces radio, video, and multimedia content in northern Ontario, Canada[1]

This chapter provides a review of technologies used to provide connectivity in rural, remote, and Indigenous regions for connectivity to the internet and access to e-services, as well as technologies for local networking, including community networks. It also points out how rural users can blend traditional activities with applications of digital technologies.

Overview: Transmission Technologies

Digital connectivity for voice, data, and video can be provided over various communications technologies:

- *Fiber optics*: convert electrical signals into light and then back into electrical signals. Typically installed in backbone networks in regional, national, and international networks; increasingly installed for local connections such as to homes or businesses.

DOI: 10.4324/9781003431602-10

- *Wireless*: transmits data using radio waves to portable devices (for example, mobile phones), and for coverage of small communities or within fixed locations such as residences or businesses.
- *Satellites*: receive and transmit radio signals from locations in space.
- Broadband over Powerline (BPL): uses low and medium voltage electric powerlines to distribute broadband services.[2]

"Last mile" transmission of digital services requiring high capacity within communities or to households or businesses may use:

- *Digital subscriber line* (DSL): transmits data over copper telephone lines.
- *Cable modem*: transmits data over coaxial cables; typically used to deliver video or internet to residential customers.
- *Fixed wireless*: Transmits signals with limited range to cover a neighborhood or village.
- *Optical fiber*: connecting buildings or households.

Mobile Communications

Increasingly, people are accessing voice and other services on smartphones and other devices over mobile networks, especially in developing regions without previously installed communications infrastructure. Mobile networks are cellular, with adjacent cells providing coverage from towers or repeaters that are typically connected to a fiber backbone network. The number of smartphone mobile network subscriptions worldwide has reached about 6.4 billion[3] – though smartphone users may have more than one subscription with SIM cards from multiple providers, depending on their pricing or coverage. In Africa, more than 73 percent of webpage views were generated via mobile in 2025, whereas in North America, the majority of web traffic still took place via desktop connections, with mobile accounting for 45.5 percent of total web traffic.[4]

The growth of mobile internet use has accelerated with the installation of high-speed mobile networks, particularly 5G (fifth generation) networks, although many developing countries provide access to 4G (fourth generation) or slower networks, particularly in rural areas. 5G upgrades are particularly expensive for rural areas as the coverage of these frequencies is more limited, requiring more towers and transmitters to be installed. Frequencies for 6G (sixth generation), promoted for Internet of Things (IoT) applications, such as connecting and monitoring devices in manufacturing and logistics, have very limited range.

Hong Kong has the world's highest 5G penetration rate, with 74 percent of its population subscribing to the 5G mobile service, followed by mainland China with 60 percent and South Korea with 59 percent. The high uptake of 5G in China and several other Asian countries may be attributed to availability of affordable next-generation devices, widespread fiber-optic backbone infrastructure, and government policies that encouraged broad 5G cellular coverage. As the most populous nations in the world, India and China also have the most smartphone users. Companies in both countries have designed relatively low-cost smartphones that are not only sold domestically but are also exported to developing countries, particularly in Africa. For example, one Chinese smartphone provider has a 43 percent market share in Africa. In India, telecommunications companies have committed tens of billions of dollars to the latest network technology and are producing ultra-cheap smartphones. The goal of India's Reliance Industries through its Jio brand is "to connect everyone and everything, everywhere."[5]

In many of the world's poorer economies, where a latest-generation 5G-capable smartphone is out of reach to all but the very rich, a 5G network is seen as a luxury rather than a requirement. An alternative is to concentrate on access to 4G networks, which can also handle broadband. Offering "4G for all, not 5G for few" has been the goal of Veon, a network operator that serves low-income markets from Ukraine to Bangladesh. Its chief executive states:

> Some areas lack the fiber-optic-cable infrastructure to support 5G-capable cellphone towers, and roughly half of the population in those markets lacks even a smartphone, let alone one capable of picking up 5G connections. Some countries also impose high taxes on smartphones, which puts the devices out of reach for many consumers. This is really matching the needs of the markets with the technologies that are available.[6]

Optical Fiber

Cables consisting of bundles of optical fiber have become the predominant means of providing international connectivity, surpassing satellite communications except in some remote regions of the Arctic and the Pacific Islands. Optical fiber has generally replaced other technologies such as microwave for "middle mile" networks linking communities to major hubs, and for backbone networks connecting these hubs. For international networks, fiber offers greater capacity than satellites with minimal latency (delay), which is important for interactive digital services. About 95 percent of intercontinental data traffic is carried on submarine cable,[7] with international satellite facilities now primarily maintained for television and for backup, such as when a submarine fiber is cut or electrical power to the cable is lost. Cable cuts may result from ice scouring near cable landings in the Arctic (such as in Alaska), anchors dragged by fishing boats, volcano eruptions on the ocean floor (such as near Tonga), and possibly sabotage by agents of hostile countries.

In addition to submarine cables linking continents, there are numerous regional cables, such as those linking countries in East and Southeast Asia, and cables with links to many countries on the east and west coasts of Africa.[8] Although traditionally international cables have been owned by a consortium of telecommunications operators, Google has now become the biggest investor in its own submarine cables.[9] Google, Amazon, and Meta are installing submarine cables to connect their data centers, to speed performance and reduce latency for their "cloud" customers, and to connect previously underserved developing regions.

Satellites

GEO Satellites

Geostationary satellites (or GEOs) are placed into orbit 36,000 km above the equator. At that distance, the satellites appear stationary because they take 24 hours to revolve around the Earth, the same time that it takes the Earth to rotate once on its axis. The advantage is that the satellites appear stationary so that earth stations can remain fixed once pointed at the satellite, rather than having to track the satellite across the sky. Three satellites located 120 degrees apart above the Atlantic, Pacific, and Indian oceans can cover the Earth's surface. Satellite beams can also be shaped to cover a country such as Indonesia or India or a region such as the South Pacific. Domestic U.S. and Canadian GEO satellites provide communications services in Alaska and in the Canadian Arctic.[10] A disadvantage of GEOs is that their distance from Earth results in a quarter-second delay in each direction to and from the satellite, or a half-second round trip. This latency can be tolerated but is frustrating for interactive voice, data, and video users.

An example of a relatively recently launched GEO is Kacific, which is designed to cover the South Pacific Islands and parts of Asia such as Bhutan, Myanmar, Nepal, and Pakistan. Its high power levels allow use of 75 cm to 1.2 m Very Small Aperture Terminals (VSATs). These small terminals offer speeds up to 200 Mbps downstream with low DC power consumption, so that they can be operated on low-cost solar power systems. Typical offerings are up to 30 Mbps downstream and 10 mbps upstream; for enterprises, 100 Mbps downstream, 20 upstream.[11] The satellite services are provided through existing operators that also set the prices in each country.

LEO Satellites

Low Earth Orbiting satellites have orbits in multiple planes ranging from 300 km to 2,000 km above the Earth's surface. At these elevations, latency is greatly reduced, and smaller antennas can be used. However, numerous LEO satellites are needed to provide seamless connectivity as the electronics in the small antennas switch between satellites.

The most widely adopted LEO system to date is SpaceX's Starlink, which offers low latency broadband connectivity to individual households, as well as to businesses, maritime customers, including fishing boats and ships, and government services in remote regions. Starlink states that it has more than 6 million users in more than 140 countries, territories and "other markets."[12] Starlink typically sells pizza-box size terminals directly to end-users, who then pay a monthly fee for connectivity. Starlink has become popular in Alaska and northern Canada, and is expanding in other remote regions that do not have access to broadband networks. Starlink terminals have also been purchased as backup to existing terrestrial or submarine connections, such as in Alaska villages on the coast of the Bering Sea that lost connectivity when a submarine cable was cut under the sea ice and could not be repaired for several months.

In southwest Alaska, a Native corporation has purchased Starlink terminals for several villages, rather than waiting for terrestrial providers to upgrade their networks. A corporation leader said, "To go from nothing to having this type of speed in our communities is life changing."[13] Some rural school districts have installed Starlink terminals in remote schools without broadband. The Alaska state government has deployed Starlink terminals on its ferries to run back-office functions such as credit card processing. State emergency responders employ Starlink to feed real-time drone footage of disasters to coordinators in city offices. Construction crews use Starlink terminals at remote sites, while commercial fishing crews now use Starlink for updated weather reports, access to repair manuals, and potentially life-saving medical information.[14]

In Africa, many Sudanese in war-ravaged areas have been relying on Starlink connections to receive remittances from relatives abroad, allowing them to purchase food and other necessities. Some aid groups have also relied on the service to communicate with local staff. In South Africa, a teacher said he had bought a Starlink device while vacationing in Canada to bring the internet to his school in a small rural town. The teacher said, "The kids are more interested in school since we've modernized it."[15] Tongans living overseas have bought terminals for their relatives at home in the South Pacific so that they can stay connected.

Sympathizers in the West helped to get Starlink terminals into Iran when the Iranian government shut down internet access in response to citizen protests. An organizer explained: "The main goal is not really equipping all Iranians with satellite [terminals], but basically sending a few thousand devices and getting them to the right people, so an Internet shutdown is not a problem."[16] In Ukraine, Starlink effectively replaced the internet network that was taken down during the Russian invasion, with the U.S. government and its allies and SpaceX contributing thousands of Starlink antennas.

Thus, in addition to providing connectivity for individuals, businesses, and public services in rural and remote regions, Starlink can function as a political disruptor by providing connectivity in countries where existing networks have been disabled. Starlink has also functioned as an industry disruptor, challenging existing operators by offering more reliable and/or less expensive broadband services in underserved regions. In some countries, Starlink services must be offered through existing providers to prevent customers from avoiding use of existing networks. In June/July 2024, the Tongan islands of Vava'u and Ha'apai were without internet service for more than two weeks after an undersea cable linking them to the capital was damaged in an earthquake. The government ordered all Starlink terminals (which had been purchased directly from offshore sources) to be disabled on July 10 because Starlink did not have a license. After numerous complaints from residents and businesses, the government issued a temporary permit to Starlink for six months. In December 2024, the Tongan government announced that the license had been approved and that Starlink services could now be accessed through authorized resellers, including majority government-owned Tonga Communication Corporation (TCC).[17]

Some other countries also impose permits and fees for directly imported Starlink equipment. For example, in Vanuatu, equipment ordered online for personal or business use must have a type-approval import permit approved by the regulator. Further, "If you are purchasing for personal use then it's free but if it's business related then one has to pay VT1,000 [about US$8] fee for each model regardless of the quantity."[18]

Other LEO satellite systems include OneWeb, Amazon Leo (formerly Project Kuiper), China's planned Guowang LEO network, and Telesat's planned Lightspeed network. OneWeb's LEO satellite network utilizes more than 630 satellites in 12 orbital planes 1,200 km above the Earth. It launched its first satellites in December 2020 and began commercial service in 2022. Its connectivity is typically used for enterprise, maritime, aviation, government services, and disaster recovery. OneWeb is now owned by Eutelsat, which also operates GEO satellites.

Amazon Leo plans to increase global broadband access through a constellation of 3,236 LEO satellites in orbit between 590 and 630 km above the Earth, to provide broadband to unserved and underserved communities around the world. It appears to be targeting individuals and households "for uses like video calls, gaming, and high-definition streaming."[19]

Canada's Telesat, which has operated GEO satellites covering Canada since the 1970s, also plans to offer services through a LEO network of 198 satellites called Lightspeed. It intends to provide "enterprise class" high-speed broadband services to businesses and government agencies and telecommunications operators in Canada's remote regions, rather than to individual households. Although a private sector enterprise, it has received a C$2.14 billion (about US$1.5 billion) investment from the government of Canada.[20]

China is planning a LEO network known as Guowang with a "mega-constellation" of about 13,000 satellites. It is seen as a response to Starlink and other LEO constellations. According to ITU regulations, China is required to launch at least half of the 13,000 satellites by 2032.[21]

LEOs may be considered disruptive not only because they leapfrog existing technologies to reach unserved and underserved populations, but also because they can avoid existing operators, reaching customers directly. However, some LEO systems such as OneWeb and, apparently, Lightspeed have chosen to provide services through incumbent providers. It is unclear what business model will be adopted by future LEO systems.

As demand increases for more high-bandwidth services, more LEO satellites will be required. For example, an analysis of Starlink's capacity estimates that where there are more than 7 households per square mile (about 3 households per sq km) within a Starlink beam's coverage area, Starlink may fail to deliver the minimum service level (100/20 Mbps) to qualify as a broadband service in the

United States.[22] Starlink also plans to provide connectivity for mobile phones, which could be particularly useful for people living in remote areas as well as for those working or traveling in regions without cellular coverage. Preliminary service is only for text or limited data, but SpaceX is working with chip manufacturers to get satellite-compatible chips installed in mobile phones and is planning a new system of up to 15,000 satellites to "provide ubiquitous connectivity to ordinary mobile handsets and a range of other devices and user terminals."[23] Future LEO systems will likely compete to offer mobile phone connectivity.

There are concerns that the numerous existing and planned LEO satellites will contribute to space debris. Although the satellites are designed to de-orbit and then burn up in the Earth's atmosphere when decommissioned, they may not always do so. The many rocket launches required to place these thousands of satellites and their replacements in orbit may also result in damage to launch areas and create distant debris fields over oceans. Astronomers have also complained that the LEO satellites are blocking views of space from some telescopes, an issue being addressed by the ITU.[24]

Fixed Wireless

Rather than requiring installation of coaxial cable or optical fiber to each household, fixed wireless can be a low-cost means of covering a village with a central transmitter and inexpensive equipment in each home or business. Some examples of fixed wireless networks covering rural Indigenous communities in the United States are discussed in Chapter 11, "Digital Policy Issues and Strategies." Another application of fixed wireless using different frequencies is for networking within homes, businesses, and schools. Known as Wi-Fi, it is based on the Institute of Electrical and Electronics Engineers (IEEE) wireless communication standard 802.11. The industry trade association, Wi-Fi Alliance, estimates that there are 23.3 billion Wi-Fi devices in use for applications ranging from connecting computers to the internet, security cameras, wireless printers, and videoconferencing systems as well as, in industrial settings, automated machinery and sensors.[25]

Niche Technologies

Several other technological solutions designed to provide cheap internet access for people in rural and remote regions have been piloted. For example:

- **TV white space (TVWS)**: This utilizes frequencies between TV channels to provide broadband access. These white space frequencies have been deployed in some community networks and rural regions. For example, in mountainous regions in Colombia, TVWS has been used to connect rural schools and coffee plantations.[26]
- **High altitude platform service (HAPS)**: Google's Loon project launched a network of hot-air balloons to provide connectivity to unserved locations. Loon was used during floods in Peru in 2017 as well as in Kenya to provide internet access to a region covering 50,000 square km. Meta's Aquila was a high-altitude unmanned solar-powered airplane designed to circle a region up to 60 miles in diameter, beaming connectivity down from an altitude of more than 60,000 feet.[27] Loon, which stopped operating in 2021, and other experimental networks including Aquila did not prove to be commercially viable.[28]
- **Networked tethered flying platforms (NTFP)**: These could be tethered balloons or drones. During communications outages or where connectivity is insufficient, rapidly deployable and flexible solutions are needed to establish communications. In Australia, first responders tested a tethered drone functioning as an aerial mobile tower, carrying an LTE base station, a Wi-Fi access point, and a repeater. Through tethering, the drone was connected to a cable that provided a fiber-optic feed down to a Starlink terminal. The drone could operate for several hours because it was connected to a generator on the ground. The demonstration concluded:

  > The Broadband Connectivity Drone can serve as a repeater for public mobile networks or establish a private mobile network for emergency services. It can also accommodate advanced network equipment, … two-way radios, floodlights and cameras, making it invaluable in places where traditional infrastructure is lacking or compromised.[29]

Community Networks

At the local level, community networks offer broadband connections to households and businesses, which can then be linked to national networks through existing infrastructure. In North America and Europe, community networks began as email and electronic bulletin board systems (BBSs) in the mid-1980s; they evolved into networks as amateur users connected dial-up modems with low-cost personal computers. With the growth of the internet and creation of the World Wide Web, some of these amateur networks became "freenets" offering free access to basic services, and eventually evolved into community ISPs (internet service providers). Others were supplanted by commercial ISPs.[30]

In Sweden in the 1990s, approximately 1,000 rural communities adopted a "village fiber" approach, forming cooperatives to build and operate their own local fiber networks where local connectivity was not available. Residents contributed volunteer labor and paid up-front fees to connect their dwelling to the network; some government grants were available, with funding from a European Union rural development program.[31]

Precursors to community networks were telecenters, various community access sites such as community centers, libraries, local government buildings, or stand-alone locations where people could access the internet. Telecenters provided a means of going online in communities without local connectivity or where the price of individual access was too expensive for most residents. With the support of development agencies and other sources, telecenters were installed in communities from Timbuktu in Mali to Bario in Sarawak (Malaysian Borneo). Some telecenters did not survive because of lack of sustainable business models to cover costs; others evolved into community services in libraries; others were phased out with the expansion of mobile services and eventually smartphones. Numerous studies were conducted on telecenters and their contribution to rural development.[32]

The community network model has been adapted to provide local connectivity in remote villages in North America and in developing regions of Africa, Latin America, and some remote regions of

Southeast Asia such as Sarawak.[33] These networks often use fixed wireless to minimize installation costs, although some have now installed optical fiber, either trenched or on poles, to each building.

These networks face similar problems to versions using earlier technologies. They often rely, at least to some extent, on volunteer labor to install and maintain the facilities. Community members therefore require what McMahon and colleagues call "infrastructure literacy training"[34] to gain necessary technical skills. New users may also benefit from digital literacy training to take advantage of the newly available online services. A longer-term issue is sustainability. In addition to turnover in volunteers, community networks face costs for maintaining, replacing, and upgrading equipment. They may also need to pay for access to middle-mile networks. Some rely on grants from governments and non-profit organizations or foundations; others try to raise funds within the community. In some cases, they intend to transition to a user-pay model, but residents may be reluctant or unable to pay user fees.

Community or regional ISPs that have managed to sustain operations may also be challenged by the introduction of competing services, such as Starlink. During the COVID-19 pandemic, many First Nations in northern Ontario received Starlink terminals, subsidized through limited-term federal and provincial infrastructure projects. An Indigenous non-profit ISP serving these communities previously held 95 percent of the local market. The subsidized Starlink services split the consumer market and weakened the business case for local ISPs. When the free period on Starlink ended, those who were cut off had not budgeted to pay for service from Starlink or from the Indigenous ISP.[35]

Cloud Computing and Data Centers

Innovations in cloud computing, big data, and applications of artificial intelligence have created demand for scalable data storage and computing resources. Cloud services used by businesses and governments have accelerated as big data analysis is increasingly taking place over distributed cloud networks. Increased broadband connectivity and data processing speeds have reduced delays in accessing data centers for remote storage, processing, and analysis of data. The Internet of Things is generating vast amounts of data on connected inventory, smart appliances, vehicles, cargo, and other items. Also, high-performance computers powerful enough to run AI programs are frequently only available in the cloud. As noted above, global platform providers such as Amazon, Google, and Meta are investing in their own submarine cables to connect their data centers.

Data centers provide space, power, and cooling for servers hosting data and network cabling. They contribute to the digital economy by storing data and by local hosting of domestic content. In addition, data centers offer a significant advantage when processing large volumes of data and in the development of big data services. The ITU points out that the presence of data centers is also an indicator of the digitalization of the economy, reflecting "demand from the [ICT] sector and other services such as finance and insurance, transportation, legal and accounting activities, research and development, advertising and the public sector."[36]

However, data centers are costly to build and require enormous amounts of energy for operations and cooling. Many low- and middle-income countries lack the capital and necessary expertise to build them. The private sector has funded some data centers (for example, by Huawei in Senegal) and the World Bank has provided some development funding (such as for a data center in Togo).[37] Some northern countries, such as Iceland and Finland, with cool climates and inexpensive thermal or hydropower are attracting investment in data centers.

Commentary

Digital connectivity is available through numerous technologies, primarily fiber-optic cable in terrestrial and submarine networks, satellites, and wireless facilities for both fixed and mobile connectivity. New entrants such as LEO satellites may disrupt legacy services and business models while offering reliable and affordable connectivity, especially in rural and remote regions.

However, challenges remain. While technological capacity continues to increase, users may face costs of replacing obsolete devices and prices for access, and rural service providers may struggle to maintain sustainable services in areas with relatively high costs and low user demand. Also, wireless services continue to require additional spectrum, which may be costly for small and rural providers. These and other issues such as user privacy and network security are discussed in Chapter 11, "Digital Policy Issues and Strategies."

References

1. Wawatay Native Communications Society. https://www.wawataynews.ca/.
2. Federal Communications Commission (2014), *Types of Broadband Connections*. https://www.fcc.gov/general/types-broadband-connections.
3. https://www.statista.com/forecasts/1146962/smartphone-user-by-country.
4. https://www.statista.com/statistics/306528/share-of-mobile-Internet-traffic-in-global-regions/.
5. Purnell, Newley (2023, October 12), Billionaire Bets that a $12 Mobile Phone Can Get More of the World's Most Populous Country Online, *Wall Street Journal*. https://www.wsj.com/business/telecom/jio-bharat-phone-india-84db73d0.
6. Fitzgerald, Drew (2023, October 14), After More than Four Years, Has 5G Lived Up to Expectations? *Wall Street Journal*. https://www.wsj.com/business/telecom/how-5g-changed-world-752b13ee.
7. https://www.networkcomputing.com/enterprise-connectivity/amazon-meta-google-plan-subsea-cable-expansion.
8. For a map of global submarine cables see https://www.submarinecablemap.com/.
9. https://www.submarinenetworks.com/en/nv/insights/complete-list-of-google-s-subsea-cable-investments.
10. For more information on the roles and impacts of GEO satellites, see Hudson, Heather E. (1990), *Communications Satellites: Their Development and Impact*, Free Press.
11. https://kacific.com/.
12. https://www.starlink.com/stories.
13. Hughes, Zachariah, DeMarban, Alex, & Naiden, Alena (2023, August 20), In Just a Few Months, Satellite Internet Has Reshaped Web Access in Rural Alaska, *Anchorage Daily News*, August 20.
14. Hughes, Zachariah, DeMarban, Alex, & Naiden, Alena (2023, August 20), In Just a Few Months, Satellite Internet Has Reshaped Web Access in Rural Alaska, *Anchorage Daily News*, August 20.

15. Bariyo, Nicholas, Steinhauser, Gabriele, Wexler, Alexandra, & Maidenberg, Micah (2024, April 16), Musk's Starlink Cracks Down on Growing Black Market, *Wall Street Journal*. https://www.wsj.com/tech/elon-musk-spacex-starlink-satellite-access-crackdown-e09f3e4e?mod=Searchresults&pos=1&page=1.
16. Vick, Carl (2023, January 23), Inside the Clandestine Efforts to Smuggle Starlink Internet Into Iran, *TIME*, January 23. https://time.com/6249365/iran-elon-musk-starlink-protests/5.
17. Islands Business (2024, December 24), Starlink Approved to Revolutionise Tonga's Internet Business. https://islandsbusiness.com/news-break/starlink-approved-in-tonga/.
18. Massing, Adorina (2024, October 19), TRBR Confirms Two Network Resellers for Starlink in Vanuatu, *Daily Post Vanuatu*.
19. https://www.aboutamazon.com/what-we-do/devices-services/project-kuiper.
20. https://cdev.gc.ca/telesat-lightspeed/.
21. https://spacenews.com/china-launches-third-batch-of-guowang-megaconstellation-satellites/.
22. Meinrath, Sascha, Grindal, Karl, Fishbine, Glenn, & DeGidio, Nancy (2025, July 16). *Starlink Capacity Analysis*. https://thexlab.org/wp-content/uploads/2025/07/Starlink_Analysis_Working_Paper_v0.2.pdf.
23. Space Exploration Holdings LLC (2025, September 17), Application for Launch and Operating Authority for the SpaceX NGSO MSS Satellite System, Filing with the Federal Communications Commission.
24. ITU (2023), *Handbook on Small Satellites*. https://www.itu.int/hub/publication/r-hdb-65-2023/.
25. See https://www.wi-fi.org/beacon/the-beacon/powering-connected-world-wi-fi-momentum-2025.
26. ITU (n.d.), *Adopting TV White Spaces in Colombia*. https://www.itu.int/net4/wsis/archive/stocktaking/Project/Details?projectId=1514859321.
27. https://about.fb.com/news/2016/07/aquilas-first-flight-a-big-milestone-toward-connecting-billions-of-people/.
28. GSMA (2021, January 27), *Intelligence Brief: End of Loon Highlights Economic Issues*. https://www.mobileworldlive.com/gsma/intelligence-brief-end-of-loon-highlights-economic-issues/.
29. New South Wales Government (2024, May 15), Broadband Connectivity Drone Creates a Canopy of Wireless Connectivity. https://www.nsw.gov.au/broadband-connectivity-drone-creates-a-canopy-of-wireless-connectivity.
30. Song, Steve, Rey-Moreno, Carlos, Esterhuysen, Anriette, Jensen, Mike, & Navarro, Leandro (2018), The Rise and Fall and Rise of Community

Networks, *Global Information Society Watch 2018: Community Networks.* Alliance for Progressive Communications (APC).

31. OECD (2018), Bridging the Rural Digital Divide, *OECD Digital Economy Papers 31.* https://www.oecd.org/content/dam/oecd/en/publications/reports/2018/02/bridging-the-rural-digital-divide_34e688e4/852bd3b9-en.pdf.
32. See, for example, Latchem, Colin & Walke, David (2001), *Telecentres: Case Studies and Key Issues*, The Commonwealth of Learning; and references cited in Hudson, Heather E. (2006), *From Rural Village to Global Village: Telecommunications and Development in the Information Age*, Routledge.
33. E-Bario. https://www.isiti.unimas.my/about/isiti-ebario-history.
34. McMahon, R., Gurstein, M., Beaton, B., O'Donnell, S., & Whiteduck, T. (2014), Making Information Technologies Work at the End of the Road, *Journal of Information Policy*, 4, 250–69.
35. McMahon, Rob (2025, May 2), Forget Starlink. Indigenous Innovation Is Canada's Best Bet for Rural Internet, *Macleans* 2. https://macleans.ca/economy/forget-starlink-indigenous-innovation-is-canadas-best-bet-for-rural-Internet/.
36. ITU (2022), *Global Connectivity Report 2022*, p. 74. https://www.itu.int/itu-d/reports/statistics/global-connectivity-report-2022/.
37. ITU (2022), *Global Connectivity Report 2022*, p. 76. https://www.itu.int/itu-d/reports/statistics/global-connectivity-report-2022/.

11

DIGITAL POLICY ISSUES AND STRATEGIES

> "Neither universal connectivity with poor quality nor meaningful connectivity for the few will yield significant, society-wide benefits."
>
> – United Nations (2020)[1]

This chapter reviews digital connectivity policy issues with particular relevance to rural, remote, and Indigenous regions, such as universal connectivity, affordability, digital literacy, access to spectrum, and privacy and security. It includes examples of strategies to address these challenges.

Meaningful Connectivity

The United Nations has adopted the term "meaningful connectivity" to describe "the possibility for everyone to enjoy a safe, satisfying, enriching, productive and affordable online experience" as key for enabling digital transformation and meeting the Sustainable Development Goals. It points out that universality and affordability are complementary: "neither universal connectivity with poor quality nor meaningful connectivity for the few will yield significant, society-wide benefits." It identifies several "connectivity enablers": infrastructure, affordability, devices, skills, and safety and security.[2]

The ITU/UN target for affordability specifies that prices for entry-level broadband services should be below 2 percent of monthly

DOI: 10.4324/9781003431602-11

gross national income (GNI) per capita in developing countries by 2025. Yet lack of affordability continues to be a key barrier to digital connectivity, particularly in low-income countries. A wide gap between high-income economies and the rest of the world persists: compared to prices in high-income countries, the mobile-broadband basket (an estimate of fees for subscription and usage) is 5.5 times less affordable in lower- to middle-income economies and more than 20 times less affordable in low-income countries. A fixed-broadband subscription, if available, costs the equivalent of a third of the average monthly income.[3] In measuring progress toward the target of cost of entry-level broadband services of less than 2 percent of monthly GNI per capita, the Broadband Commission for Sustainable Development includes prices of both mobile and fixed entry-level broadband subscriptions, but also adds "Tier 2" indicators of smartphone affordability and affordability of other internet-enabled devices such as computers and tablets.[4]

Pricing of digital connectivity depends on many factors, including geography, population size and distribution, infrastructure investment, and extent of competition, as well as legal, policy, and regulatory frameworks. ITU data show a close association between a well-developed regulatory environment and affordability of broadband services; median prices for ICT services are highest in economies with limited regulatory maturity, and lowest in economies that are leaders in terms of having "a holistic, multi sectoral, collaborative national regulatory framework for digital transformation."[5] Correlation does not demonstrate causality, but it does indicate the importance of the policy and regulatory environment in successfully addressing affordability. For example, national policymakers may set targets for universally available and affordable connectivity and digital transformation, while regulators may allow and monitor competition in digital services, and mandate subsidies where deemed necessary, to help achieve these goals.

Competition

Although competition may seem unrealistic in rural and remote regions with generally high costs to provide services and relatively small populations and/or low incomes, it may be feasible if appropriate regulations are implemented and enforced. There are two types of competition: facilities-based and services-based. Facilities-based competition requires separate networks, either duplicating similar facilities, such as mobile networks, or installing different technologies, such as satellite antennas or fixed wireless. Services-based competition allows competing service providers to access existing networks such as optical fiber to reach customers.

It was the decision by government regulators or policymakers to allow competition by mobile providers that first resulted in lower prices and extended coverage in many African countries. Initially, monopoly mobile operators targeted primarily business customers. Prices were high, and uptake of mobile service was also limited to those who could pay for monthly service and usage charges. There was little or no attempt to attract customers with modest incomes, who often lacked access to any telephone service. New private-sector operators built networks to compete with the monopoly, generally government-owned mobile networks, and stressed affordability through the introduction of prepaid or "pay-as-you-go" pricing and less expensive devices. Customers could pay small amounts to "top up" their minutes at local shops rather than having to qualify for monthly billing. In turn, operators who collected revenue in advance eliminated financial risk from unpaid bills.

Now most of sub-Saharan Africa, including many rural areas, have coverage by multiple mobile operators. To reduce costs of extending competing networks, regulators may approve or require sharing of transmission towers by several operators; in some jurisdictions competing providers may lease capacity on incumbents' networks. This option can be attractive for small operators unable to finance construction of their own networks, but may be challenged by incumbents claiming that they will lose incentive to extend and upgrade their networks if they are forced to resell some of their capacity to lower-cost competitors. Alternatively, incumbents may compete by offering packages to target various markets on their own networks with different branding, sometimes called "flanker brands."[6]

Universal Service Funds

Strategies to address the need for investment in rural infrastructure and for affordable connectivity include the establishment of funds intended to bridge these gaps. Infrastructure funders, such as governments, development banks, and/or commercial lenders, tend to provide funds only for financing costs of equipment and installation (capital expenditure, "Capex"). They typically do not provide ongoing operating support (operating expenditure, "Opex"), and therefore do not address funding that may be required for sustainability of the networks. Typically, communication networks cover these costs from operating revenues, but high costs in rural areas and low revenues from scattered and lower-income populations may not generate sufficient revenue. As an operator serving rural Africa stated: "You can't spend $6,000 or $7,000 a month on a site that gives you only $200."[7]

The means of setting prices in high-cost and/or low-income regions traditionally involved internal cross-subsidies by the operator from high-margin services to loss-making services. Typically, a regulator would authorize tariffs designed to generate revenue from services such as international calls or monthly subscription charges that could then be directed to subsidizing expansion of networks or pricing of services in rural areas. However, with the introduction of competition, internal cross-subsidies had to be eliminated; otherwise, incumbent providers could simply absorb losses to drive out competitors by cutting their rates in targeted regions.

Some of the first Universal Service Funds (USFs) were established in the mid-1990s in Latin America (Colombia and Peru, 1994; Chile and Mexico, 1995; Guatemala, 1996). Among industrialized countries, the United States expanded its universal service subsidies to include "advanced services" for schools and libraries in the Telecommunications Act of 1996. In Africa, the first USF was established in South Africa in 1998. By 2022, 49 percent of all countries had established a USF, with Africa having the highest percentage at 70.5 percent, followed by the Americas at 60 percent, the Arab states at 54.6 percent.[8] However, as discussed below, not all these funds became or remained operational.

Funding of USFs is typically from levies on operators. Most countries with USFs now require contributions from both fixed and mobile operators; some also include ISPs. Revenue from spectrum auctions (see below) may also be used for subsidies. When the first USFs were established in developing countries in the mid-1990s, teledensity (at that time fixed lines per 100 inhabitants) was very low, and in most rural and isolate areas, telephone service was nonexistent. Thus, funds prioritized coverage for regions without access to voice telephony (traditionally provided over fixed lines and public pay phones); now definitions have been expanded to include mobile telephony and, increasingly, internet access.

Some countries have included subsidies or discounts for public institutions that make internet services available to the public, such as post offices and libraries, and schools that provide public access (such as through Wi-Fi that is accessible outside the school or after school hours). In the United States, the E-Rate (short for "education rate") created by the Telecommunications Act of 1996 provides discounts on telecommunications, internet access, and internal connections for schools and libraries. The applicable discount rate is based on indicators of student families' incomes and whether the facility is located in an urban or rural area. Approved schools and libraries post their requirements online, where they are open for competitive bids.[9] The E-Rate program creates incentives by designating schools as paying customers that use the subsidy to take bids from providers, rather than freeloaders that must be served as a condition for a license. Yet the paperwork requirements may be difficult for school districts. In some states, state-wide coordinators or consultants have been hired to manage grant applications and management.

In Alaska, the E-Rate subsidy was a vital vehicle to bring internet access to village schools and libraries. The operational subsidy for these "anchor tenants" has helped to make a business case to upgrade connectivity to the entire village. A federal Rural Health Care fund supports connectivity for rural hospitals and clinics. In rural Alaska, where Indigenous people live in more than 200 isolated villages, most without road access, the AFHCAN telemedicine program, discussed in Chapter 4, relies on this subsidy to connect more than 150 village clinics and regional hospitals.[10]

Traditionally, through their own budgets or USF resources, governments have identified unserved or underserved regions and provided subsidies to incumbents or "carriers of last resort" to extend facilities and, in some cases, to subsidize prices in these areas. Although this approach can extend connectivity, it has several potential flaws. Typically, the incumbent or designated operator has no incentive to be efficient or innovative in its choice of technology and its installation and maintenance if these costs are directly subsidized. Second, the operator may have no incentive to maintain adequate quality of service (QoS) if it assumes these areas are unlikely to generate significant revenue. And third, the operator may demand special treatment or concessions in a liberalized environment because of its universal service obligations.

An alternative approach adopted in several countries to create incentives for efficient investment in rural areas is the reverse auction, a form of "smart subsidy." Licenses to install and operate facilities in designated unserved or unserved areas are put to competitive bid. The operator requesting the lowest subsidy wins the right to serve the territory. Terms may include performance by specific roll-out dates, maintenance of approved QoS, and multi-year licenses (in some cases with exclusivity for a specified period). Chile's success with reverse auctions is the best-known example. In the 1990s, Chile's Telecommunications Development Fund used competitive bids to extend payphones in rural and low-income areas. Any firm could bid, and the winner got a 30-year license. The resulting average subsidy was $3,600 per payphone, compared to estimated costs of $10,000 to $20,000. Chile managed to cover 66 percent of designated villages using only 54 percent of financing available – 656 villages required no subsidy.[11] More recently, to achieve its digital connectivity goals, Chile is using its Telecommunications Development Fund for subsidies for the most vulnerable users to pay for internet access.[12]

At the national level, USF management may require expertise in implementation and monitoring of regulatory policies and public-sector funds that is lacking or committed to other government priorities. Thus, some developing countries have established USFs but have not implemented them, failing either to collect or to disburse funds. Arakpogun and colleagues identify institutional and organizational constraints that help to explain why USFs have been largely unsuccessful in African countries. Institutional constraints can include lack of clear, realizable, and measurable universal connectivity objectives and ineffective governance including political interference. Major organizational factors include lack of institutional capacity, including regulatory skills and financial capacity.[13] They propose developing universal service and access policies and regulatory frameworks that are suitable locally through wide engagement with both private sectors and local communities to allow continuous learning and adaptation.[14]

Affordability

As discussed above, competition may reduce prices for connectivity, but there may be few or no competitive providers in some rural regions. Where operating costs are high because of isolation, climate, or difficult terrain, pricing to recover these costs may make services unaffordable for rural households or institutions. Some countries have subsidy programs to reduce the costs of connectivity for low-income residents.

In the United States, the Lifeline Program, which has provided a subsidized voice service for low-income subscribers since 1985, now also provides subsidies for broadband access.[15] Lifeline provides a monthly discount on service prices for eligible low-income subscribers and a higher discount for eligible subscribers on Tribal lands.[16] The High Cost Fund (which subsidizes costs for carriers in order to reduce the prices they charge to subscribers) is being replaced by the Connect America Fund (CAF). Eligible providers must offer both voice and broadband (previously, only voice services were required). During the COVID pandemic, the FCC's Emergency Broadband Benefit Program also implemented additional subsidies for broadband services to low-income and Tribal households.[17] It was later extended as the Affordable Connectivity Program (ACP). Participating providers were to make available discounts of up to $50 per month for internet service and associated equipment to eligible households; on Tribal lands, the monthly discount was up to $75 per month. Participating providers could also receive a discount of up to $100 for supplying an eligible household with a laptop or desktop computer.[18] The ACP was discontinued in 2024 due to a lack of appropriation of additional funds from Congress.[19]

These programs have not been totally successful. As noted, some, such as those implemented during the pandemic, provide only short-term assistance. Some may be difficult to qualify for, or may not have been publicized effectively. And fraud has been a problem with Lifeline as some unscrupulous companies have secured subsidies for Tribal community members without providing telecommunications services in return.[20]

Canada has no national subsidies for low-income users, or for health or education services, although some government departments (provincial/territorial and federal) may provide funds in their budgets for telemedicine, internet for schools and libraries, etc. But these funds are not part of any overall policy and, typically, depend on annual allocations from federal or provincial/territorial budgets. In 2025, the national regulator, the Canadian Radio-television and Telecommunications Commission (CRTC), approved the introduction of a retail internet subsidy to improve affordability in the Far North, where the cost of living is already higher than elsewhere in Canada. All households in the Far North (Yukon, Northwest Territories, and Nunavut) will be eligible for the subsidy. The subsidy is intended to help reduce the price gap between internet services offered in the region and elsewhere in Canada.[21]

The Australian government invested A$13.7 million in a School Student Broadband Initiative to boost education opportunities and narrow the digital divide. About 30,000 qualifying families with school-age children will receive free internet access until 30 June 2028. No more places are available under the current initiative. The government states that an evaluation will assess the Initiative's impact on families and students.[22]

Engagement: Consultation, Training, and Jobs

Earlier chapters have discussed the importance of engagement with residents in planning, implementing, and operating networks for rural digital connectivity. For example, consultation is necessary to ensure that Indigenous and other communities in rural and remote regions are aware of the potential impacts and opportunities of publicly funded broadband infrastructure projects in their regions. Regulations that require consultation as a condition to receive government funding or subsidies may create incentives to comply.

Canada's first Indigenous female communications commissioner has stated that relevant Indigenous entities must be meaningfully consulted prior to the approval of a broadband funding application in accordance with their [Canadian] constitutional rights and their rights under the United Nations Declaration on the Rights of Indigenous Peoples (the UN Declaration).[23] She notes:

> The UN Declaration provides that, among other things, Indigenous peoples have the right to maintain and strengthen their distinct political, legal, economic, social and cultural institutions … (Article 5); participate in decision-making in matters which would affect their rights, through representatives chosen by themselves … (Article 18); and that States shall consult and cooperate in good faith with the indigenous peoples concerned through their own representative institutions in order to obtain their *free, prior and informed consent* before adopting and implementing legislative or administrative measures that may affect them (Article 19).[24] [emphasis added]

Infrastructure providers and others applying for public sector funding should be required to include a summary of who was consulted, how the consultation was carried out, and relevant findings. Original Canadian Broadband Fund guidelines in 2019 stated only that applicants should show that they "attempted to consult" with communities to be served. Such a requirement could be fulfilled by a letter never received or a telephone call never answered. Further, an example of acceptable consultation was a market study that could be done using available information (such as population, average income, public institutions, local businesses, etc.) without any interaction with the community.[25] More recently, Canadian federal agencies have issued more specific requirements for evidence of consultation with Indigenous communities.

In the United States, the FCC must "send any public notice seeking comment on any petition for designation as an eligible telecommunications carrier on Tribal lands, at the time it is released, to the affected tribal government and tribal regulatory authority, as applicable, by the most expeditious means available." Also the FCC requires a *Tribal Government Engagement Obligation* from carriers receiving subsidies to provide services on Tribal lands. These carriers must demonstrate that they have coordinated with the Tribal government and provide a report documenting their compliance. The FCC determined that, at a minimum, the annual Tribal engagement obligation … must include: (1) needs assessment and deployment planning; (2) feasibility and sustainability planning; (3) marketing services in a culturally sensitive manner; (4) rights-of-way processes, land-use permitting, facilities siting, environmental and cultural preservation, and review processes; and (5) compliance with Tribal business and licensing requirements.[26]

However, Indigenous connectivity advocates point out the limitations of this process. According to interviews with Indigenous representatives, although regulations require carriers to meet with Tribes, consultation is typically limited to a letter sent to a generic email box of the Tribal government (whose staff may not have telecommunications expertise or access to consultants or advisors). After 60 days, the carrier can check the box stating that it did consult with Tribes even if it received no reply. As one interviewee put it: "Less than one percent [of carriers] are truly doing consultation … it's a very small number of people who are actually doing consultation." Another person noted that many Tribal communities are learning that funding for connectivity in their communities has been secured by external providers who may not have engaged with (or even informed) them about their plans.[27]

Digital Literacy and Skills

Lack of awareness of the internet and lack of digital skills can discourage interest as well as discourage internet use. In surveys on mobile phone and internet access in 16 developing countries in Asia, Latin America, and Africa, results showed that affordability of devices and lack of awareness were the main barriers to internet use in the countries surveyed.[28] In addition to lack of digital skills in many developing regions, Russian researchers also found that the population of the Russian Federation possessed these skills to a minimum degree, and the rural population to an even lesser degree. According to a 2017 survey, among households not using the internet, the main factor was unwillingness and lack of interest (22 percent) and the second factor was absence of internet usage skills (8.9 percent).[29]

Effective utilization of new services may require a digital literacy strategy to ensure that residents understand how to use online services and to handle issues such as fake content and threats to privacy. For example, McMahon and colleagues describe training of Indigenous residents to access community networks in Canada's North.[30] Similar training has been provided by members of Hawai'i's Broadband Hui (an organization of community stakeholders, government, and the private sector, committed to digital equity goals),[31] and by organizations in other countries.

Governments and NGOs can also raise awareness about connectivity benefits for persons with disabilities, and use USFs and other sources to provide equipment and customized training. Regulators can also require that online public services are accessible to those with disabilities. For example, many governments require voice services to be accessible for deaf and blind users. Accessibility standards have been developed for websites, but adoption is typically voluntary.[32] In China, availability of barrier-free internet access devices, free training in how to use the internet, and easy access to special information were found to be major motivators to go online among non-adopters. By the end of June 2024, almost 2,800 websites and apps closely related to the lives of the elderly and people with disabilities were updated for accessibility.[33]

Barriers to installing community networks can include lack of skilled local people to build and maintain the facilities. Public-sector funders seek to ensure that the facilities get built, but rarely include requirements for training and hiring of local residents. The result is typically higher installation and maintenance costs (including travel and lodging as well as wages for outside crews) and no transfer of skills or income to the community. Local employees of digital networks and services will also contribute to local and regional economies, in turn creating additional demand for digital services.

The Internet Society has organized workshops in several regions to provide training in skills needed to install, operate, and maintain community networks. Commercial operators can also be encouraged to provide training and jobs in rural communities they serve. Indigenous participants in Canadian regulatory proceedings have urged that commercial recipients of federal broadband funding be required to hire and train local residents to install and maintain their equipment.[34] To date, no such requirements have been imposed, but Indigenous applicants may also include budgets for training in broadband funding proposals. In the United States, guidelines for federally funded broadband projects include references to workforce development. For example, the Tribal Broadband Connectivity Program (TPCP) states: "Project proposals must include a plan for workforce training and development."[35] However, it does not specifically require local hiring.

Some commercial operators do provide training and jobs besides manual labor for installations such as digging trenches for optical fiber. A satellite services provider in the Canadian Arctic has trained local community service providers (CSPs), most of whom are Inuit, in each settlement. They work as commissioned contractors to sign up accounts, process monthly payments, and provide technical support to customers. Other local residents are also trained as infrastructure support agents (ISAs), learning maintenance skills and providing on-site assistance to company technicians as required, often following directions by phone and completing tasks that would otherwise require costly travel arrangements. The company states that this CSP-ISA model delivers more than C$1 million into the Nunavut economy annually.[36]

The Frequency Spectrum

As discussed in Chapter 10, "Technologies to Extend Digital Connectivity," wireless technologies are vital to the expansion of digital connectivity, including broadband in rural and developing regions. Most of the population in the Global South now relies on mobile devices, increasingly smartphones, for personal communications and access to commercial and public services. Satellites provide connectivity to rural communities, as well as to individual households, schools, and businesses as LEO satellite terminals proliferate. Fixed wireless can provide an inexpensive means to cover villages.

These technologies make use of available frequencies allocated for each type of service by the International Telecommunication Union (ITU), a UN agency with 194 member states. Within countries, spectrum is administered by a national regulatory agency, which may issue spectrum licenses to qualified applicants. These procedures are designed to avoid interference in use of frequencies for various services, ranging from aviation to radio and TV broadcasting to mobile telephony, and to set standards that enable industries to design and manufacture equipment that can be used in multiple countries. (Some frequencies such as those used for Wi-Fi are generally unlicensed and therefore unprotected from interference.) As demand grows, for example for broadband, ITU members also identify additional frequency bands for services or allow frequencies to be shared among various services.

There may be advantages as well as trade-offs in moving to higher frequencies. For example, next generation 6G mobile frequencies can accommodate more data transmission, such as is required for IoT applications, but have very limited range, so require many more transmitters than 3G or 4G. Frequencies that can transmit over a greater range are less costly to cover rural areas. Higher frequencies allocated to satellite systems to meet demand for more data and more users are also prone to interference from heavy rain or dust storms that can affect developing regions. Rural users may therefore be forced to adopt technologies with frequencies that are not optimized for their circumstances of lower demand and geographic dispersion.

These issues are addressed at ITU conferences where national delegations propose and decide upon frequency allocations. Rural development proponents within a country therefore should be represented on their national delegations or should convince their delegates to represent rural spectrum needs, which may differ from requirements for urban and peri-urban areas. The ITU's Development Bureau also includes experts who provide advice on rural spectrum issues.[37]

In some cases, domestic frequencies may be reallocated to meet rural needs. For example, some spectrum in the 2.5 GHz band, which the United States and Canada have made available for 5G mobile services, is also used to for local fixed broadband. Before conducting an auction of this spectrum for 5G use, the FCC in the United States opened a "priority window" to allow federally recognized rural Tribes and Alaska Native villages to obtain this spectrum to serve rural Indigenous lands. While the window was open for seven months during 2020, more than 350 Tribal and other Indigenous entities applied, some to serve multiple locations or communities.[38]

There are several examples of use of 2.5 GHz to serve U.S. Indigenous communities. As discussed in Chapter 3, the Havasupai Tribe, located at the base of the Grand Canyon, uses 2.5 GHz spectrum for wireless broadband connectivity for Head Start (preschool), teachers, and K-12 students. A fixed wireless community network is installed in the Native Hawai'ian community of Pu'uhonua o Waimānalo on Oahu.[39] The Alaska Tribal Spectrum consortium with the support of 85 Tribal members reserved 2.5 GHz spectrum covering a large area of rural Alaska.

The Canadian government has also developed a new draft spectrum policy framework called the Indigenous Priority Window (IPW) with the aims of improving Indigenous access to spectrum and supporting Indigenous-led connectivity solutions.[40] The proposed IPW could enable Indigenous applicants to obtain spectrum licenses in a particular spectrum band, on a first-come, first-served basis to enable wireless solutions, such as the provision of mobile phone or wireless home internet services.

Some governments may assess one-time or annual fees to use spectrum. In the United States and some other countries, some spectrum, such as for mobile services, is auctioned. Revenue from such auctions may be designated to cover the costs of a communications ministry or regulator, or considered revenue contributed to the government as a whole.[41] Although a potentially lucrative contributor to public funds, auctions may include financial and other prerequisites that make it difficult or impossible for small and rural operators to obtain spectrum. In some cases, they may obtain licenses through secondary market transactions, through buying or leasing the license from another provider.

Although spectrum is considered a nationally administered resource, a spectrum sovereignty movement,[42] led by Indigenous connectivity advocates in the United States[43], Canada,[44] and New Zealand,[45] argues that Indigenous people should have the right to claim and use spectrum covering Tribal and other Indigenous lands. In 2022, Māori reached an agreement with the New Zealand government that included establishment the Interim Māori Spectrum Commission, with Māori "receiving an ongoing allocation of 20 percent of future national commercial spectrum allocations, at no cost."[46] A Māori company, Tū Ātea, now holds long-term spectrum management rights in New Zealand for a range of frequency bands (*tū ātea* means to stand in space). Its mission is to "increase Māori participation and opportunities in spectrum-related industries [...] and leverage the radio spectrum to enable Māori economic, cultural, environmental and social wellbeing."[47] Additionally, the government agreement includes funding designated for training so that Māori can manage their spectrum resources.

In Mexico, Indigenous rights to spectrum are recognized in its telecommunications act, based on an argument that the rights are essential to the preservation and promotion of Indigenous culture and language. In 2014, Mexican Indigenous advocates won the right to have community spectrum licenses guaranteed in the constitution, specifically Indigenous-use licenses for any kind of network or service, including wireless telecommunications and broadcast media. The act states:

> Concessions for Indigenous social use purposes may be granted to Indigenous peoples and communities throughout the country in accordance with the guidelines issued by the [Federal Telecommunications] Institute and shall target the promotion, development, and preservation of their languages and culture, knowledge promoting their traditions, internal rules and principles respecting gender equality, allowing Indigenous women to participate in the objectives for which the concession was requested, and other elements constituting Indigenous cultures and identities.[48]

Privacy and Security

Rural participants in the digital economy face challenges similar to those faced by their urban counterparts who have become increasingly dependent on digital connectivity for finding work, funds transfers, government services, and personal communications. While governments should be responsible for regulations to protect individuals' identity and security of data transactions and their enforcement, rural users also need to be aware of threats to their privacy and security from digital communications.

Digital Identification

Digital identity technologies are evolving rapidly. The GSMA states:

> "Continuous behavioural authentication is one trending technology that verifies a user's identity on an ongoing basis by using a combination of data such as IP address, location, biometrics, device details, and calling/messaging behavioural patterns, *in accordance with privacy regulations*.[49] [italics added]

The GSMA points out that successful adoption of digital identity solutions involves factors including "compliance with local laws and regulatory frameworks, especially data protection and privacy." It cites a case in Southeast Asia where ride-hailing app Grab, which needed higher identity verification standards for transactions such as e-payments and delivery, implemented frequent mobile identity checks (for example, selfies, location checks, and route geofencing) for onboarding drivers in markets including Indonesia, Malaysia, the Philippines, Thailand, Singapore, and Vietnam.[50] The drivers had no choice but to trust the company with their frequently monitored personal data.

Biometric data (such as fingerprints, facial features, voice identification, and iris identification) differentiate between people based on their physical characteristics. Owners can now use facial recognition to unlock their mobile phones. CCTV cameras linked to facial identification databases track individuals in public places in many countries. Biometrics may be used to identify individuals by comparing biometrics against an individual's stored record and to eliminate duplicate data records by comparing biometrics with all or a subset of records. The ability to accurately and uniquely identify individuals is considered important for fraud prevention, but intrudes on people's privacy, often without their knowledge.

The World Bank points out that identification systems capable of establishing unique, official identities for individuals help to enable development of e-government and e-commerce, but that today's modern society creates new demands on identity: "identity has to be mobile, transactional, interoperable, portable, and social – in addition to being secure."[51] In many developing regions, governments lack the regulatory capacity or authority to oversee such digital identity applications.[52] Rather than developing their own regulations, governments could adopt existing models such as the General Data Protection Regulation (GDPR) implemented by the European Union in 2018. The GDPR contains enforceable provisions to support users including requiring companies to design and build systems that protect personal data, ensuring the informed consent of the user, and allowing users to request a portable copy of their data. Companies are also required to report breaches within 72 hours, with penalties for violations up to €20 million or up to 4 percent of global turnover, whichever is greater.[53] Of course, countries that adopt this model to protect their citizens must also be able to enforce it.

E-Signatures and Contracts

Many online documents require digital or e-signatures to signify a legally binding agreement, rather than a physical signature on a hard copy document that must then be delivered to the sender (or in some cases, transmitted by facsimile). Contracts, including those required to access some websites or download software, may also be difficult to understand or unavailable in local languages. Rural residents, especially in developing regions, may experience digital inequalities both because they do not have access to sufficient reliable or affordable bandwidth to comply with digital requirements and because they may not have sufficient time or skills to read and understand these requirements.

Cybersecurity

Cybersecurity refers to "defensive mechanisms put in place by government, the private sector, or individuals to protect themselves from malicious online behaviour."[54] Encryption of data is a means of protecting user privacy and transactions such as mobile payments and other e-commerce activities. These protections are relevant for rural users of e-commerce websites and services, as well as rural businesses that establish their own digital presence. However, businesses in developing regions may not prioritize cybersecurity or have the budgets to implement security measures such as updating software or contracting with cybersecurity providers, leaving their organizations and their users subject to malware and hacking.

As essential goods and services such as banking, energy, and health care become more reliant on digital technologies, the impact of cybersecurity incidents is increasing significantly. The World Bank notes that developing countries are particularly vulnerable because they often lack the institutional and technical capacity to effectively protect data collected in their digital transformation. Between 2014 and 2024, the World Bank assisted 64 countries in building the foundations of cyber resilience. Establishing and enhancing Computer Security Incident Response Teams (CSIRTs), or "digital firefighters," has been a fundamental capacity-building strategy. However, only 5 countries out of 22 in Western and Central Africa and 10 out of 26 countries in Eastern and Southern Africa had at least one operational CSIRT as of 2024.[55]

Cryptocurrencies

Cryptocurrencies can be defined as a type of private-sector digital asset that depends primarily on cryptography and distributed ledger or similar technology such as a blockchain, a form of distributed ledger in which details of transactions are held in the ledger in the form of blocks of information, with a repeated digital copy of data available at multiple locations.[56] As no single place controls that record, the currency is impossible to counterfeit. Cryptocurrencies are not controlled by a central reserve bank.

Cryptocurrencies may seem irrelevant for most residents of remote and developing regions, but they can be an attractive alternative to cash. Purported benefits of cryptocurrencies include cheaper and faster cross-border payments, increased financial inclusion, greater operational resilience, and increased transparency and traceability of transactions. However, there are many risks associated with crypto assets, including macroeconomic risks, legal risks, consumer protection, and market integrity. Some of these risks stem from a lack of policies or their enforcement, especially in many developing countries. Also, enforcement could be particularly challenging as many crypto-asset service providers are located in offshore jurisdictions but market their services globally. Specifics for a crypto-assets policy framework have been proposed by agencies such as the International Monetary Fund (IMF).[57]

Virtual Barriers

Totalitarian regimes may attempt to restrict access to information from digital sources. The "great firewall" of China blocks access to many Western news and commercial sites,[58] as well as to banned content in Uyghur and Tibetan languages.[59] Governments may also cut off access to mobile connectivity to prevent coverage of controversial events[60] or hinder efforts to organize political opposition. Although clever workarounds exist, these barriers are likely to continue to hinder access, especially to less digitally savvy rural populations.

Commentary

Digital policies can be effective in extending access to digital networks and services and in increasing affordability in rural regions. Requirements for training and hiring of local employees for digital networks and services may build skills and create jobs. Regulatory reform is required to combat market dominance by incumbents and to remove barriers to entry by small and rural connectivity providers.

National regulations may also help to protect privacy of rural users and security of their data. As governments and businesses increasing rely on collecting electronic data, data privacy and security are critical. Yet these and other policies discussed in this chapter require effective national governance, which in turn requires public institutions staffed by professionals with up-to-date expertise and with mandates to manage and enforce these policies.

References

1. United Nations, Office of the Secretary-General's Envoy on Technology (2022), *Achieving Universal and Meaningful Digital Connectivity Setting a Baseline and Targets for 2030*. https://www.itu.int/itu-d/meetings/statistics/wp-content/uploads/sites/8/2022/04/UniversalMeaningfulDigitalConnectivityTargets2030_BackgroundPaper.pdf.
2. United Nations, Office of the Secretary-General's Envoy on Technology (2022), *Achieving Universal and Meaningful Digital Connectivity Setting a Baseline and Targets for 2030*. https://www.itu.int/itu-d/meetings/statistics/wp-content/uploads/sites/8/2022/04/UniversalMeaningfulDigitalConnectivityTargets2030_BackgroundPaper.pdf.
3. Broadband Commission for Sustainable Development (2024), *The State of Broadband 2024: Leveraging AI for Universal Connectivity Part One*. https://www.broadbandcommission.org/publication/state-of-broadband-2024/.
4. Broadband Commission for Sustainable Development (2025), *State of Broadband Advocacy Targets*. June. https://www.broadbandcommission.org/wp-content/uploads/dlm_uploads/2025/06/State-of-Broadband-Targets-2025.pdf.
5. ITU (2024), *ITU Policy Brief. The Affordability of ICT Services 2023*. https://www.itu.int/en/ITUD/Statistics/Documents/publications/prices2023/ICTPriceBrief2023.pdf.
6. See, for example, https://crtc.gc.ca/eng/publications/reports/Policy-Monitoring/comm.htm.
7. Arakpogun, Emmanuel Ogiemwonyi, Whalley, Jason, Wanjiru, Roseline, Elsahn, Ziad, & Kummitha, Rama Krishna Reddy (2023), Bridging the Digital Divide in Africa via Universal Service Funds: An Institutional Theory Perspective, *Information Technology & People*, 36(8). 126-154 DOI 10.1108/ITP-01-2023-0042.
8. ITU (2024), *Challenges and Opportunities for Using Universal Service Funds to Bridge the Digital Divide*, ITU-D Study Group 1. https://www.itu.int/hub/publication/d-stg-sg01-04-05-2024/.
9. For details on U.S. federal universal service funds, see www.usac.org.

10. Hudson, Heather E. (2016), *Connecting Alaskans: Telecommunications in Alaska from Telegraph to Broadband*, University of Alaska Press.
11. Hudson, Heather E. (2011), Rural Broadband: Strategies and Lessons from North America, *Intermedia*, 39(2).
12. Government of Chile (2024, April 15), Internet Access as a Public Service Will Be A Reality in Chile. https://www.gob.cl/en/news/Internet-access-as-a-public-service-will-be-a-reality-in-chile/.
13. Arakpogun, Emmanuel Ogiemwonyi, Whalley, Jason, Wanjiru, Roseline, Elsahn, Ziad, & Kummitha, Rama Krishna Reddy (2023), Bridging the Digital Divide in Africa via Universal Service Funds: An Institutional Theory Perspective, *Information Technology & People*, 36(8). 126-154 DOI 10.1108/ITP-01-2023-0042.
14. Arakpogun, Emmanuel Ogiemwonyi, Whalley, Jason, Wanjiru, Roseline, Elsahn, Ziad, & Kummitha, Rama Krishna Reddy (2023), Bridging the Digital Divide in Africa via Universal Service Funds: An Institutional Theory Perspective, *Information Technology & People*, 36(8). 126-154 DOI 10.1108/ITP-01-2023-0042.
15. https://www.fcc.gov/general/lifeline-program-low-income-consumers.
16. FCC, Lifeline Support for Affordable Communications (n.d.). https://www.fcc.gov/lifeline-consumers.
17. Consolidated Appropriations Act, 2021, H.R. 133, 116th Cong. (2020) (enacted). Available at https://www.congress.gov/bill/116th-congress/house-bill/133/text (Consolidated Appropriations Act) (enrolled bill).
18. See https://www.fcc.gov/broadbandbenefit.
19. FCC, Affordable Connectivity Program (n.d.). https://www.fcc.gov/affordable-connectivity-program.
20. Interview conducted by Rob McMahon, Associate Professor, Communications and Technology, University of Alberta, for a research project in progress.
21. CRTC (2025, January 16), Telecom Regulatory Policy CRTC 2025-9: Telecommunications in the Far North. https://crtc.gc.ca/eng/archive/2025/2025-9.htm.
22. Australian Government. School Student Broadband Initiative (SSBI). https://www.infrastructure.gov.au/media-communications/Internet/national-broadband-network/school-student-broadband-initiative-ssbi.
23. Anderson, Claire (2024, July 4), Dissenting Opinion. Telecom Decision CRTC 2024-149 Ottawa Public Record: 1011-NOC2022-0325 Broadband Fund – Project Funding Approval for the Government of Nunavut's Transport Fibre Project in Nunavut. https://crtc.gc.ca/eng/archive/2024/2024-149.htm.
24. Anderson, Claire (2024, July 4), Dissenting Opinion. Telecom Decision CRTC 2024-149 Ottawa Public Record: 1011-NOC2022-0325

Broadband Fund – Project Funding Approval for the Government of Nunavut's Transport Fibre Project in Nunavut. https://crtc.gc.ca/eng/archive/2024/2024-149.htm.

25. CRTC (2019), Telecom Notice of Consultation CRTC 2019-45: Call for Comments – Application Guide for the Broadband Fund, Section 6.2.1(d). https://crtc.gc.ca/eng/archive/2019/2019-45.htm.
26. Form available at https://www.usac.org/wp-content/uploads/high-cost/documents/Forms/FCC-Form-481-Template.pdf.
27. Quoted in Hudson, Heather E. (2025), Remote and Indigenous Broadband: A Comparison of Canadian and U.S. Initiatives and Indigenous Engagement, *Journal of Information Policy*, forthcoming.
28. Razzano, Gabriella, with Gillwald, Alison, Aguera, Pablo, Ahmed, Shamira, Calandro, Enrico, Matanga, Cecilia, Rens, Andrew, & Van Der Spuy, Anri (2020), *The Digital Economy and Society*, Research ICT Africa. https://researchictafrica.net/research/sadc-pf-discussion-paper-the-digital-economy-and-society/.
29. Aleksandrov, I., Fedorova, M., & Parshukov, A. (2020), E-commerce in Russian Rural Areas as a Tool for Regional Development.
30. See, for example, McMahon, R., McNally, M., Fraser, C., Pearce, H., & Fontaine, T. (2018), Supporting Digital Literacy Learning and Resources with Gwich'in Tribal Council, *Northern Public Affairs*, 6(2); and McMahon, R., Gurstein, M., Beaton, B., O'Donnell, S., & Whiteduck, T. (2014), Making Information Technologies Work at the End of the Road, *Journal of Information Policy*, 4(1).
31. https://broadband.hawaii.gov/broadband-hui/.
32. Web Content Accessibility Guidelines (WCAG) 2.1. https://www.w3.org/TR/WCAG21/.
33. Broadband Commission for Sustainable Development (2025, June), State of Broadband Advocacy Targets. https://www.broadbandcommission.org/wp-content/uploads/dlm_uploads/2025/06/State-of-Broadband-Targets-2025.pdf.
34. First Mile Connectivity Consortium (FMCC) (2020, July 10), Reply comments in Telecom Notice of Consultation CRTC 2019-406: Call for Comments Regarding Potential Barriers to the Deployment of Broadband-Capable Networks In Underserved Areas in Canada, paras 67–72. http://firstmile.ca/fmcc-submits-reply-comments-to-crtc-on-barriers-to-the-deployment-of-broadband-capable-networks-in-underserved-areas/.
35. National Telecommunications and Information Administration (NTIA), U.S. Department of Commerce (2024), Notice of Funding Opportunity Tribal Broadband Connectivity Program, Tribal Broadband Connectivity

Program Funding Opportunity Number NTIA-ICG-TBCPO-2023-2008098.

36. Veniot, David (2018, October), Qiniq: A Northern Success Story, *Northern Public Affairs*.
37. See, for example, the ITU's Development Bureau, World Radio Conference (WRC), and World Telecommunication Development Conference (WTDC) at www.itu.int.
38. Based on analysis of data reported at https://www.fcc.gov/25-ghz-rural-tribal-window-submitted-applications.
39. McMahon, Rob, Buente, Wayne, Hudson Heather E., Maka'awa'awa, Brandon, Garcia, John Kealoha, & Kanahele, Dennis "Bumpy" (2023), Indigenous Community Networking in Hawai'i: A Case Study, *Social Inclusion*, 11(3), 286–297. https://doi.org/10.17645/si.v11i3.6638.
40. ISED, Spectrum and the Indigenous Priority Window. https://ised-isde.canada.ca/site/spectrum-management-telecommunications/en/spectrum-allocation/spectrum-and-indigenous-priority-window.
41. For examples of revenues from U.S. FCC spectrum auctions, see https://www.fcc.gov/auctions-summary.
42. Couture, Stéphane, Toupin, Sophie, & Baños, Alejandro Mayoral (2025, January), Resisting and Claiming Digital Sovereignty: The Cases of Civil Society and Indigenous Groups, *Policy & Internet*. https://onlinelibrary.wiley.com/doi/10.1002/poi3.434.
43. Blackwater, Darrah (2021, July/August), Spectrum Sovereignty: The U.S. Must Recognize Indigenous Rights to Spectrum, *Arizona Attorney*. Available at: https://www.azattorneymag-digital.com/azattorneymag/20210708/MobilePagedArticle.action?articleId=1712103&app=false#articleId1712103.
44. Indigenous Connectivity Institute. Spectrum and ISED's Indigenous Priority Window in Canada. https://indigenousconnectivity.org/spectrum-and-iseds-indigenous-priority-window-in-canada/.
45. Howell, Bronwyn & Tang, Xin (2023, November), Using spectrum allocations to address indigenous rights claims: The case of New Zealand, *Telecommunications Policy*, 47(10).
46. Māori Spectrum Working Group and Government of New Zealand (2022, 2 February), Memorandum of Understanding on Radio Spectrum. https://www.mbie.govt.nz/dmsdocument/18702-memorandum-of-understanding-maori-spectrum-agreement#:~:text=In%202020%20M%C4%81ori%20agreed%20to,claims%20to%20spectrum%20remain%20unresolved.
47. Tū Ātea. https://www.tuatea.nz/about.

48. Quoted in Cocullo, Jenna (2022, September 30), Spectrum Unceded: How Indigenous people are Fighting for Digital Sovereignty in a Wireless World, *Wire Report*. https://www.thewirereport.ca/2022/09/30/spectrum-unceded-how-indigenous-people-are-fighting-for-digital-sovereignty-in-a-wireless-world/.
49. GSMA (2025, June), *Introduction to Mobile Identity*. https://www.gsma.com/solutions-and-impact/technologies/mobile-identity/wp-content/uploads/2025/06/GSMA-Introduction-to-Mobile-Identity.pdf.
50. GSMA (2025, June), *Introduction to Mobile Identity*. https://www.gsma.com/solutions-and-impact/technologies/mobile-identity/wp-content/uploads/2025/06/GSMA-Introduction-to-Mobile-Identity.pdf.
51. Atick, Joseph J., Gasol Ramos, Elena, Gelb, Alan Harold, Pahlavooni, Seda, & Safdar, Zaid (2014), *Digital Identity Toolkit: A Guide for Stakeholders in Africa* (in English). World Bank Group, Washington, DC. http://documents.worldbank.org/curated/en/147961468203357928.
52. See IMF (2025, June 27), Digital Payment Innovations in Sub-Saharan Africa. https://www.imf.org/en/Publications/Departmental-Papers-Policy-Papers/Issues/2025/06/27/Digital-Payment-Innovations-in-Sub-Saharan-Africa-529198.
53. Regulation (EU) 2016/679 of The European Parliament and of The Council of 27 April 2016 on the protection of natural persons with regard to the processing of personal data and on the free movement of such data, and repealing Directive 95/46/EC (General Data Protection Regulation). https://eur-lex.europa.eu/legal-content/EN/TXT/PDF/?uri=CELEX:02016R0679-20160504. See also, *What Is GDPR, the EU's New Data Protection Law?* https://gdpr.eu/what-is-gdpr/.
54. Razzano, Gabriella, with Gillwald, Alison, Aguera, Pablo, Ahmed, Shamira, Calandro, Enrico, Matanga, Cecilia, Rens, Andrew, & Van Der Spuy, Anri (2020), *The Digital Economy and Society*, Research ICT Africa. https://researchictafrica.net/research/sadc-pf-discussion-paper-the-digital-economy-and-society/. For a more detailed definition see ITU Study Group 17. https://www.itu.int/en/ITU-T/studygroups/com17/Pages/cybersecurity.aspx.
55. World Bank (2025, January 29), Enhancing Cyber Resilience in Developing Countries. https://www.worldbank.org/en/results/2025/01/29/-enhancing-cyber-resilience-in-developing-countries.
56. Aquilina, Matteo, Cornelli, Giulio, Frost, Jon, & Gambacorta, Leonardo (2025, April), *Cryptocurrencies and Decentralised Finance: Functions and Financial Stability Implications*, Bank of International Settlements. https://www.bis.org/publ/bppdf/bispap156.pdf.

57. IMF (2023, February 23), *IMF Policy Paper: Elements of Effective Policies for Crypto Assets*. https://www.imf.org/en/Publications/Policy-Papers/Issues/2023/02/23/Elements-of-Effective-Policies-for-Crypto-Assets-530092#:~:text=The%20paper%20presents%20a%20policy,and%20market%20and%20financial%20integrity.#:-~:text=The%20paper%20presents%20a%20policy,and%20market%20and%20financial%20integrity.
58. Wu, Mingshi, Zohaib, Ali, Durumeric, Zakir, Houmansadr, Amir, & Wustrow, Eric (2025, May), A Wall Behind a Wall: Emerging Regional Censorship in China, *Great Firewall Report*. https://gfw.report/publications/sp25/data/paper/paper.pdf.
59. https://www.hrw.org/news/2025/04/13/china-police-arrest-tibetans-for-Internet-phone-use.
60. Chentemirov, Georgiy (2025, August 25), Northern Russia Troubled by Mobil[e] Internet Shutdowns, *Barents Observer.* https://www.thebarentsobserver.com/news/northern-russia-troubled-by-mobil-Internet-shutdownsnbsp/435576.

12

THE ERA OF ARTIFICIAL INTELLIGENCE

> "As technology advances, artificial intelligence is becoming increasingly pervasive and has revolutionized sectors such as agriculture, healthcare and transportation."
>
> – Nathaniel Ofori, Digital Innovation Manager, Farm Radio International[1]

The Coming AI Era

In 2016, Klaus Schwab, founder of the World Economic Forum, predicted that a "fourth industrial revolution" (following steam power, electricity, and computing) would transform society, combining advances in biology and computing with connectivity to the internet.[2]

This "fourth" revolution may become known as the era of artificial intelligence, or perhaps a more inclusive term signifying the combined intelligence of humans and machines. The transformative technical elements of this revolution are enormous increases in capacity of computing and in digital networks that can connect computers with data centers. These centers store data that high-powered computers can analyze to find answers and solve problems that would be impossible – or impossibly time-consuming – for humans alone to solve.

The AI era began to emerge from theories and science fiction with the invention in 1999 of the graphics processing unit (GPU) by tech

DOI: 10.4324/9781003431602-12

company Nvidia.[3] Originally designed for 3D graphics in multimedia and gaming, the parallel processing capabilities of GPUs were recognized to have potential for science and research and eventually for applications ranging from logistics to medicine to weather forecasting. As Nathaniel Ofori of Farm Radio International points out, there are already pioneering applications that suggest future opportunities to harness AI for rural development. The following sections discuss some of these applications and experiments as well as concerns about the potential negative consequences of AI.

Agriculture

As discussed in Chapter 5, "Agriculture, Natural Resources, and the Environment," Farm Radio International developed a suite of services (called Uliza, meaning "to ask" in Swahili) that combines radio, mobile phones, and interactive voice response systems to enable listeners to communicate and exchange information with their radio station quickly, easily, and free of charge. By 2021–2022, more than 400,000 listeners used Uliza to interact with FRI-supported radio programs, making it difficult for staff and volunteers to transcribe the responses, let alone to analyze listeners' feedback.

To make transcription easier and more efficient, FRI turned to AI to test the use of automatic speech recognition (ASR) to transcribe voice recordings from listeners. Using AI-based "On Air Dialogues," Farm Radio can gather thousands of rural people's perspectives from radio and mobile phones. Using their mobile phones, listeners answer a series of multiple-choice and open-ended questions; AI tools then analyze and disaggregate responses by country, age, and gender. FRI points out:

> Uliza Interactive enables the participation of individuals whose voices might not otherwise be listened to, including women, youth and people with disabilities … Playing a variety of voices on air ensures that diverse perspectives and experiences are heard and respected in their community.[4]

During the COVID pandemic, Farm Radio also used AI to provide answers to frequently asked questions about COVID from African broadcasters. Broadcasters could record their own questions for experts and could write to an AI chatbot for answers about the virus. In six months, the service handled 3,050 interactions with broadcasters, who in turn could share accurate information with their listeners.

Global development organization Digital Green is building an AI-powered assistant to help small-scale farmers around the world to improve their productivity and incomes by providing timely localized advice. Digital Green supports government public extension systems in India, Ethiopia, Kenya, Nepal, and Nigeria. The platform's users are extension agents (EAs), who act as educators and facilitators. They are typically college-educated government employees from the regions they serve and have expertise in crops, livestock, and horticulture. AI tools have become integral in various tasks such as document drafting, brainstorming, and research, with significant usage in technical tasks like data analysis and forecasting.

Digital Green states that these tools not only streamline processes but also foster a culture of innovation and continuous learning; and they have resulted in reduced costs and increased incomes for farmers.[5] However, more than half the respondents to a survey they conducted expressed a lack of understanding about the risks associated with using AI tools; there were also concerns about keeping pace with rapid AI integration, which could lead to disparities in skill levels and job security. To address these concerns, Digital Green has committed to providing equitable access to AI technologies and upskilling opportunities.[6]

Precision agriculture refers to farming that harnesses technologies such as drones, satellite imagery, and AI to improve yields, save money, and reduce environmental harm. It can also be extended to include innovations for "precision conservation." Satellite imagery can identify where to use fertilizer, and where more fertilizer would go to waste, polluting the air and water. It can also identify areas that do not thrive; taking those areas out of production could improve biodiversity and environmental health.

Computer vision and machine learning could identify weeds in real time to spray only where needed, reducing herbicide use by up to two-thirds. Also, AI can provide real-time analysis of the soil.

Traditionally, farmers send topsoil samples to a lab to have them analyzed.

> New technology that uses sensors to scan the soil on-site is enabling a precise diagnosis covering large areas of farms rather than spot checks … Rather than spraying or irrigating an entire field, the farmer can pinpoint where to spray, which dose to use, and the best timing for intervention.[7]

At present, these techniques are being piloted and adopted on large farms, primarily in North America. Cost remains a major barrier, with prices for equipment and data processing beyond the means of small farmers. Connectivity is another barrier. Moving data to a cloud and receiving results require broadband internet, likely using wireless to cover fields; gaps in rural digital coverage remain, especially developing regions.

The Environment

More timely and accurate weather forecasts are increasingly important as extreme weather events have become more deadly and more costly in destroying forests, buildings, and infrastructure. For years meteorologists have derived weather forecasts using equations and data from measurements taken by weather stations, high-altitude balloons, ocean buoys, and satellites and fed into supercomputers. Instead, AI looks for patterns in weather data to make predictions using algorithms trained on decades of weather data. In 2024, Microsoft and Google released forecasting tools that produce global air-pollution predictions and 10-day weather forecasts 5,000 times faster than existing models run by U.S. and European government forecasters.[8]

AI is also helping to detect wildfires, which are becoming increasingly frequent and devastating in many regions because of climate change. ALERTCalifornia is a public safety program working to understand wildfires and other natural hazards and to determine impacts on humans and the environment. The program manages a network of monitoring cameras and sensor arrays built on towers, observatories, and buildings. The cameras, which operate 24 hours a day, are coupled with an AI system that provides early wildfire confirmation and actionable real-time data to quickly scale fire resources, provide information to assist evacuations, and monitor fire behavior. The AI platform provides data that help firefighters make decisions, with the potential to save lives and to protect habitats and infrastructure. In its first season, the AI platform detected more than 1,200 fires across California. It can spot anomalies in remote locations and is effective at night. The program, based at the University of California San Diego, shares research and open-source data.[9]

AI-assisted technologies are also playing a crucial role in helping scientists detect and contain invasive species before they cause irreversible ecosystem damage. Machine-learning models are being developed even with limited data to detect invasive species, such as plants that can drive out crops. Scientists are also using environmental DNA to test water samples for traces of invasive organisms. While sifting through this genetic data previously took weeks, with machine learning it now takes hours, allowing near real-time detection of invasive pathogens before they spread to critical water infrastructure.[10]

Education

In a collection of essays on AI and the future of education, UNESCO states:

> Artificial intelligence is entering education not quietly, but as a disruptive force, stirring hope, unease and tension. It unsettles familiar rituals of teaching and learning … Classrooms once anchored in the slow work of pedagogy now contend with algorithms that accelerate, predict and reshape the very nature of knowledge … Now for the first time, machines are no longer only passive tools. They are fast becoming interactive actors and agents that talk back, respond and engage us as personalized tutors, companions and even professors, reshaping what it means to learn and teach.[11]

AI-guided instruction can tailor content and pace of learning for individual students, enhancing learning and potentially improving efficiency over traditional classroom instruction. Students are quickly learning to let AI help them with research, and with writing and other assignments. However, some researchers have emphasized the importance of human interaction: "it appears that even with AI's facilitation, human components from both teachers and peers are still important in cultivating a successful learning environment."[12] Teachers may find that their workload is not reduced, but redirected to detecting plagiarism and teaching digital literacy skills such as evaluating sources and identifying misinformation.

For distance learning, AI can become a personalized tutor, such as Khan Academy's Khanmigo, designed to help students with practice exercises and structured problem solving.[13] AI translators, now available in hundreds of languages, can help learners to understand materials written in foreign languages. Translation of spoken languages in real time is becoming accessible through smartphones.

Minority Languages

Google has implemented voice typing for several African languages by working closely with researchers and organizations in Africa to create and publish data. In South Asia, it is working with local governments, NGOs, and academic institutions to eventually collect representative audio samples from across all the regions' dialects and languages. Google states that it intends to support 1,000 languages ultimately through the use of AI.[14] Other AI platforms and developers are likely to provide alternatives to Google in the future.

AI can also help to preserve and develop content in minority languages. As discussed in Chapter 8, "Languages, Cultures, and Gender," RobotsMali has used AI to produce children's stories in Bambera for students in rural Mali who had never seen their language in writing.[15] As RobotMali has shown, AI can also help to generate content, with the guidance of local language educators, social service providers, and creatives. The next steps should be producing more, and more relevant, content in local languages to meet the needs of minority-language speakers.

Health Care

In health care, AI could also herald a "transformative moment in human history."[16] AI could aid or improve many facets of health care – such as early detection of illnesses, personalizing of medicine, handling of administrative tasks, and development of new drugs. Neural networks and generative AI, which can swiftly uncover difficult-to-discern patterns in massive quantities of data, could revolutionize how physicians are trained, how biomedical research is conducted, and how health care is delivered. Generative AI could help to break down barriers to access and dramatically improve the quality and efficiency of healthcare. For example, a rural physician could access the same analytic diagnostic information as a physician in an academic medical center.[17]

AI could become an important tool in early detection of breast cancer, for example. Researchers and companies are designing AI models to predict a woman's near-future breast-cancer risk, as well as risks of lung cancer and other diseases. The AI algorithms are trained on mammograms from past patients, enabling the AI to identify patterns in breast tissue that would predict future cancer.[18] Another tool for early detection is the digital stethoscope, which can be paired with AI software to identify murmurs, atrial fibrillation, or other life-threatening conditions that may be overlooked. Wearable digital stethoscopes for sound recording and visualization also offer real-time, wireless monitoring, and can be paired with smartphone applications for continuous auscultation monitoring.[19] "This is an elegant example of how the humble stethoscope, invented more than 200 years ago, can be upgraded for the 21st century."[20]

AI may also help with early diagnosis of tuberculosis (TB). Researchers at Stellenbosch University in South Africa are developing and testing an algorithm that will enable health care workers at primary care facilities to detect likely TB cases using a hand-held ultrasound device and smartphone. The goal is to improve access to TB screening among symptomatic adult patients at the primary health care level. The project involves ten institutions in Africa and Europe, with field trials in Benin, Mali, and South Africa, and funding from the European Union.[21]

AI can also help to improve efficiency of health care tasks and administration. Ambient-listening software runs on devices from desktops to mobile phones and tablets, using speech recognition and AI language models to capture and process conversations between a clinician and a patient during a visit. "By the time a doctor's appointment is done, an AI scribe can generate a comprehensive note for the electronic medical record, create a concise after-visit summary for the patient and provide data for coding and billing purposes."[22] AI-powered systems can also be used to update medical records, draft care plans, and create discharge instructions.[23]

e-Business

Rural e-business is increasingly likely to incorporate AI tools – such as for managing supply chains, expanding mobile money services, and overseeing gig workers. As discussed in Chapter 6, "e-Commerce," one of the most valuable assets Alibaba and other e-commerce operators collect is transaction data. Each transaction contributes to better knowledge about the economy and consumer behavior, enabling its subsidiaries to innovate in offering other products such as consumer finance, wealth management, and insurance.[24] Blockchains that act as decentralized digital ledgers combining the reach of the internet and the power of cryptography could help to eliminate the need for financial intermediaries in banking and increase transparency in opaque food supply chains and other trade involving rural populations.

AI-driven chatbots and virtual assistants are being integrated into customer service, including in the telecommunications sector to reduce reliance on human agents and decrease waiting times. For example, in 2023, African operator MTN launched Zigi, an AI-powered chatbot to interact with customers in Nigeria and South Africa. In 2024, the operator upgraded Zigi to manage more complex customer-service tasks, and integrated it with billing systems for real-time account updates. A case-study evaluation of Zigi in Nigeria found that it could provide useful responses, had shorter response time, and was easy to use, but customers stated that it often required repeated inputs, did not feel engaging, and was too time-consuming for simple actions and queries.[25]

While creating jobs, AI-managed platforms have largely relegated gig workers to low-paying insecure tasks. Ride-hailing and delivery services in Indonesia and elsewhere are able to monitor their employees as well as to expand into providing on-demand, e-commerce, and digital payments services based on analysis of their consumer data. Location-based platforms offer workers some positive features, such as gainful employment and income, which are the top two motivating factors for many workers. However, as Castel-Branco and Dawson note:

> While informal employment has always been the norm in the Global South, the proliferation of digital labour platforms has extended labour insecurity into new sectors and imposed new forms of labour control through algorithmic management. Platform workers work long hours for little pay, have no access to labour or social protections, must absorb the full risk of activities and can be terminated with no due process.[26]

Government and Non-Profit Organizations

Some governments and municipalities are introducing AI tools for e-government services ranging from simple redundant task automation to more advanced chatbots to serve citizens and as decision support tools to improve public policies, investment, and services. In India, for example, the Civil Services' Capacity Building Commission is developing "Amrit Gyaan Kosh," a repository of case studies on best practices in public administration.[27] The United Nations Development Programme (UNDP) helped researchers in Kyrgyzstan to develop Mildet, a Telegram chatbot trained on family law issues such as dissolution of marriage, division of property, and determination of paternity. This virtual "lawyer-bot" provides basic advice on alimony, tax regimes, and labor and consumer issues, and has the ability to draft basic legal documents such as application for alimony recovery and promissory notes.[28]

Many governments are not prepared to integrate AI in delivery of government services. The UNDP's AI Landscape Assessment (AILA) is a tool to evaluate a country's readiness to integrate AI technologies within governmental frameworks, focusing on the dual role of governments as both facilitators of technological advancement and users of AI in the public sector. It prioritizes ethical considerations surrounding AI use through policies, infrastructure, and skills. This assessment can serve as a useful first step to developing national digital or AI strategies.[29]

AI Governance

Several countries in the Global South are preparing to address the governance and other challenges of AI. The Global AI Summit on Africa held in Rwanda in 2025 resulted in the Africa Declaration on Artificial Intelligence.[30] It received endorsements from 49 African countries, the African Union, and Smart Africa, an alliance of 40 countries and more than 50 private sector entities committed to providing leadership in accelerating socioeconomic development through ICTs.[31] The declaration affirms the continent's vision on AI, as outlined in the African Union's Continental AI Strategy[32] released in 2024, and makes commitments to grow seven key areas: talent, data, infrastructure, market, investment, governance, and institutional cooperation. The declaration also announced the creation of an AI Fund and an Africa AI Council,[33] which is intended to promote AI initiatives throughout the continent, particularly in governance.[34]

Commentary

Artificial intelligence appears to have the potential to contribute to rural development in many ways, but it also poses challenges that cannot be ignored. Privacy concerning personal data will be a key concern. As more digital services use personal information, challenges to user privacy are likely not only to proliferate, but to accelerate. As examples above demonstrate, delivery services monitor their drivers, e-commerce sites collect data from mobile phone use to evaluate credit worthiness, and medical applications share identifiable patient data. In health care, patient data collected for AI analysis must be kept anonymous and meet safeguards such as those mandated by HIPAA (the Health Insurance Portability and Accountability Act) in the United States. HIPAA includes a Privacy Rule that applies to all forms of individuals' protected health information and a Security Rule that requires security for health information in electronic form.[35] If such safeguards do not exist, they must be implemented. Enforcement will be required if laws are to be effective. There is also currently a lack of uniformity in data protection laws and regulations, where they do exist around the world, which can create conflicts when data are shared across jurisdictions.

The data that users provide for banking, health care, shopping, and other e-services are increasingly stored "in the cloud," i.e. transmitted to distant data centers. During transmission the data may be intercepted by cybercriminals. Data that remain on host organizations' servers are also vulnerable to hacking, leading to the theft of financial data and user identities. Rural and small digital services providers need the latest updatable cybersecurity protection, including strong encryption. However, they may not have the technical skills to implement essential security or funds to pay for cyber services from third-party vendors.

Governments must also confront the challenges of misleading and inappropriate AI content, and how such a fast-evolving technology can be regulated. Perhaps more important, digital literacy training will be needed to help their citizens learn to identify false information online, and to take steps to protect their own digital privacy. Educators will also need training in how to incorporate AI tools while encouraging critical thinking.

Extending access to digital technologies, including broadband, must also remain a priority, as well as ensuring affordable access to digital services including AI. As UNESCO points out:

> While one-third of humanity remains offline, access to the most cutting-edge AI models is reserved for those with subscriptions, infrastructure and linguistic advantage. These disparities not only restrict who can use AI, but also determine whose knowledge, values and languages dominate the systems that increasingly influence education.[36]

References

1. Farm Radio International (2024), Using Automatic Speech Recognition to Transcribe Voice Messages from African Farmers. https://www.comminit.com/policy-blogs/content/using-automatic-speech-recognition-transcribe-voice-messages-african-farmers.
2. Quoted in Bauer, Jean-Martin (2024, July 18), Food, Water, Wifi: Is This the Future of Humanitarian Aid? *Guardian*. https://www.theguardian.com/news/article/2024/jul/18/food-water-wifi-is-this-the-future-of-humanitarian-aid.
3. https://www.nvidia.com/en-us/about-nvidia/corporate-timeline/.
4. Farm Radio International (2024), Using Automatic Speech Recognition to Transcribe Voice Messages from African Farmers. https://www.comminit.com/policy-blogs/content/using-automatic-speech-recognition-transcribe-voice-messages-african-farmers.
5. https://digitalgreen.org/about-us/.
6. https://digitalgreen.org/embracing-ai-a-leap-towards-enhanced-productivity-and-skill-development-at-digital-green/.
7. Boston, William (2025, July 16), Drones, AI and Robot Pickers: Meet the Fully Autonomous Farm, *Wall Street Journal*. https://www.wsj.com/tech/autonomous-farming-ai-95657bd1?mod=series_foeevergreen.
8. Niiler, Eric (2024, August 2), How AI Is Learning to Predict Our Extreme Weather, *Wall Street Journal*.
9. https://alertcalifornia.org/about/.
10. Khokhar, F.A., Shah, J.H., Saleem, R., et al. (2025), Harnessing Deep Learning for Faster Water Quality Assessment: Identifying Bacterial Contaminants in Real Time, *Visual Computer*, 41, 1037–48. https://doi.org/10.1007/s00371-024-03382-7.
11. Giannini, Stefania (2025), *AI and the Future of Education: Disruptions, Dilemmas and Directions*. UNESCO. https://www.unesco.org/en/articles/ai-and-future-education-disruptions-dilemmas-and-directions-0
12. Warschauer, M. & Xu, Y. (2024), Generative AI for Language learning: Entering a New Era, *Language Learning & Technology*, 28(2), 1–4. https://hdl.handle.net/10125/73569.
13. https://www.khanmigo.ai/.
14. https://blog.google/technology/ai/ways-ai-is-scaling-helpful/.
15. Chason, Rachel (2024, April 13), With French Under Fire, Mali Uses AI to Bring Local Language to Students, *Washington Post*.
16. Matheny, M., Thadaney Israni, S., Ahmed, M., & Whicher, D. (Eds.) (2019), *Artificial Intelligence in Health Care: The Hope, the Hype, the Promise, the Peril*. NAM Special Publication, National Academy of Medicine, Washington, DC.

17. McGinty, Jo Craven (2023, October 6), Why AI Is Medicine's Biggest Moment Since Antibiotics, *Wall Street Journal*. https://www.wsj.com/tech/ai/artificial-intelligence-medicine-innovation-6739b4f8.
18. Abbott, Briana (2025, September 23), Want to Know Your Future Breast-Cancer Risk? Just Ask AI, *Wall Street Journal*. https://www.wsj.com/health/ai-breast-cancer-screening-tool-8d3ac976?mod=djemfoe.
19. Seah, J.J., Zhao, J., Wang, Y., & Lee, H.P. (2023), Review on the Advancements of Stethoscope Types in Chest Auscultation, *Diagnostics*, 13(9), 1545. https://doi.org/10.3390/diagnostics13091545.
20. Allen, Vicky (2025, August 30), *AI Stethoscope Can Detect Three Heart Conditions in 15 Seconds*, British Heart Foundation. https://www.bhf.org.uk/what-we-do/news-from-the-bhf/news-archive/2025/august/ai-stethoscope-can-detect-three-heart-conditions-in-15-seconds.
21. Stellenbosch University (2025, 20 June), *AI Making it Easier to Diagnose TB in Sub-Saharan Africa*. https://www.su.ac.za/en/research/statistical-consultation/news/ai-making-it-easier-diagnose-tb-sub-saharan-africa.
22. Landro, Laura (2025, May 27), Why AI May Be Listening In on Your Next Doctor's Appointment, *Wall Street Journal*. https://www.wsj.com/health/healthcare/ai-ambient-listening-doctor-appointment-e7afd587?mod=series_foeevergreen.
23. Lee, DonHee & Yoon, Seong No (2021), Application of Artificial Intelligence-Based Technologies in the Healthcare Industry: Opportunities and Challenges, *International Journal of Environmental Research and Public Health*, 18(1), 1–18.
24. https://www.antgroup.com/en/business-development?tab=finance.
25. Akintola, Omolola (2025), Evaluating Usability: A Case Study on MTN's Chatbot (Zigi). https://medium.com/@omololaabike/evaluating-usability-a-case-study-on-mtns-chatbot-zigi-e5a67f0e5def.
26. Castel-Branco, R. & Dawson, H.J. (2023), The Remaking of Working Classes: Digital Labour Platforms and Workers' Struggles in the Global South, *Work in the Global Economy*, 3(2), 109–15. https://doi.org/10.1332/27324176Y2023D000000008.
27. Broadband Commission for Sustainable Development (2024), *The State of Broadband 2024: Leveraging AI for Universal Connectivity Part One*. https://www.broadbandcommission.org/publication/state-of-broadband-2024/.
28. ITU/UNESCO (2023, September), The State of Broadband 2023: Digital Connectivity A Transformative Opportunity, ITU/UNESCO Broadband Commission for Sustainable Development. https://www.itu.int/dms_pub/itu-s/opb/pol/S-POL-BROADBAND.28-2023-PDF-E.pdf.

29. UNDP (n.d.), *Artificial Intelligence Landscape Assessment*. https://www.undp.org/digital/aila.
30. Africa Declaration on Artificial Intelligence (2025). https://c4ir.rw/docs/Africa-Declaration-on-Artificial-Intelligence.pdf.
31. https://smartafrica.org/who-we-are/.
32. African Union (2024), *Continental Artificial Intelligence Strategy*. https://au.int/sites/default/files/documents/44004-doc-EN-_Continental_AI_Strategy_July_2024.pdf.
33. https://smartafrica.org/smart-africa-steering-committee-convenes-in-kigali-and-endorses-the-establishment-of-the-africa-artificial-intelligence-council/.
34. Munga, Jane & Quansah, Sylvester (2025, September 11), Understanding Africa's AI Governance Landscape: Insights From Policy Practice and Dialogue. Carnegie Endowment. https://carnegieendowment.org/posts/2025/09/understanding-africas-ai-governance-landscape-insights-from-policy-practice-and-dialogue?lang=en&utm_source=carnegieemail&utm_medium=email&utm_campaign=announcement&mkt_tok=ODEzLVhZVS00MjIAAAGc8nMaSjCK8ErRqdnf71AB5Iz_V09jzYgnt-AL2gblDSBOJDo-J3l3qmiSApB3TeBb6wZ9m-RqUIMcxlWM9aNS9zUYLWiypx6lB6KnGXZ1ILdf.
35. The Health Insurance Portability and Accountability Act of 1996. https://www.cdc.gov/phlp/php/resources/health-insurance-portability-and-accountability-act-of-1996-hipaa.html.
36. Giannini, Stefania (2025), *AI and the Future of Education: Disruptions, Dilemmas and Directions*. UNESCO. https://www.unesco.org/en/articles/ai-and-future-education-disruptions-dilemmas-and-directions-0

EPILOGUE

Lessons and Future Directions

> "While technology can be a transformative factor in serving the most vulnerable groups, addressing the deeper, interlinked problems of the digital age will require solutions that extend far beyond digital technologies. It will take time to achieve the cultural shifts and digital mindset needed to take optimal advantage of e-government and other digital offerings."
>
> – United Nations e-Government Survey, 2024[1]

The previous chapters identify research findings and lessons from case studies and observations that contribute to our understanding of the role of digital connectivity in rural development. They address how digital technologies and services can contribute to development including to the Sustainable Development Goals, and how effective policies are needed to maximize rural access and minimize threats. As the UN's *E-Government Survey on Accelerating Digital Transformation for Sustainable Development* points out, solutions to problems of the digital age will require remedies beyond those provided by digital technologies.

Access and Affordability

Some 1.9 billion people remain on the wrong side of the digital divide. Although digital connectivity is reaching more rural and developing

DOI: 10.4324/9781003431602-13

regions, network capacity is often too limited to support digital services. Also challenges of affordability persist. Gaps in government development of digital services remain and are particularly wide in Africa and Oceania.[2]

Digital skills

As Research ICT Africa points out: "The ability of citizens to deploy … technologies and digital services to enhance their livelihoods and wellbeing will be determined not only by affordable access or even their digital literacy to consume the service, but the education and skills to do so productively."[3] Many of the projects and services in previous chapters identified the need for digital literacy, including understanding not only how to use digital technologies, but how to protect privacy and evaluate content. With rapid technological change including adoption of AI, there will also be requirements for upskilling of those engaged in e-services and e-commerce.

Interactivity

Interaction with users such as farm groups and students can increase both learning and willingness to adopt new practices or skills. Interaction via mobile phones and online tutors can improve learning outcomes and completion rates of e-education and training courses.

Context

Contextual factors must be considered in understanding potential impacts of digital technologies in rural development, ranging from access to loans for purchasing farming inputs, to availability of electric power, to cultural considerations.

Engagement and Inclusion

It is important to involve users in planning, implementation, and evaluation of digital networks and services. Engagement can contribute to building trust and increasing adoption. Outreach to women, the disabled, and vulnerable populations can help to encourage them to become involved and to provide feedback on their specific needs. Also, in health care and other services, AI training must be inclusive. For example, care-delivery models trained on a specific demographic group without inclusion of other demographic groups can potentially generate models that could be harmful to the groups whose data were excluded.[4]

Sustainability

Whether intended to be non-profit or for-profit, digital initiatives must be financially sustainable if they are to survive a trial period or transition from start-up funding. Digital solution providers must include a convincing business model with a long-term economic perspective.[5] A user-centered approach can also help to make digital services sustainable.

Energy use

In confronting the challenges of climate change to environmental sustainability, the ICT sector is a major contributor to transport substitution and economic efficiency. However, the sector itself must prioritize technical efficiency and also accelerate its transition to renewable energy to meet the computing demands of data centers that will be critical in the era of "big data" and artificial intelligence.

Policy and Regulation

National governments must implement or update laws to protect privacy and security of data and adopt policies to ensure equitable and affordable access to digital technologies and services. However, to be effective, these laws and regulations must be enforced by agencies with sufficient staff with high levels of, expertise as well as recognized official legitimacy.

The Need for Research

It is important to evaluate digital experiments, projects, and other initiatives so that we can increase our understanding of the role of digital technologies and services in rural development, and identify lessons learned for future activities. Economic and other methodologies of social science research should also be carried out to add to our knowledge about digital impacts.

Since the early days of research on ICTs in rural development, we have learned about the benefits of connectivity, but many questions remain unanswered. Today, in the era of broadband digital connectivity and the emergence of AI, we need to understand more about how and under what conditions use of digital networks and services can contribute to rural social, economic, and cultural development.

For example:

- Can short-term outcomes of digital projects contribute to long-term benefits?
- What is known about the demographics of users of various digital applications?
- What is known about characteristics of early adopters and laggards? Do profiles of adopters change over time as their numbers increase?
- Under what conditions is digital connectivity necessary but not sufficient to achieve socioeconomic benefits?
- What conditions are necessary for digital networks and services to be sustainable?
- How should externalities or indirect benefits be assessed?
- How should we measure the health benefits and cost savings of rural telemedicine?
- How can local residents be involved in planning and evaluation of digital networks?
- How can digital skills be incorporated in network implementation, both in user skills and in installation and operation of digital networks?
- How effective are the various online tools for teaching and preserving minority languages?
- Can the availability of digital services in rural communities create incentives for young people to remain in these communities or for those who have left to return?

More generally, how can digital connectivity and services contribute to the achievement of the UN's Sustainable Development Goals?

Answers to these questions are important not only for researchers but also for policymakers and funding agencies in the digital era where governments, development agencies, and private industry are investing in infrastructure to extend access to broadband digital connectivity to rural, remote, and Indigenous communities.

Future Directions

In 2024, world leaders at the Summit of the Future convened by the United Nations adopted a Global Digital Compact with the following objectives:

1 Close all digital divides and accelerate progress across the Sustainable Development Goals.
2 Expand inclusion in and benefits from the digital economy for all.
3 Foster an inclusive, open, safe, and secure digital space that respects, protects, and promotes human rights.
4 Advance responsible, equitable, and interoperable data governance approaches.
5 Enhance international governance of artificial intelligence for the benefit of humanity.[6]

Words in UN documents are far from guarantees that goals will be achieved, but these objectives reflect priorities that must be addressed if the benefits of digital connectivity are to become available to all.

References

1. United Nations Department of Economic and Social Affairs (2024), *United Nations e-Government Survey 2024: Accelerating Digital Transformation for Sustainable Development*. https://publicadministration.un.org/egovkb/en-us/.
2. United Nations Department of Economic and Social Affairs (2024), *United Nations e-Government Survey 2024: Accelerating Digital Transformation for Sustainable Development*. https://publicadministration.un.org/egovkb/en-us/.
3. Razzano, Gabriella, with Gillwald, Alison, Aguera, Pablo, Ahmed, Shamira, Calandro, Enrico, Matanga, Cecilia, Rens, Andrew & Van Der Spuy, Anri (2020), *The Digital Economy and Society*, Research ICT Africa. https://researchictafrica.net/research/sadc-pf-discussion-paper-the-digital-economy-and-society/.

4. McGinty, Jo Craven (2023, October 6), Why AI Is Medicine's Biggest Moment Since Antibiotics, *Wall Street Journal* https://www.wsj.com/tech/ai/artificial-intelligence-medicine-innovation-6739b4f8.
5. *Harnessing the Chances of Digitalization for Rural Development: Lessons-Learnt in German-Funded Rural Development Projects* (2018), Deutsche Gesellschaft für Internationale Zusammenarbeit (GIZ) GmbH, Bonn, p. 13.
6. See https://www.un.org/global-digital-compact/sites/default/files/2024-09/Global%20Digital%20Compact%20-%20English_0.pdf.

INDEX

Note: Locators in ***bold-italic*** indicate boxes.